BTEC FIRST

Business
Level 2

Editor: Ian Marcousé

Authors: Charlotte Bagley
Michelle Billington
Andrew Dean
Louise Stubbs

Published by Collins Education
An imprint of HarperCollins Publishers
77–85 Fulham Palace Road
Hammersmith
London
W6 8JB

Browse the complete Collins Education catalogue at
www.collinseducation.com

ISBN 978 0 00 734268 6

British Library Cataloguing in Publication Data.
A Catalogue record for this publication is available from the British Library.

Commissioned by Emma Woolf
Project managed and edited by Jo Kemp
Design and typesetting by Thomson Digital
Text design by Nigel Jordan
Cover design by Angela English
Index by Christine Boylan
Picture research by Geoff Holdsworth/Pictureresearch.co.uk
Printed and bound by L.E.G.O. S.p.A.

Contents

About the authors

Charlotte Bagley qualified as a teacher in 2007. After progressing at Harris Academy, South Norwood, from a business teacher and teacher in charge of enterprise, she was promoted to head of the Business and Enterprise specialism in 2009. She has been program leader of BTEC Business since September 2007.

Michelle Billington is an experienced and successful teacher of Business and ICT, as well as being a published author. Michelle is currently Director of the Business and Enteprise specialism and the Director of Learning for Business, ICT and Enterprise at Moor Park Business and Enterprise School in Preston.

Andrew Dean is Head of Economics and Careers at Harris Academy, South Norwood, where he teaches BTEC at both Level 2 and 3. Andrew has been teaching BTEC for 3 years, with over 250 students currently undertaking this award, and this year he has introduced the Level 2 Diploma.

Ian Marcousé is a well-known author of Business books. He was Chief Examiner for A Level Business Studies for 13 years and is now a consultant to Edexcel, as well as the Director of A–Z Business Training Ltd. In 1994 he launched the magazine Business Review, for which he remains the Editor.

Louise Stubbs is Assistant Head Teacher at Great Sankey High School, in charge of Vocational Learning. Louise is an experienced BTEC teacher at Levels 2 and 3 and has been the Centre Quality Nominee for five years.

Photographic acknowledgements

Fishburn Hedges (3/www.talktofrank.com); iStockphoto (5/lisafx); Rex Features (6/Hatami Collection); Alamy (8/Chris Howes/Wild Places Photography); Alamy (10/Roberto Herrett); iStockphoto (10l/Lisa F. Young); iStockphoto (10c/Michael DeLeon); iStockphoto (10r/Konstantinos Kokkinis); Alamy (12/Marion Kaplan); iStockphoto (14l/Alex Varlakov); iStockphoto (14cl/AVTG); iStockphoto (14cr/Francesco Rossetti); Alamy (14r/uk retail Alan King); Alamy (27/Image Source); Rex Features (28/Offside); iStockphoto (30/Peter Cox); iStockphoto (32/Andrew Martin Green); Alamy (33/Kevin Britland); iStockphoto (37/Anastasia Pelikh); iStockphoto (39/Dainis Derics); Alamy (40/Alex Segre); iStockphoto (43/Wojtek Kryczka); iStockphoto (44/webphotographeer); iStockphoto (51/Bart Broek); The One Foundation (52/One Water – The One Foundation, Registered Charity Number 1118810, www.onedifference.org); iStockphoto (53/alxpin); iStockphoto (55/Kaupo Kikkas); iStockphoto (59/Neustockimages); iStockphoto (62/Sandra O'Claire); iStockphoto (66/Sean Locke); Carl Halliday (76); iStockphoto (79/Alexander Raths); iStockphoto (80/Ashwin Kharidehal Abhirama); iStockphoto (84/Doug Berry); Rex Features (87/Back Page Images); iStockphoto (93t/Kohlerphoto); iStockphoto (93c/Anna Khomulo); iStockphoto (93b/Edgaras Marozas); Alamy (94/D. Hurst); iStockphoto (95t/vm); Alamy (95c/fStop); iStockphoto (95bl/Andrew Reese); iStockphoto (95bcl/thumb); iStockphoto (95bcr/Amanda Rohde); Alamy (95br/image100); Geoff Holdsworth (96t); iStockphoto (96b/Lise Gagne); iStockphoto (99t/Anton Brand); iStockphoto (99b/Alex Slobodkin); iStockphoto (101/Dean Mitchell); Photos.com (102); iStockphoto (107/Vyacheslav Shramko); iStockphoto (108/Chris Schmidt); iStockphoto (110/Stephan Zabel); iStockphoto (112/David Anderson); iStockphoto (114/Jacob Wackerhausen); iStockphoto (116/Neustockimages); iStockphoto (118/Izvorinka Jankovic); iStockphoto (125/quavondo); iStockphoto (127/PeskyMonkey); iStockphoto (129/Vyacheslav Shramko); iStockphoto (132/Pali Rao); iStockphoto (134/Andrzej Podsiad); iStockphoto (136/Chris Schmidt); iStockphoto (140/Jacob Wackerhausen); Photos.com (149); iStockphoto (154/TommL); Alamy (160/Lee Martin); Rex Features (162/Graham Chadwick / Daily Mail); CartoonStock (166/www.CartoonStock.com/Clive Goddard); iStockphoto (169/Chris Schmidt); Alamy (175/Roger Bamber); iStockphoto (176/Duygu Ozen); Rex Features (178/David Pearson); iStockphoto (182/diego cervo); Rex Features (193/Alex Segre); iStockphoto (195/Justin Horrocks); Photos.com (196); Alamy (201/croftsphoto); Alamy (203/adam james); iStockphoto (204/Gene Chutka); CartoonStock (206t/www.CartoonStock.com/ Stephen Hutchinson,); Alamy (206b/Dan Atkin); iStockphoto (213/AquaColor); Alamy (214/Michael Kemp); www.gabeandgrace.co.uk (216, 219); iStockphoto (222/paul kline); Alamy (231/Hugh Threlfall); Rex Features (233/Alex Segre); Rex Features (234/Philippe Hays); BoBelle London (242); iStockphoto (244t/Guillermo Lobo); Mars (244b/Reproduced by kind permission of Mars. ®BOUNTY and the BOUNTY logo are trademarks. ©Mars 2010); iStockphoto (246/YinYang); iStockphoto (248/Mark Hatfield); Alamy (256/Mike Booth); Alamy (264/Jason Cox); iStockphoto (266/Paul Piebinga); iStockphoto (268/Robert Pernell); Alamy (270/Andrew Butterton); Alamy (274/Peter Titmuss).

Introduction

These are exciting times in business, with more companies starting up than ever, even though the country has been through a tough recession. This book is focused on your need to gain your BTEC qualification, but it never loses sight of the real world of businesses – big, small, brilliant and hopeless. By rooting the text in the real world, we authors think we've made the subject more fun to study.

This book provides the knowledge and understanding you need to complete your BTEC First in Business. In addition, it gives the pointers to help you achieve a Merit or Distinction. You will be working towards one of the following titles, depending on how many credits you obtain overall:

▶ Edexcel BTEC Level 2 Certificate in Business (15 credits)
▶ Edexcel BTEC Level 2 Extended Certificate in Business (30 credits)
▶ Edexcel BTEC Level 2 Diploma in Business (60 credits)

Your tutor will create a learning programme that gives you opportunities to explore a wide range of business topics. This book will help you obtain the credits you need for the qualification you wish to achieve. At the start of your course, make sure to find out which BTEC First qualification you are aiming to achieve and which units you will be studying.

Each chapter in this book covers one BTEC First Business unit. The chapters help develop the knowledge and understanding you need to successfully complete the assignments that are essential to your BTEC First award.

Features of the book

The book follows the BTEC First specification (syllabus) closely. This means that all of the topics and issues referred to in the course specification for the units in the book are fully covered. You will find the following features in the book:

▶ **Chapter introduction** – this is a short, introductory section at the start of each chapter that tells you what the chapter is going to focus on.
▶ **Key terms** – briefly explaining the language of business.
▶ **Over to you!** – these are short activities that aim to get you thinking about an issue or topic. They can usually be completed on the spot without doing any more research.
▶ **Activities** – these are designed to extend your knowledge and understanding by encouraging you to find out a bit more about a key business topic.
▶ **Case studies** – these are short examples of real business issues and problems. From iPhone to Woolworths. They encourage you to apply your knowledge and understanding to real situations that you might face in business.
▶ **Topic check** – this is a list of questions about the topic you have been studying. You should try to answer as many of these as you can.
▶ **Chapter checklist** – you will find this feature at the end of each chapter in the assessment summary. It encourages you to think about what you have been studying and to check that you have covered everything. The chapter checklist also explains how the topics you have been studying are assessed.

Assessment

BTEC First Level 2 awards are assessed through coursework assignments. You are required to demonstrate that you have met assessment and grading criteria for each unit. The Pass, Merit and Distinction grade criteria for each unit are outlined at the start of each chapter in the book. They are then listed again at the end of each chapter so that you can check that you have covered all of the criteria you need to.

Our book should help you succeed in your BTEC and also gives you a taste of what to expect from a career in business – whether as an employee or in starting your own venture. Taking a BTEC First Business course enables you to think about both the theory and practice of business. We hope you'll think about taking your interest in business further when you've worked through the book and completed your BTEC First qualification.

Good luck with your course!

Ian Marcousé

1 Understanding the purpose and ownership of business

Unit outline

Business is about people, often extraordinary people who use business to change their lives. Many dream about winning the lottery (a 1 in 14 million chance), while others start up businesses from restaurants to low-cost airlines. For example, Julian Dunkerton, whose Superdry clothing brand has made him a multimillionaire, started up with a market stall.

Learning outcomes

1 **Understand the purpose and ownership of business.**
2 **Understand the business context in which organisations operate.**

Grading guide

To achieve a **pass**, you must show you can:	To achieve a **merit**, you must show you can:	To achieve a **distinction**, you must show you can:
P1 Identify the purpose of four different business organisations	**M1** Contrast the ownership and purposes of two different business organisations	**D1** Evaluate how an organisation has responded to changes in the business environment
P2 Describe the different types of business ownership, linking this to the size and scale of four different organisations		
P3 Explain how businesses are classified using local and national examples	**M2** Compare areas of growth or decline in the primary, secondary and tertiary classifications of business activities	
P4 Outline the role of government in creating the business climate		
P5 Explain the characteristics of the local business environment		

The purpose and ownership of business

 Getting started

Most businesses are started for financial reasons. In most cases it is not to 'get rich', but simply to make a living (without having a bossy boss). There are also some who start a 'business' to achieve a social purpose such as renewable energy or clean water in Africa.

When you have completed this topic, you should:

- understand the reasons why people start businesses
- understand the different ways a business can be started.

 ## Key terms

Articles of Association: the legal document that shows how the business is to be run

Certificate of Incorporation: the legal document showing that a limited liability company has been formed

Cost price: the price charged by a supplier, which is therefore the cost to the purchasing company, e.g. a car manufacturer buying tyres from Pirelli

Deed of Partnership: a legally binding agreement between all the partners in a business partnership

Income: the revenue generated by selling items to customers

Limited liability company: all companies have limited liability, i.e. the owners (the shareholders) have control, yet cannot be held responsible personally for any business debts

Market share: the percentage of all sales held by one brand or business, e.g. Wrigley's has 90% of the UK market for chewing gum

Memorandum of Association: the legal document giving details about what the company does and how it has been financed

Multinational: multinational businesses operate in many, or perhaps all, countries around the world, such as Coca-Cola, McDonald's and BP

Private sector: organisations that operate without any government funding, including sole traders, companies and charities

Profit: revenue from sales minus all the costs to the business involved in making those sales

Public sector: organisations financed by government, such as the NHS and state schools

Unlimited liability: the business owner is limitlessly liable for any business debts, and may therefore have to sell personal assets (house, car) to repay debts

What are businesses for?

Every business exists to supply a product or a service to the public (its customers). In most cases, the owners of the business are trying to make a living – perhaps even become seriously rich. But that is not possible without customers – who are usually free to go elsewhere if they are not happy with what's on offer. In simple terms: a business creates a product or service and then sells it to the customer.

Products and services

A product is anything that has been made by labour through a process. For example, the iPhone is a product which has been made through the labour of humans and machines. In 2009 Apple's sales of iPhones amounted to $6,754 million – probably generating $3 billion of **profit**.

A service is work done by a single person or an organisation (e.g. travel agents) to help other people. If a service has no prospects of making a profit, and therefore is unlikely to be provided by private business, it may be set up or funded by the government. Some businesses, such as charities and not-for-profit services (e.g. *Talk to Frank*, a drugs advice service set up to give youngsters access to information), are formed to provide products and services free of charge. For example, the NHS gives free advice (service) via its website and phone line, as well as free contraception (product).

Source: www.talktofrank.co.uk

Profits and prices

Most businesses, whether large companies like Apple or state-owned corporationslike the BBC, aim to make a profit. Profit is the money left over when all the costs are taken from the **income** made. For private businesses, unless a profit is made it will be impossible to maintain the business and cope with any changes that require extra investment, so the business will not survive.

In some circumstances, businesses may sell their products at **cost price**. This means that they do not make any profit on that particular sale. They do this in the hope of making profit in other ways (e.g. through customer support, product parts or additional extras). Some firms go further, and may choose to sell below cost, charging the customer less than the cost of making the item. Sony did this when it launched its PS3 – its gamble was that later software sales would bring in more profits than the money lost on the hardware. Selling below cost can also be a way for an established company to try to drive a new competitor out of business.

Over to you!

Visit the Business Link website (www.businesslink.gov.uk).
- What does this website offer?
- Give examples of some of the advice you can receive.

Business ownership

There are millions of businesses in the world, ranging from the local convenience store to the global giants such as Tesco and Google. It is estimated that there are 4.7 million businesses in the UK alone. Many people dream of one day owning their own business, and TV programmes like *Dragons' Den* make the dream seem possible. Yet what is 'a business'?

Businesses are also known as organisations. An organisation meets the needs of its customers by providing a good or service. All organisations have to meet certain requirements and will:

- have a legal structure
- have a specific function
- use resources
- try to achieve their objectives
- be accountable for their actions.

Private sector companies

We have all heard of companies like Cadbury and McDonald's, but you may not have not realised that they are in the **private sector**. The private sector includes all businesses set up by an individual or group of individuals. Although most businesses are in the private sector, the type of business within the sector can vary enormously. Some are small, independent, family-run shops. Others are large **multinational** companies such as BP and HSBC. The most important thing to remember is that the type of business ownership will vary from business to business in the private sector (see pages 4–12).

> **? Did you know?**
>
> 'Despite the myth, the average weekly wage in the public sector is greater than that of the private sector.'
>
> *Source:* Hudson HR (www.hudson.com), 18 August 2009

Public sector companies

Whether it's your love of the cars reviewed on *Top Gear*, Sir Alan Sugar's arguments on *The Apprentice* or the full coverage of the men's 100 m Olympic final, the BBC has programmes for all. This is a good example of a **public sector** organisation. You may be surprised how many public sector businesses affect you each day – below are just a few examples:

- The Post Office
- Network Rail
- The Met Office (public weather service)
- Academy schools.

Types of business organisation

As has already been mentioned, there are a variety of different types of business, which are discussed below.

Sole trader

Of all the businesses set up and run in the private sector, the most common is the sole trader, with around 2.8 million trading in the UK. Sole traders are thought of as 'one-person businesses', though many are family run, such as corner shops. This doesn't mean that the business cannot employ other people, but it is unlikely that employees will have much influence on decisions, control or financing.

You may have family or friends who own their own sole trader business, for example if they are plumbers, hairdressers, shopkeepers, taxi drivers or electricians. Some young people also start their business this way, perhaps helped by grants from local government and charities such as the Prince's Trust.

Sole traders are classified as small businesses as they employ few people and have relatively low sales. They normally operate on a local scale (e.g. a painter and decorator may only work in the area where they live). You will see from the advantages and disadvantages listed below, starting your own business is not as simple as it may seem, and you are unlikely to make millions of pounds overnight.

Advantages of being a sole trader

- This sort of business is easy to set up – there are no complicated forms or procedures.
- The owner of the business keeps all the profits that the business is making.
- The owner has total control of the business and therefore makes all key decisions.
- The business is very flexible, for example, hours worked or stock bought can be altered on a daily basis. (Imagine you could decide what time you went to and from school or college!)

Disadvantages of being a sole trader

- Sole traders have **unlimited liability**. This means that the owner is personally responsible for any debts the business creates, so may be forced to sell personal belongings, including the family home, to cover these debts. If they cannot cover their debts they may be declared bankrupt. To avoid this, a limited company can be formed (see page 7).
- If the owner is the only person working in the business, illness will mean that no money is being made. This may lead to debts piling up and missing out on future custom.
- Sole traders are unincorporated, which means there is no legal difference between the owner and the business. All work will be carried out in the owner's name and if a dispute arises, it is the owner who could be sued.
- Some sole traders struggle with some of the aspects of running a business due to limited skills in areas such as finance.

 ## Activity

Glenn had always wanted to start his own plastering business but didn't know the best way to go about it. In 2007, he became self-employed as a sole trader and started to pick up a lot of plastering work. The following year he bought a new Ford Transit van to transport all of his tools and equipment. He is now busy, starting work at 7.30 every morning. In the evening he does his own accounts and comes up with special offers to attract new customers.

Explain why Glenn loves being a sole trader.

Partnerships

A partnership is a business set up by two or more people who may or may not have a written agreement about who owns what. Partnerships are common among professionals such as doctors, accountants and dentists. Some of the world's largest businesses, such as Google and Apple, started as partnerships.

Partnership solves some of the problems faced by sole traders:

▶ It allows the business to keep running if one owner is ill or needs a holiday.

▶ Decision-making can be shared, reducing the pressure on each individual.

▶ It can allow the business to offer other services. For example, a plasterer, electrician and bricklayer may form a partnership to offer full building services (e.g. building an extension).

▶ All profits are shared equally among the partners if they have all invested equal amounts at the start.

 ## Case study

In 1924, 3 years after creating her fragrance Chanel No. 5, Coco Chanel and Pierre Wertheimer, a successful French businessman, established Parfums Chanel. While Chanel had the name and the fame, she lacked Wertheimer's finances and connections. Wertheimer took a 70% stake in the new partnership and Chanel received 10%.

Although the deal made Chanel a wealthy woman, she soured on the business partnership and unsuccessfully tried to restructure the terms. Today, the Wertheimer family owns 100% of the company, including worldwide rights to the Chanel name. Chanel No. 5 remains one of the best-selling perfumes in history.

1. Was Coco Chanel right to join a partnership instead of going it alone?

2. Why do you think Coco Chanel was unhappy with the terms of the partnership?

Coco Chanel

In legal terms, the partners are the business and, like a sole trader, have unlimited liability. This means that if one partner runs up large debts, then all the partners will be liable for it. This can cause great tension, so it is wise for all partnerships to draw up a **Deed of Partnership**. A deed of partnership is a legally binding agreement between all the partners of the business. It will give details of:

▶ how the profits and losses of the business are to be shared

▶ the duties of each partner, including the amount of time they should contribute to the business

▶ the procedures for adding or removing a partner

▶ how much money each partner is expected to put into the business at the start.

Partnerships are often small to medium-sized businesses. They normally have more employees than a sole trader, but usually no more than 50. They operate on a local or regional scale, depending on how large the business is. For example, a dentist partnership may serve the local area, whereas a solicitor partnership may have customers from all over a region.

Advantages of partnerships

- A partnership is easy to set up.
- The business can expand and improve by taking on an experienced or qualified partner.
- Having partners in the business brings with it extra capital as well as expertise.
- The decision-making and workload can be shared, making the day-to-day running of the business easier.

Disadvantages of partnerships

- A partnership still has unlimited liability, meaning that each partner could lose their personal belongings, even if the debt is created by another partner.
- Profits have to be shared between the partners.
- Partners may disagree on how the business should be run, which can make it difficult to progress.

 Case study

Dr Penfold and Dr Keen set up Silvertooth Dentistry in 2008. Both had a great deal of experience as dentists and they decided they could make a lot of money from opening their own practice. They each invested in the partnership as follows:

Dr Keen   £20,000

Dr Penfold   £10,000

They decided that they didn't need to draw up a deed of partnership, as they had been friends for years. However, within a year, things were going very badly. Dr Keen was working half the hours he was supposed to but was demanding half the profits. Dr Penfold had to work the extra hours to cover Dr Keen

and was unhappy about Dr Keen's demands. The situation worsened when Silvertooth Dentistry was sent a letter from the bank saying they owed £12,000 in tax. This had occurred because Dr Penfold had forgotten to send in the tax records.

1. Discuss the benefits to Silvertooth Dentistry of a deed of partnership.

2. Dr Keen wants half the profits. Explain whether you agree with this demand.

3. Write a letter to Silvertooth Dentistry outlining why you recommend they draw up a deed of partnership.

Limited companies

Many businesses start as either a sole trader or partnership, but then struggle to expand due to a lack of capital. They also have to accept unlimited liability, which means every decision has added risks attached to it. The solution to this is to form a **limited liability company**. A limited company will have its own legal identity, so that any debt is tied to the company and not an individual, thus giving the business limited liability. This means that investors can put money into the company in the hope it will succeed, but without the threat of unlimited liability. There are two types of limited company.

Private limited company (Ltd)

A private limited company is often owned by friends and family. Each owner becomes a shareholder in the business by buying shares. A share can be seen as a small piece of the business, which is exchanged for a capital investment. These shares are sold to a few individuals and cannot be sold to the public. Each time a share is sold, the existing shareholders have to agree to the sale. The shareholders will meet up once a year at an Annual General meeting (AGM) at which they will discuss the business's progress and any other issues.

Case study

On 19 April 2009, Red Bull's Sebastian Vettel won the Chinese grand prix in Shanghai. It was a true victory for a truly enterprising company. Since its formation in 1987, Red Bull Ltd has grown at a staggering rate, with $4.3 billion in sales predicted for 2009 worldwide. The company was set up by Chaleo Yoovidhya and Dietrich Mateschitz, with both receiving 49% of the shares for a $500,000 investment. The other 2% was given to Chaleo Yoovidhya's son Chalerm. In 1992, Red Bull was sold for the first time in Hungary, followed shortly afterwards by the United States. Today, Red Bull is sold worldwide, with both

Yoovidhya and Mateschitz on the 'World's Billionaires list' created by Forbes. They estimate that the two entrepreneurs have a joint fortune of around $3.7 billion.

However, Red Bull is still banned in some countries. The company is constantly coming under scrutiny from pressure groups concerned about its effect on health.

Using Red Bull as an example, explain why choosing to be a private limited company is a better idea than being a partnership in this case.

To set up a limited company, two documents must be produced: the **Memorandum of Association** and **Articles of Association**. The Memorandum of Association gives details about the company, such as:

▶ the company's name and address

▶ the amount of share capital raised

▶ the purpose of the company (what is its main activity, e.g. retail furniture)

▶ a statement of limited liability.

The Articles of Association outline how the company will be run, for example:

▶ how new directors will be appointed.

▶ rules and regulations for the AGM (e.g. what will be covered, how shareholders will vote)

▶ the rights of the shareholders, depending on how many shares they own.

Once these two documents are completed, they are sent to the Registrar of Companies which, when happy, will issue a **Certificate of Incorporation** allowing the business to start trading. The company will then have to produce its financial accounts once a year.

Despite its size, IKEA is still a private limited company

Private limited companies are usually small to medium-sized businesses. They employ people other than the owners, sometimes having hundreds of employees. The sales revenue of a private limited company is usually greater than that of a sole trader.

Private limited companies normally operate on a regional scale, but some, such as IKEA, can be national (operating all over the country, through retail outlets or sales employees) or even international (operating in more than one country). This means they have more customers and are often well known.

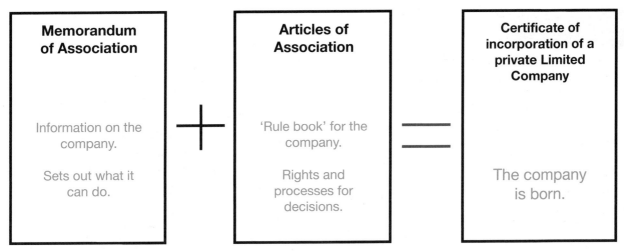

Figure 1.1 Requirements for setting up a private limited company

Advantages of private limited companies

- Limited liability – the shareholders can only lose the value of the shares they have bought, not their own possessions.
- Control – the shareholders can keep tight control over who buys shares in their company.
- The company can raise extra capital by selling more shares.
- The business has its own legal 'identity'.

Disadvantages of private limited companies

- Each year the business must produce a set of financial accounts to be checked by an independent accountant. This is sent to the Registrar of Companies and is available for the public to see.
- They are more expensive to set up than a sole trader or partnership.
- Profits have to be shared with other shareholders.

Public limited company (plc)

Public Limited companies tend to be larger than private limited companies, and their name will always end in plc. They can make huge profits and tend to employ large numbers of people. Public limited companies include Apple, Pepsi, Wal-Mart and Google.

The major difference between a public limited company and a private limited company is that the shares in a public limited company are bought by the general public and other organisations. The shares are bought and sold on the stock exchange at a particular price, which can be found in major newspapers and on the London Stock Exchange website. The general public buy shares in the hope that they will make a profit on the share price, and also receive an annual dividend income. Since a plc can offer its shares to the public, it has more possibilities for investment than a private limited company.

? Did you know?

Google's daily sales revenue is more than $70 million.

The wealthiest woman in the world is Christy Walton who is worth $20 billion. She is the widow of Wal-Mart founder Sam Walton.

Activity

Mary received £250 for her 18th birthday. She wanted to invest the money, and her parents suggested that she could buy some shares. After discussing it with a financial advisor and some friends, she decided to buy some shares in Cineworld plc. She knew that many people love films, so she thought it would be a good investment. She purchased 10 shares, each costing £25. A few months later, Mary received a cheque from Cineworld plc for £25. This was her dividend – her share of the profit being made by Cineworld plc. She was delighted. In addition, the stock market value of her shares had risen to £30 each!

1. How much are Mary's shares worth now?

2. Would you describe Mary's investment as a success? Why?

A year later, Cineworld plc started to lose customers to Vue Cinemas, resulting in no dividend being paid to the shareholders. The share price also dropped to £20.

3. How much are Mary's shares worth now?

Advantages of public limited companies

- Limited liability – the shareholders only lose the value of the shares they have bought, not their own possessions.
- The company can raise extra capital by selling more shares.
- The business has its own legal 'identity'.
- Banks are more willing to lend to larger businesses that are well-established and less of a risk.

Disadvantages of public limited companies

- An annual report and accounts have to be drawn up and sent to all shareholders. These can be seen by competitors as well.
- It is expensive to set up, as the legal side to it is very complicated.
- Profits have to be shared with other shareholders.
- There is a risk that, in tough times, another firm can buy up your business on the cheap.

Unincorporated businesses ⟶ **Incorporated businesses**

Sole trader

Partnership

Limited company

The individual owner is the business.
Unlimited liability!

Partners are the business.
2–20 partners
Unlimited liability!

Private (Ltd)
Public (plc)
Limited liability

The owners are the business.

Limited liability – the business is separate from the shareholders.

Figure 1.2 The difference between incorporated and unincorporated businesses

THOMAS TALLIS SCHOOL LIBRARY

Co-operatives

A co-operative is normally formed when a group of people or organisations come together to work towards a common goal. The members of a co-operative will vote on the decisions being made, so they have a say in the running of the business. There are two main types of co-operative: employee co-ops and customer co-ops. Most co-ops are small businesses, but there are two big co-ops in the UK:

▶ John Lewis (which includes Waitrose), is an employee co-operative – the business is owned by its staff. There are no outside shareholders. At the end of each year the directors decide how much of the year's profit should be reinvested into the business. The rest is paid out to staff. In a good year staff receive a bonus worth 20% of their salary.

▶ The Co-op chain is a customer co-operative. It includes a bank and many retail outlets. All of these are owned by its customers. Perhaps because of this, the Co-op focuses heavily on Fairtrade and other forms of ethical marketing.

Over to you!

Log on to the London Stock Exchange website at www.londonstockexchange. com. Try to find out the price of shares in:

• Debenhams

• Barclays

• another company of your choice.

Over to you!

1. Go to the Co-op's website: www.co-operative.coop.

   a) Find out how many shops the Co-op owns and runs in Britain.

   b) Identify two of the main issues the Co-op is campaigning about in the Ethics in Action part of its website.

2. Type 'John Lewis staff bonus' into your search engine to find out the latest bonus payments given to John Lewis's staff.

Advantages of co-operatives

• Members have a real impact on the running of the business; this may inspire staff or customers to get more involved.

• Less focus on profit may lead to better customer service.

• It is easier for co-ops to focus on business ethics than for businesses generally.

Disadvantages of co-operatives

• Decision-making can be long winded.

• It may be hard to agree on tough decisions in tough times, e.g. staff cutbacks.

• Medium-sized, democratically run co-ops have proved very difficult to manage.

Charity and voluntary organisations

Despite the phrase 'money makes the world go round', not all organisations aim for profit alone. Many important organisations within the business world are run as charities. These can range from pressure groups, such as Greenpeace, to charities with a presence in many high streets, such as Oxfam and Cancer Research.

Charities work to raise money, which can then be used to help achieve their aims. This money is normally raised by donations, but some charities have moved on to the high street, setting up shops that sell mainly second-hand goods.

Unlike sole traders, those who fund the charity will not be liable for any debts that are created. So, charitable status can provide protection for the owners against financial liability.

The aims of these charities differ from those of conventional businesses as they focus on achieving their charitable purpose. For example, Save the Children states: 'Our hunger, health, education and protection work aims to come up with long-lasting solutions to these ongoing problems affecting the poorest children. Our work on rights and economic justice looks to research and explain the underlying reasons for the hardship so many children suffer.'

The aims of charities like Save the Children differ from those of conventional businesses.

Size and scale

In the same way as businesses can vary greatly in their type, they can also vary greatly in size and scale.

Size

In some cases it is obvious whether a business is small or large, but it is useful to know exactly how small, medium and large businesses are categorised.

- ▶ *Small businesses*: different government departments have different ways of defining what a small business is. The Treasury usually regards a small business as one with fewer than 250 employees. Yet that could easily mean a company with annual sales of £10 million. The Inland Revenue has a special category of small business: one with a turnover of less than £200,000 a year (which might imply about four members of staff). Most small businesses are sole traders, partnerships or private limited companies.

- ▶ *Medium-sized businesses*: the government regards these as businesses with 250–999 employees. This includes major organisations such as Manchester United, Harrods and Oxfam.

- ▶ *Large businesses* should really be divided into two categories: those that operate mainly in Britain (e.g. Sainsbury's, the Co-op and ITV) and those that are **multinational**, including Tesco, HSBC, the BBC, BP and Shell. Massive businesses such as Tesco employ as many as 250,000 staff.

Figure 1.3 The number of small, medium and large businesses in the UK, 2009

Number of employees	Number of businesses
0–4	1,734,345
5–49	728,490
50–249	73,850
250–999	10,480
1,000+	1,285

Source: Office for National Statistics, 2009

Scale

When analysing a business, it is vital to look at the geographical scale of its operations. A business might have a turnover of just £150,000 a year, yet if it operates within a single village, it may be in a very strong position. The same turnover spread over UK and European sales might give the business a tiny **market share**.

▶ *Local*: a strong local business might be in a secure, profitable position, because it is too successful for a competitor to find a way into the local market. However, to be 100% dependent on one town or village is risky – 1,700 people lost their jobs in Redcar, in the north east of England, in December 2009 when a steelworks was mothballed. Imagine the effect of this on local businesses such as travel agents and builders.

▶ *Regional*: many businesses have succeeded in one region before spreading nationwide. ShakeAway milkshakes was based entirely in the south of England before breaking into new territory in 2010. Businesses can build up sales based on regional pride – and then use the regional 'heritage' elsewhere. Good examples include Ginsters Cornish Pasties, Devon cream and Yorkshire Tea.

▶ *National*: some businesses are inevitably national, such as Network Rail or the Post Office. Others build up from local to regional and then choose to go national. Sainsbury's and Waitrose could only be found in southern England until recent years, while Morrisons was limited to the north of England until it bought Safeway Food Stores. A business operating nationally is likely to be able to bulk-buy materials at much lower unit costs than local competitors.

▶ *European and global*: operating internationally provides opportunities to find skilled, but lower-cost, labour plus markets much bigger than Britain alone. The population of the whole European Union is nearly ten times that of Britain. This gives massive scope for building a much bigger, better business. Global business opportunities are even more exciting, with the rapidly growing, high-population China and India being the most obvious places to start.

Classification of business sectors

There are three different sectors of the economy in which businesses operate. In the primary sector, raw materials are extracted and food is grown (e.g. farming, mining and forestry). This is the first stage of production as these businesses create the resources to be used by other businesses.

In the secondary sector, the raw materials are transformed into goods (e.g. steel production and motor manufacturing). This stage creates the goods ready to be sold. Although this sector is small and shrinking in Britain, it still provides a high proportion of British exports.

The tertiary sector provides services such as transport, leisure and education. Retail (shops) is also a big part for this sector. The raw materials that have been transformed into a product are then sold through tertiary sector businesses. Voluntary and not-for-profit services such as Oxfam are also included in this sector.

Some businesses operate in more than one sector, for example BP, which extracts oil (primary sector), refines it (secondary sector) and sells it as petrol (tertiary sector).

Over to you!

Below is an example of how the three business sectors link together. Explain the process in this case.

Over the last 20 years, there has been a decline in the primary and secondary sectors, which have seen a shift of employment to the tertiary sector. As one industry declines another one starts to grow, and spare labour can be used by the new industry to support growth. In the UK, there was a large rise in unemployment when the coal mines closed during the 1980s and 1990s. The shift towards tertiary sector businesses made it very hard for the unemployed to find a job in which they could use the skills they had developed.

With the rise in technology, labour forces in the secondary sector have also been falling for many years. Car manufacturing factories are now largely automated with a reduced labour force needed to create the cars. The government has a crucial role to play in situations like these, when training and support are needed to help reduce unemployment.

In some countries, such as the Congo, primary sector businesses still provide the largest source of income. Mining is one of the Congo's biggest industries. However, in the UK the growth has been in the tertiary sector, with supermarkets, restaurants and high street shops leading the way.

Activity

Link each of the statements below to the most suitable business type.

1. Must have 'plc' after the company name.

2. The owner receives all of the profit.

3. Its main aim is to raise money.

4. It is often owned by friends or family.

5. The owner has unlimited liability.

6. A dentist is an example of this type of business.

7. The shares are sold on the stock exchange.

8. It can have between 2 and 20 'owners'.

9. It cannot sell shares to the general public.

Sole trader
Private limited
Partnership
Public limited company
Charity

Assessment activity 1.1 (P1, P2, P4)

The National Trust was set up in 1985 to protect historical buildings, coastlines and countryside. Since then it has grown and grown, now looking after over 200 buildings and 612,000 acres of countryside. As a registered charity, this is all made possible by a combination of paying visitors and donations. Each year, many of its properties open to the public run at a loss! Without large donations each year, charities like the National Trust would cease to exist.

In contrast, HSBC continues to grow as it trades its shares in over 119 countries with over 220,000 shareholders. As a PLC, HSBC aims to grow into the largest banking organisation in the world. The success of HSBC and other banks in the UK would not have been possible without the recent help from the government.

1. Using The National Trust and HSBC as examples, identify the purpose of each business.

2. Using follow-up research, find examples of a public limited company, a private limited company, a franchise and a partnership. Describe the different types of business ownership, linking in their size and scale.

3. Outline the role of government in creating the business climate.

Topic check

1 Three brothers are thinking of opening a clothes shop.

   a) Suggest one reason why they might want to form a company rather than a partnership.

   b) Identify whether the business is in the primary, secondary or tertiary sector.

   c) Is the business in the private or public sector?

   d) Briefly explain why it will be important that the business makes a profit.

2 What is the difference between revenue and profit?

3 Outline two possible problems for a business operated as a sole trader.

4 Explain why a co-operative such as John Lewis might be more successful than a public company such as Marks & Spencer.

5 What is the main difference between a company and a charity?

Understanding the context in which businesses operate

Getting started

Even at the best of times, it's hard to run a business. The problem becomes much worse when the business context changes unexpectedly. In September 2008 neither economists nor business leaders knew that 2009 was to see the worst economic downturn since 1921.

When you have completed this topic, you should:

- understand the meaning of the term 'business context'
- know why a changing business context can be hard to cope with.

Key terms

Grants: business funding provided by government that does not have to be repaid

Inflation: a measurement of the rate of increase in prices throughout an economy

Infrastructure: the basics of modern life such as water, electricity, broadband, motorways and fast rail links

The role of government

For long-term success, businesses must operate in a world of rules and regulations. The government sets the legal context in which they operate. There are many requirements set by the government, which businesses have to follow in order to avoid punishment or – in extreme cases – closure. The government's aim is to support business growth so that they continue to produce goods, employ staff and pay taxes.

Whether it is the European, national or local government, all will try to support innovation, risk taking and entrepreneurship. At the same time, governments want to protect workers, customers and local residents from damage that can arise from business activity. Striking the right balance can be difficult.

The European Union

The UK is part of the European Union (EU), which means it can trade with any of the other 26 member countries without any barriers to trade. This means that there are no restrictions on employment or setting up a business in the EU. The fact that the UK is in the EU gives many benefits to the business owner.

▶ *Increase in the size of the potential market*: businesses can now trade with the entire EU, thus increasing the potential number of customers from 60 million to 500 million.

▶ *Cheaper resources from Europe*: the availability of cheaper resources from parts of Europe has helped UK businesses to grow. Ford imports car parts from Portugal and Spain, and many companies hire engineers and labourers from Poland and Lithuania.

▶ *Access to EU contracts*: Businesses now have the opportunity to bid for contracts all over Europe. They are no longer forced to bid only in the UK. This has been a welcome boost for construction firms around the UK that have been hit hard by the decline in the housing market.

European Union Member States

Figure 1.4 European Union member states

The European government has an influence over other issues that directly affect the business environment. A large number of **grants** and subsidised loans are available to UK businesses. These can be used to help the business expand, focus on research and development (R&D), train its staff or acquire new premises. The main factor behind the level of funding available is the number of jobs the business will create. In a recession, the level of unemployment rises, putting pressure on the government.

? Did you know?

The UK has the third largest economy in the European Union (EU) behind Germany and France.

Source: CIA World Factbook, 1 January 2010

National government

The government runs the country. Its main focus is on maintaining a high level of employment, low **inflation** and solid growth of the economy. The overall decisions it makes reflect the environment in which businesses will have to operate.

Governments will help local regions attract multinational companies to the country. The British government has been very successful at attracting foreign investment with Nissan, Honda, Toyota, BMW, IBM and Intel all operating from the UK.

 Case study

Honda, Japan's third largest car maker, is going to switch most of its production of the Honda Civic from Japan to Swindon in the UK. This move will save thousands of jobs and help local businesses that supply Honda survive the recession. For the first time, Honda cars made in the UK will be exported to Japan.

Discuss the benefits to the UK government of this decision.

The national government is in charge of the tax levels. It will decide on the amounts businesses should pay, depending on their revenue. This can affect where businesses want to set up, as they may be able to save lots of money by setting up in a low-tax country.

The UK government will try to keep the country's economy growing. This means that it is increasing its production, unemployment is low and standard of living is high. When the country's economy starts to slow or falls into a recession, the government may choose to sit back and wait for recovery, or may intervene to try to put things right.

In 2009, the government cut VAT and started the 'scrappage scheme' for old cars. Customers were offered £2,000 towards buying a new car in exchange for scrapping cars that were over 10 years old. This helped the car manufacturing companies to increase their flagging sales, keeping thousands of people in jobs. All governments try to maintain their country, avoiding disruptions to business.

? Did you know?

By the end of March 2010 over 400,000 customers had taken advantage of the government car scrappage scheme.

Source: BIS Department for Business, Skills and Innovation

Local government

Local government aims to support the businesses in its district. It may offer advice to businesses on such matters as:

▶ how to find suitable grants and funding from the EU or national government

▶ planning permission for new business premises

▶ helping to find suitable employees in the local area.

Local governments may try to attract businesses to the area by offering reduced local taxes and other incentives. When large businesses open up in the area, this not only creates jobs for the local people, but also provides other benefits. For example, trade for other local businesses may increase, bringing more money into the economy as well as contributing to the local **infrastructure**.

All levels of government will have key goals which will depend on their location, the state of the economy and the resources available. However, the main goals for the government are low unemployment and low inflation.

Full employment

The government tries to encourage everyone to find a job. If unemployment is high, the government has to spend a lot of money on benefits. This is money paid to the unemployed to help support them while they look for another job. This is very expensive, and can put a huge strain on the government's bank account. To stop the number becoming too high, the government will put money into training schemes aimed at helping the unemployed develop a new skill. It must try to offer equality for the population, so that everyone can find employment.

As shown in the graph below, unemployment rose sharply as recession hit during 2008 and 2009. In August 2009, unemployment in the UK was measured at 7.9%. With businesses struggling, it was a pleasant surprise that the figure rose no higher than 8.0% by March 2010.

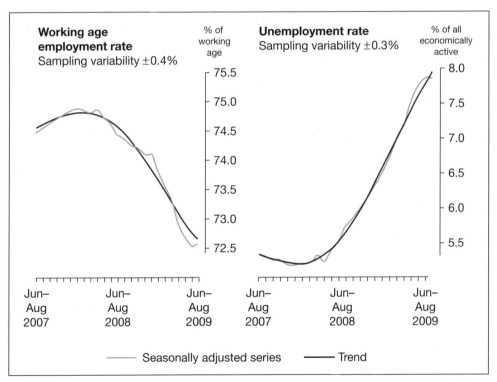

Figure 1.5 Unemployment figures 2007–09

Activity

At the end of March 2010, unemployment had reached 2.5 million. The government was urged to focus on reducing this figure in the coming months.

1. Why does the government want unemployment to be lower?

2. How can the government reduce the number of people out of work?

Inflation

The term inflation means a sustained increase in the level of prices. The government will always try to keep inflation low because if it increases, then the value of money will decrease. There is always going to be a certain level of inflation. If you look at the price of bread 20 years ago it was 12p; it is now around £1.00.

If inflation rises:

Then the cost of raw materials for businesses will increase.

↓

Businesses will then have to raise their prices to cover the extra costs.

↓

The workers will then want a pay rise to keep up with this increase in the cost of living.

↓

Higher wage bills force businesses to increase prices again.

Figure 1.6 The effects of rising inflation

The government wants the country to compete effectively with other countries. It can do this by reducing unemployment and inflation. If the country is producing a lot of goods, it can export these to other countries. Selling goods abroad boosts the level of income and jobs in this country.

Over to you!

Go to the government's statistics website: www.statistics.gov.uk.

From the home page, identify the latest inflation rate.

Assessment activity 1.2 (P3, M2)

The 2010 World Cup marked a great opportunity for England to regain the trophy for the first time since 1966. This was in stark contrast to the British primary and secondary sectors, which have continued to decline. The shift of manufacturing from the UK to other parts of the world has become more apparent, with the 'Jabulani' football being produced in China. UK producers and manufacturers are struggling to compete with cheaper alternatives in countries such as China, Thailand and India, where costs are much lower.

1. Using the information provided, as well as your own research, explain the relationship between the primary, secondary and tertiary sectors.

2. Explain, using local and national examples, how businesses are classified.

3. Using in-depth research, compare areas of growth in the primary, secondary and tertiary classifications of business activities.

Assessment activity 1.3 (M1, D1)

In 2007 Waitrose and Marks & Spencer (M&S) Food were neck and neck in the food sales market. M&S advertising was using the line, 'It's not just food, it's M&S food', and sales were doing well. Both businesses target wealthy, middle-class shoppers, and both were enjoying a boom.

Then came the banking crisis and recession. By the second half of 2008 sales were falling at both store chains. Customers were switching to Asda, Morrisons and Aldi. Things were no better in the first part of 2009. The boss of M&S, Sir Stuart Rose, started to feel the heat from unhappy shareholders, but M&S policy stayed unchanged. At Waitrose, discussions had been going on since June 2008, when sales started to slip badly. Because Waitrose is a worker co-operative, every manager and shopfloor worker could have their say. And in Spring 2009 discussion turned into action.

In March 2009 Waitrose launched its 'Essentials' range of high-quality but lower-priced products. This was followed up in April when Waitrose became the first UK supermarket to offer free delivery for online orders. Both actions proved a success. From May 2009 onwards, Waitrose's sales grew by more than £10 million a week! By 2010 Waitrose outsold M&S food for the first time ever.

1. Use the information provided, plus follow-up research on the websites of M&S and Waitrose, to contrast the ownership and purposes of these two different business organisations.

2. Evaluate how Waitrose responded to the changes in its business environment. Consider the length of time it took to respond, and whether there may be any drawbacks to its response.

Topic check

1 How might a business such as Innocent Drinks benefit from Britain's membership of the European Union?

2 How might a new business benefit from the availability of a government grant?

3 Why might a small grocery business find it hard to cope with a sharp rise in inflation?

4 Are the following true or false?

a) When unemployment rises it's easier for school-leavers to get a job.

b) Low inflation means prices are going up, but not by much.

c) Most members of the European Union have the Euro as their currency.

d) Britain's economy is the third largest in the EU, after Germany and France.

Assessment summary

The overall grade you achieve for this unit depends on how well you meet the grading criteria set out at the start of the chapter (see page 1). You must complete:

- all of the P criteria to achieve a **pass** grade
- all of the P and the M criteria to achieve a **merit** grade
- all of the P, M and D criteria to achieve a **distinction** grade.

Your tutor will assess the assessment activities that you complete for this unit. The work you produce should provide evidence which demonstrates that you have achieved each of the assessment criteria. The table below identifies what you need to demonstrate to meet each of the pass, merit and distinction criteria for this unit. You should always check and self-assess your work before you submit your assignments for marking.

Remember that you MUST provide evidence for all of the P criteria to pass the unit.

Grading criteria	You need to demonstrate that you can:	Do you have the evidence?
P1	Identify the purpose of four different business organisations	
P2	Describe the different types of business ownership, linking this to the size and scale of four different organisations	
P3	Explain how businesses are classified using local and national examples	
P4	Outline the role of government in creating the business climate	
P5	Explain the characteristics of the local business environment	
M1	Contrast the ownership and purposes of two different business organisations	
M2	Compare areas of growth or decline in the primary, secondary and tertiary classifications of business activities	
D1	Evaluate how an organisation has responded to changes in the business environment	

Always ask your tutor to explain any assignment tasks or assessment criteria that you don't understand fully. Being clear about the task before you begin gives you the best chance of succeeding. Good luck with your Unit 1 assessment work!

2 Business organisations

Unit outline

This unit gives an overview of what drives businesses on, and how they work. You will consider the different types of aims and objectives of different businesses. This may depend on which sector they operate in, including charities and voluntary organisations.

You will look at the sense of mission that some organisations develop, and understand the importance of SMART objectives in focusing the organisation and its staff. The businesses discussed in this unit help provide a context so that you can develop a good understanding of business activity.

Learning outcomes

1 **Understand business aims and objectives and how they are set.**
2 **Know how and why businesses are organised into functions such as marketing, finance and operations.**

Grading guide

To achieve a **pass**, you must show you can:	To achieve a **merit**, you must show you can:	To achieve a **distinction**, you must show you can:
P1 Define aims and objectives	**M1** Compare the aims and objectives of different businesses	**D1** Assess whether a selected organisation meets its aims and objectives
P2 Describe the purpose for a business in setting aims and objectives		
P3 Write aims and objectives for a selected business		
P4 Describe the functional areas in two contrasting business organisations	**M2** Compare the interaction of functional areas and how they relate to each other in two selected businesses to support the business objectives	
P5 Explain how these functional areas link in one of these organisations		

Setting business aims and objectives

▶ Getting started

This topic introduces you to the different types of business aims and objectives, and discusses how and why they are set. When you have completed this topic, you should:

- understand what aims and objectives are
- know about the different business sectors.

Key terms

Aim: where a business wants to be in the future

Market share: one firm's sales as a percentage of total sales in the whole market

Mission statement: an aim that is intended to inspire

Objectives: the specific targets that must be achieved in order to reach the long-term aims

Profit: sales minus the costs paid to make the sale

Sales: the money collected from customers, i.e. selling price times quantity sold

Aims and objectives

Mission statements, **aims** and **objectives** are used by businesses to help them achieve their long-term ambitions. The mission statement is the dream, the ultimate goal of the business. Aims are the long-term achievements that are required for the dream to come true. Objectives are the specific steps needed to achieve each aim. Essentially, they provide the targets to help staff know that they are heading in the right direction.

Think of your own hopes and dreams. For example, you may want to be your own boss and have your own business one day – this is your aim. However, in order to achieve this you need to get the best qualifications and work experience you can, so that you have the skills you need to start a business. So, your objective might be to get a Distinction in this BTEC, as well as GCSEs in Maths and English. You may then set yourself short-term targets such as doing your homework and completing relevant work experience.

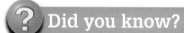

Did you know?

Mission statements can be quite general. For example, the British Army's is to 'Be the best!' and Audi's is, 'Vorsprung Durch Technik', which translates as, 'Progress through technology'.

Did you know?

Coca-Cola's mission statement is to 'refresh the world', and once led them to contemplate putting Coke taps in people's homes!

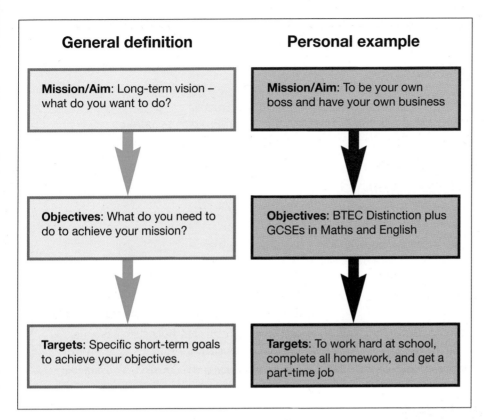

Figure 2.1 Mission statements, aims and objectives

 Over to you!

Create your own personal mission statement, aims and objectives flow chart. Think about your future career and the steps you need to complete to get there.

The different aims of businesses

The aim of all businesses is to be successful, but at what? This depends on:

▶ the mission of the business (i.e. what does it dream to be?)

▶ the size and age of the business

▶ the sector the business operates in.

For example, a new business will be looking to survive its first year. An established business might be looking to become the market leader. A business working in the public sector should be focused on providing a good service. A private business might focus on making as much **profit** as possible.

 Over to you!

What do you think are your school's main aims?

 Over to you!

Consider the following quote from the famous car manufacturer, Henry Ford: 'A business that makes nothing but money is a poor business.' What do you think he is trying to say about the aims of business?

The most common business aims are summarised in Figure 2.2.

Figure 2.2 Common business aims

Business aims	Description
Survival	Survival is a concern for all businesses, especially when they first start trading. To survive, businesses need to work hard to find and keep customers by making sure they are better than their competitors.
Breaking even	In order for a business to survive it needs to break even. This is the point where a business becomes self-sufficient, i.e. the money it collects in **sales** is equal to the money it spends on costs.
Sales	Some businesses focus on increasing sales, perhaps because they think that big firms can compete more effectively than smaller ones.
Growth	Growth is another way of saying increasing sales. Sales can be increased by increasing **market share**, selling in new geographical areas or to new customers, or developing new products or services to sell.
Increasing market share	To increase market share a business has to sell more compared with its competitors than it has previously. It can do this by having lower prices or by developing better products or services.
Maximising profit	Profit maximisation means that a business is focused on making as much money as possible, as quickly as possible. This can be done by increasing sales or by cutting costs such as raw materials and wages.
Providing a service	Some businesses focus on providing the best service possible to customers. This could be because they want to increase sales by charging customers more, or want customers to keep coming back. Other businesses (e.g. charities and public sector businesses) are happy to break even, as the services they provide are more important to them than making money.

Setting objectives

A key reason why firms set objectives is to motivate staff. Football teams with a chance of promotion train harder and play harder. Students with a chance of a C+ grade at English GCSE will work hard during Year 11.

To be really motivating, an objective must be SMART: Specific, Measurable, Achievable, Realistic and Time-related (see Figure 2.3).

? Did you know?

Market share works in a similar way to the phone voting on TV programmes such as *Britain's Got Talent* and *The X Factor*. On these programmes the acts with the highest share of the phone votes win. Similarly, the business with the highest share of sales in a particular market is the most successful.

SMART objectives help the push for success.

Figure 2.3 SMART targets

Specific	Specific objectives can be clearly understood. For example, if a business wants to increase sales, as an employee you will want to know for which product, to which type of customer and in which geographical market.
Measurable	An objective needs to be measurable so that a business can prove it has achieved what it set out to do. For example, a measurable objective would be to increase sales by 10% or to halve the number of customer complaints.
Achievable	Objectives need to be achievable in order to be motivating. If the objectives are too hard and are unlikely to be achieved then staff will become demotivated and disheartened.
Realistic	A business must be ambitious, but also needs to set realistic objectives. For example, there is no point in a business aiming to be the number one car producer in the world if it does not know how to make cars!
Time-related	In order for an objective to be measurable it also needs to be time-related. For example, if a business wants to increase sales by 10%, when does it want to achieve this by? Next year, or in the next 5 years?

Why do businesses set aims and objectives?

There are many advantages to businesses having aims and SMART objectives, including:

▶ They help businesses develop plans to achieve their ambitions.

▶ They provide targets and milestones which businesses can use to check their progress against their aims.

▶ They provide a focus for employees and ensure that they have clear instructions on what they have to do.

▶ They help provide targets to motivate employees. This should mean they work harder and get more done.

▶ They help with team building and communication within the business, as everyone is working together towards specific goals.

Activity

There are two newsagents in your local area, called Smart News and OK News, which deliver papers in the morning. Both newsagents want to be the number one newspaper seller in the local area by offering the best service to their customers. Smart News ensures its paperboys meet the following objectives before they are paid:

- Thirty papers have to be delivered in each shift.

- All papers have to be delivered by 8 a.m.

- All papers have to be delivered in the letterbox.

- There must be no complaints from customers.

OK News does not have objectives for its paperboys; it lets them do what they want and pays them as long as they come back with an empty bag.

1. Which newsagent do you think is likely to provide the better service to its customers and why?

2. Which newsagent is able to monitor the level of service it provides its customers, and how does it do this?

? Did you know?

In 1997 the owner of Harrods, Mohammed al Fayed, bought Fulham Football Club for £30 million. The club was in football's third division and the ground was in a very run-down state. Even Fulham supporters giggled when he set the aim of becoming 'The Manchester United of the South' and set the objective of Premier League football within 5 years. In fact, in 2001 – within the timescale – Fulham gained promotion to the Premier League and stayed there. The aim has not been met, but it inspired ambitious objectives that have been met. Mr al Fayed is a very SMART man.

The importance of relationships with other businesses

It is not always possible for a business to achieve its aims and objectives on its own. It may need to form partnerships or close relations with other businesses to get where it wants to be. Consider the following examples:

▶ Tesco and Sainsbury's run voucher schemes in partnership with local schools so that they can fulfil their aim of being seen to make a positive difference to the local community.

▶ Apple uses O2's mobile phone network and shops to sell the iPhone in the UK.

▶ Barclays Bank sponsors the English Premier League so that more people know who it is.

What if businesses fail to meet their aims and objectives?

Just 13 of the bosses of Britain's Top 100 companies survived in office for the 10 years to January 2010. Of the 87 leavers, most were forced to resign or retire.

Generally this was because of a failure to meet agreed aims and objectives. Luckily for these bosses, they usually receive large pay-offs. More serious consequences of failing to achieve objectives include:

▶ The possibility of staff redundancies to cut costs and rebuild profits. For example, in 2009 Willie Walsh, boss of British Airways, looked for 5,000 redundancies following his failure to achieve the profit target he had set for the business.

▶ The failure may strengthen the hand of competitors. For example, Cadbury's 2009 disappointing sales of its Trident chewing gum brand put Wrigley's in an even stronger position (90% share of UK chewing gum sales).

▶ For a business that has a charitable purpose, failure to meet objectives will mean less money for the good causes it wants to support.

The most common reasons a business fails to meet its aims and objectives are:

▶ The aims and objectives may have been too ambitious. For example, Tesco has lost hundreds of millions of pounds trying to build a profitable grocery business in America. However, the US market is the world's most developed, so it is no wonder Tesco has struggled to achieve this aim.

▶ The aims and objectives may not be well defined. For example, Woolworths went out of business because it did not specialise in selling a particular product. There was no specific reason for people to shop there, so they stopped shopping there!

▶ Competitors may beat them to their aims and objectives. All the teams in the Premier League are trying come top. However, only one team can win each year.

Aims and objectives in different businesses

All businesses exist for a purpose. For example, they may exist to provide essential services to the community, like hospitals or schools. Or they may exist to provide people with things they like, such as their favourite chocolate bar. If you want to understand the aims and objectives of a business it is important to think about why it exists. What is its purpose? This is largely dependent on who it is owned by and what sector it operates in.

▶ *Private sector businesses* are owned and controlled by private individuals and organisations, including sole traders and limited companies. Their main purpose is dictated by the owner, but usually it is to make money by providing goods and/or services which people are willing to pay for.

▶ *Government agencies* are responsible for managing the affairs of the country. They collect money via taxes, set laws, and spend their income on services such as education and health. Their intended purpose is to ensure the country is run in the best interests of the people.

Activity

Use the internet to find out which types of organisation the following are:

a) the National Health Service

b) John Lewis/Waitrose stores

c) JCB excavators

d) Sainsbury's

e) the Post Office.

Did you know?

The website suffix will often tell you the ownership of a business: **.co.uk** and **.com** show that a company is in the private sector; **.gov** tells you that the organisation is a government agency; and **.org** usually means that the business is in the not-for-profit or voluntary sector.

▶ *Public sector services* are owned and controlled by government agencies. They receive money from the government, which they use to provide services to the general public. Their intended purpose is to provide a quality service to the local community.

Did you know?

Despite their name, public companies are not part of the public sector; they are a particular kind of private sector company that can offer their shares for sale to the general public.

▶ *Not-for-profit organisations* can be private sector or public sector businesses. The money they receive as donations from the government or the general public, or generated from sales, is used to provide services or to promote a particular cause that benefits the general public.

▶ *Voluntary sector organisations* are similar to not-for-profit organisations in that they exist to provide services or to promote a particular cause that benefits the general public. However, this is normally achieved by people working for free, rather than being paid for through donations.

 Did you know?

Because public sector businesses receive public money through taxes, their ability to achieve targets is often highlighted in performance tables, such as school and hospital league tables.

Figure 2.4 shows how these purposes affect the aims and objectives of businesses in different sectors.

Figure 2.4 The aims and objectives of businesses in different sectors

	Private sector	Government	Public sector	Not-for-profit	Voluntary
Types of business	Shops, manufacturers, builders, banks, solicitors, airlines, private hospitals, mobile phone companies, oil companies	Government departments (e.g. the Treasury, Home Office, Ministry of Defence (MOD), local councils)	State schools, NHS hospitals, police, fire service	Public sector businesses, charities, such as Cancer Research UK, Age Concern, RSPCA, Save the Children	Community groups, charities such as British Red Cross, Voluntary Service Overseas (VSO)
Possible aims	Profit maximisation, growth, increasing market share, survival	To grow the economy, to provide the best services to the public, to keep people safe, to create a fair society	To provide the best service possible to the community with the money provided by the government	To raise awareness of particular causes and to provide the best service possible with the available money	To raise awareness of particular causes and to provide the best service possible with the volunteers available
Possible objectives	Increase sales, reduce costs, develop new products/services, improve existing products/services, find new customers	To reduce crime, to set appropriate taxes, to provide the best schools and hospitals, to create new laws	To exceed customer expectations (e.g. reduce waiting times in hospitals, improve exam results in schools, lower crime rates)	To raise more money, to reduce costs so more money can be used on services, to improve services, to get more people aware of the particular cause	To get more volunteers, to improve services

Case study

Bob opened a market stall last year selling pick 'n' mix sweets in his local town. There were already two local shops selling sweets in this way, OK News, the newsagent and Watch me!, the video rental store. His main aim when he opened the market stall was to be the most popular sweet seller in his local town. He set himself the following objectives in his first year of trading to achieve this aim:

- to have a 50% share of the sweet market in his local town

- to sell a larger and better range of sweets than his competitors

- to break even.

In his first year Bob sold 10,000 sweets, OK News sold 5,000 sweets and Watch me! sold 3,000 sweets. Bob's market stall had a choice of over 100 different types of sweets, compared with 30 at OK News and 20 at Watch me! His stall also won a prize from the local newspaper for the quality of his sweets. Bob priced his sweets at 50p each. They cost him a total of £6,000.

1. How well did Bob meet his objectives? Explain your answer.

Assessment and grading masterclass

Read this account of the mission statements of two major retailers. Note the explanation of where merit and distinction grades can be achieved.

Mission, aims and objectives	Merit and distinction opportunities
Tesco plc no longer features a mission statement on its website. But boss Sir Terry Leahy has, in the past, stated it as: 'Continually increasing value for customers to earn their lifetime loyalty.' Sainsbury's plc is proud to set out that: 'Our mission is to be the consumer's first choice for food, delivering products of outstanding quality and great service at a competitive cost through working faster, simpler and together.'	Merit: 'Compare the aims and objectives of different businesses' The main difference between these aims is that Tesco's is more manageable and memorable. Sainsbury's version raises a question about the purpose of a mission statement. It is long and all-purpose, making it forgettable. Yes, almost everyone working for Sainsbury's will be able to see where they fit in, but it is easy to ignore. By contrast, the Tesco one gives two simple messages to staff and customers alike: 'value for customers' and 'lifetime loyalty'. Staff will be able to see how they can help achieve this, yet the focus is clearly on the customer.

Mission, aims and objectives *continued*	Merit and distinction opportunities *continued*
I have chosen Tesco, to examine whether it successfully meets its aims. To do this I am first going to look at what is meant by 'increasing value'. For a shopper there are two sources of value: i. obtaining what you want more cheaply ii. getting what you want at the price you expect, while enjoying extra services you hadn't expected. After that I will look at how to measure 'lifetime loyalty'. 	Distinction: 'Assess whether a selected business meets its aims and objectives': Although Tesco regularly runs price promotions, *The Grocer* magazine says that Asda regularly shows up as Britain's cheapest major supermarket. Morrisons and Tesco chop and change for second place. Although Tesco has the biggest market share, it does not always seem to have the lowest prices. As for extra services, it is hard to think what a large Tesco store offers that a large Asda does not. The key question, though, is whether Tesco's sales confirm its ability to achieve 'lifetime loyalty' among its customers. The best measure is market share. This shows:

	Tesco	Asda	Morrisons
October 2007	31.8%	16.7%	10.9%
January 2008	31.1%	16.7%	11.5%
January 2009	30.7%	16.9%	11.9%
November 2009	30.7%	17.0%	12.1%

Source: TNS Worldpanel

It seems that Tesco has not met its aims in its UK business.

Assessment activity 2.1 (P2, P3, M1)

1. Read the mission statements below and match them with the following organisations:

   a UK school, Nike Inc, Department of Transport, Cancer Research UK.

   a) *To bring inspiration and innovation to every athlete in the world*

   b) *Together we will beat Cancer*

   c) *A thriving community school committed to developing successful citizens for the future*

   d) *Transport that works for everyone. This means a transport system that balances the needs of the economy, the environment and society.*

2. Identify which of the following sectors each business in Question 1 operates in:

   private, public, government agency, and not-for-profit.

3. Write down three potential aims which each of the businesses in Question 1 will have to achieve in order to realise its mission statement.

4. For two of the businesses, select the aims you have identified in Question 3 and write a SMART objective which will have to be achieved in order for the aim to be met.

Assessment activity 2.1 *continued*

5. For the two businesses you have selected in Question 4, describe why the aims and objectives you have identified will be important to the business.

6. For the two businesses you have selected in Question 4, compare the aims and objectives you have come up with, identifying areas where the aims and objectives are both similar and different. Explain how the differences relate to the sectors the businesses operate in.

7. Repeat Questions 4 to 6 for businesses you find on the internet, where information on mission statements is readily available.

Topic check

1 Which of the following statements best describes a business objective?

   a) a long-term vision or dream

   b) the mission statement or ethos of the business

   c) the targets a business needs to set to achieve its long-term aims

   d) where a business wants to be in the future

2 Which of these is a common business aim?

   a) to minimise profits

   b) to increase sales

   c) to increase costs

   d) to reduce market share

3 Which best describes the primary aim of a new business?

   a) survival

   b) to expand overseas

   c) to increase market share

   d) to increase costs

4 Businesses set SMART objectives to ensure they meet their aims, but what does SMART stand for?

   a) Special, Measurable, Attainable, Realistic, Timed

   b) Standard, Measurable, Achievable, Realistic, Timed

   c) Specific, Mixable, Actual, Realistic, Timed

   d) Specific, Measurable, Achievable, Realistic, Timed

5 Which of the following is the most SMART objective?

   a) to increase sales

   b) to increase sales of Product A

   c) to increase sales of Product A by 10%

   d) to increase sales of Product A by 10% in the next 12 months

Topic check

6 Which of the following best describes why businesses set aims and objectives?

   a) They do it because everybody else does.

   b) They are required by law to do it.

   c) They do it to annoy employees.

   d) They provide a focus for employees and ensure that they have clear instructions on what they have to do.

7 Which of the following is a common reason why businesses fail to meet their aims and objectives?

   a) The aims and objectives are achievable and realistic.

   b) Competitors beat them to their aims and objectives.

   c) The aims and objectives are specific to a product and a geographical area.

   d) The aims and objectives are measurable and time bound.

The main functional areas in business organisations

 Getting started

Although the most important manager at a football club is the team manager, there are other business functions that must be taken care of: marketing and sales; management and maintenance of the ground; financial control. These are known as business functions.

When you have completed this topic, you should:

- understand why organisations divide themselves up into different departments (functions)
- recognise the main types of business function.

 Key terms

Commission: income dependent on the level of sales an employee makes; usually a percentage of the sales made

Computer hardware: the computer equipment that you can actually touch, e.g. the hard drive, monitor, keyboard

Functional areas: the departments responsible for completing a key operation, e.g. finance

Invoice: the bill issued by a business to a customer, indicating the products, quantities and agreed prices for products or services the business has sold to the customer

Software: computer programs and operating systems such as Microsoft Windows and Microsoft Word

Statutory accounts: the financial information (including a profit and loss account, a balance sheet and a cash flow statement) a company must submit each year to Companies' House

Functional areas in business organisations

For the aims and objectives of a business to be achieved, several key tasks have to be performed. For example, if you owned your own shop, you would have to buy stock, pay your bills, serve customers and deal with customer enquiries.

 Over to you!

Suggest the key functional areas within your school or college.

Businesses need to ensure that all employees are organised, focused and working in the best way possible to complete the key tasks. For individuals and small businesses this is fairly simple, because many tasks can be completed by one person and employees can talk to each other regularly. However, in large organisations with employees in many different locations, communication is more difficult and key tasks cannot be completed by one person. Therefore, employees are arranged into departments or teams, specialising in certain tasks. These tasks are called **functional areas**.

Functional areas vary for different businesses, depending on their purpose and what their aims and objectives are. For example, a public sector business (e.g. a hospital) will have different key tasks to perform from those of a private sector business (e.g. shop selling trainers). Functional areas can also be called different names in different businesses. However, the most common key tasks that businesses have to perform are outlined below.

Sales

People working in the sales department are responsible for ensuring that the sales targets are met. These might be to increase sales of a particular product, or to boost the company's total sales. It is common for the pay of sales employees to be linked to the objectives of the business via bonuses or **commission** payments.

The key tasks of the sales department vary depending on what the business does and the complexity of the service offered or products sold. Customers expect more help or advice if they want to buy a complex expensive item. For example, selling clothes in a high street shop is very different from travelling the world selling complex machinery to large businesses.

Regardless of what they are selling, sales employees need to be friendly, knowledgeable about the product or service, be able to describe and/or demonstrate their products and link them to customer needs and expectations.

? Did you know?

Over 6 million people are employed by government agencies and public sector businesses in the UK, which is a large portion of the UK workforce.

Over to you!

Get together in a group and discuss which functional areas you have each worked in during part-time work or on work experience.

Key tasks of sales employees
Selling the product or service to customers (i.e. taking the money or ensuring contracts are signed)
Finding new customers and maintaining relationships with current customers
Organising sales promotions such as discounts, buy one get one free or free gifts to attract more customers
Keeping current customers happy by responding to customer enquiries promptly
For specialist products and services, preparing quotations and contracts for customers
Negotiating terms, conditions and discounts for larger customers
Providing technical advice and assistance to customers
Obtaining customer details and keeping them up to date

Marketing

The marketing department is often combined with or works very closely with the sales department. Both are responsible for ensuring that the sales objectives of the business are achieved. Marketing staff are responsible for how a business and its products are perceived by customers, in other words, their image.

Marketing staff use market research to help set appropriate prices for products, to ensure that products are sold in the right shops and that products have all the necessary features to satisfy customer needs. They are also responsible for promotional activities, such as the company website, advertising, sales promotions and publicity campaigns.

Over to you!

In a group, compare your favourite television advertisements. Which do you like best and why?

Key tasks of marketing employees
Carrying out market research using focus groups, questionnaires, consumer panels etc. to obtain feedback on potential and existing products and/or services from customers
Analysing market research responses and using the findings to develop future marketing plans, promotions or product development
Promoting products and services through a variety of advertising and promotional methods, e.g. press, TV, online, direct mail, sponsorship and trade shows or exhibitions
Designing, updating and promoting the company website
Producing and distributing publicity materials, such as catalogues or brochures

Did you know?

Between 2009 and 2010 the biggest star on TV was, arguably, Aleksandr Orlov. He became the meerkat hero of comparethemarket.com partly because of the cost of Google clicking. Each Googled word has its price. And when customers put in 'Compare', Google charged £12 per click. Advertising agency VCCP needed a cheaper solution. If 'meerkat' was clicked it only cost 5p! So comparethemeerkat.com was a brilliant cost-cutting strategy, made even more brilliant by the advertisements themselves. Now Aleksandr has 670,000 Facebook fans and comparethemarket.com has gone from No 4 to the No 1 price comparison site.

Production

People working in the production department are responsible for making the products sold by the business. They take the raw materials or semi-complete products purchased by the business and assemble them to form the final product. For example, the production department at Toyota would take the car parts it gets from its suppliers and assemble them into finished vehicles.

Production staff must ensure that goods are produced on time, as efficiently as possible, in the correct quantities and are of the right quality. They must also make sure that the objectives set for the department are met, for example:

▶ If a business aims to increase sales by 10%, it will also need to increase production quantities by 10%.

▶ If a business is trying to increase market share by having better products than its competitors, it will need to ensure that its products are produced to the highest quality.

▶ If business is bad, there may be pressure to cut the time it takes to make each product; this cuts costs which means profits can be boosted.

Key tasks of production employees
Producing or assembling the finished product
Planning production so the quantity of products produced is enough to meet demand from customers or to achieve sales objectives
Checking the quality of the product throughout the production process
Checking that production is on schedule, and resolving delays or problems
Improving the production process so that it takes less time to make the products and reduces costs
Packing the final products before distribution
Inspecting and maintaining the machinery used in production

? Did you know?

Some businesses use automated production processes, which include lasers, robots and conveyor belts to reduce the time and number of people it takes to produce their products.

Purchasing

People working in the purchasing department are responsible for buying all the products, services and raw materials used by the business, e.g. the products sold by the sales department, or the raw materials and parts used by the production department to assemble the product.

? Did you know?

The purchasing department can also be called 'Procurement'.

Purchasing staff build up good relationships with suppliers and must ensure that the prices they pay are competitive, that the quality is right, and that goods are delivered on time and in the correct quantities. This should enable the aims and objectives of the business to be achieved. For example:

▶ A private sector business can only achieve the aim of maximising profits if it is paying the lowest price for its products, raw materials or parts.

▶ A charity, not for profit or public sector business can provide more services if the cost of the services, goods or raw materials it uses is minimised.

▶ If a business is trying to increase market share by having better products than its competitors, it will need to ensure that its products are made from the highest quality raw materials.

▶ Raw materials will have to be delivered on time so that the production process is as efficient as possible.

Key tasks of purchasing employees
Finding and maintaining relationships with suppliers that sell the products, services and raw materials used by the business for the lowest or most competitive price
Finding and maintaining relationships with the suppliers which provide products, services and raw materials of the required quality
Liaising with the sales and production departments to ensure enough products/raw materials/parts are purchased to meet production and sales objectives
Placing orders with suppliers including delivery dates and quantities
Ensuring that what is delivered from suppliers is the same as that ordered, i.e. right quality, quantity and delivery date
Resolving problems with suppliers, e.g. if incorrect quantity is delivered or if a delivery is late

Distribution

People working in the distribution department are responsible for the delivery of products. This may be:

▶ direct to customers, e.g. Tesco vans

▶ to storage depots owned by the big store chains

▶ to individual shops

▶ to customers overseas, perhaps requiring shipping or air freight.

Distribution staff work out the best ways to transport and store goods, and are responsible for delivering products as efficiently as possible, to the right place, on time and in the right condition. This should enable the aims and objectives of the business to be achieved. For example:

▶ A company wanting to build a reputation for great customer service will want deliveries to arrive exactly when customers expect them, 100% of the time.

▶ Improving the efficiency of distribution (i.e. the time it takes to deliver products) or changing transportation methods used can reduce costs.

Key tasks of distribution employees
Managing the warehouse and ensuring products are kept safe, secure and in the best condition, e.g. some foods need to be kept refrigerated, valuable items will have to be kept safe etc.
Working out the fastest and cheapest way to transport and store goods
Checking that all deliveries match orders precisely and notifying sales if something is wrong
Ensuring that goods are dispatched at the right time and in the right quantities
Completing the delivery documents and obtaining evidence that goods have been delivered
Dealing with distribution problems, e.g. due to bad weather or vehicle breakdown

? Did you know?

The distribution department can also be called 'Logistics'.

Customer service

Customer service staff are responsible for looking after customers who have a question or complaint about the company's products or services. Most large businesses have a phone number you can call to speak to a customer service representative. The next time you eat a chocolate bar, look on the back of the wrapper and you will see a customer helpline number.

Customer service employees need to deal with customers politely and promptly to ensure that queries or complaints are answered correctly. Keeping customers happy should mean keeping them from your competitors.

💡 Over to you!

1. Why should a worker care whether a customer is pleased with the service received?

2. How can a manager make sure that the worker cares?

Key tasks of customer service employees
Answering customer questions about products and services
Providing solutions to customer problems
Providing after-sales service, including replacing damaged goods, arranging for repairs or for spare parts to be obtained and fitted
Dealing with customer complaints in accordance with company procedures
Analysing records of customer complaints to resolve problem areas
Using customer feedback to improve customer service and satisfaction

Finance

People working in the Finance department are responsible for keeping track of the money made from sales and spent on costs such as wages and raw materials. They also make sure this money ends up in the firm's bank account. Finance staff can then tell managers:

▶ how much profit (or loss) is being made by each product or each part of the business

▶ how much money is available to do new things, e.g. to buy a new shop or factory.

Without this information the business is not able to make important decisions or to track how it is performing against its aims and objectives. This can mean the difference between success and failure. Imagine you were responsible for setting the selling price of the product but you didn't know how much it cost to make or buy? Or you were looking to buy a new factory but you didn't know how much money was available in your bank account?

The Finance department is also responsible for submitting the **statutory accounts** and the tax return to the government each year. This is a legal requirement and enables the government to calculate how much tax the business must pay on its profits.

Key tasks of finance employees
Preparing sales and cost budgets for each department (functional area) based on the aims and objectives of the business
Monitoring department (functional area) budgets to check that they are not overspending and that sales objectives are being achieved
Preparing regular financial reports on the amount of cash the business is holding (cash flow reports) and the profit being made by each product or each part of the business (management accounts), so that important decisions can be made by management
Producing sales **invoices**, checking and recording payments received from customers and chasing up overdue payments
Checking, recording and paying invoices received from suppliers
Preparing payroll and paying staff salaries (with assistance from HR)
Calculating the tax owed to the government (HMRC) on profits made by the business
Preparing the annual statutory accounts

Did you know?

In January 2010 Portsmouth FC failed to pay its wage bill on time. The finance department was not able to find the money. The wages were only paid when £3 million came in from selling the club's No 1 goalkeeper!

Human resources (HR)

People working in the human resources department are responsible for hiring new employees and looking after the existing employees of the business. HR staff try to ensure that staff are paid fairly, work in appropriate and safe conditions, have opportunities for training and promotion, and feel supported if they are ill or have personal problems.

Did you know?

HR are the people you speak to when applying for a job or when you have a problem at work.

Well-run businesses look after their employees because they are more likely to retain good experienced staff. Also, if employees are well trained, motivated and committed to the aims and objectives, the business is more likely to be successful.

Key tasks of human resources employees
Finding new employees – this includes advertising job vacancies, receiving and recording all job applications, arranging interviews and notifying candidates of the result
Induction of new employees – this includes introducing new employees to the aims, objectives and procedures of the business, and ensuring that they have a contract of employment and other essential information
Maintaining employee details and records, and ensuring that employees are paid the right amount on the right date
Supporting the professional development of existing employees by arranging training courses, professional qualifications and assisting with career management
Managing the appraisal and promotion process, ensuring that staff receive appropriate feedback on their performance, are appropriately rewarded for their efforts in terms of promotion prospects and pay
Performing research on wage levels and ensuring that employees are paid the same as those performing similar tasks in other businesses
Monitoring the work conditions, ensuring they comply with health and safety standards
Ensuring that the legal rights and responsibilities of employees in relation to health and safety, data protection and employment are not breached
Dealing with disciplinary issues and employee queries
Recording and monitoring reasons for absence, such as sick leave and holidays

Activity

A key HR task is recruitment. Cut out two job advertisements from your local newspaper. Which one do you think is the more effective? Explain why. Make sure to include the advertisements in the work you present (scanning them in would be more effective than sticking them down).

Administration

People performing administration tasks are responsible for providing support to the main functional areas of the business. This mainly consists of performing tasks such as preparing and filing documents, sending emails and faxes and organising meetings or travel arrangements.

Some senior administrators have wider responsibilities such as monitoring budgets, paying bills or interviewing new staff.

Many businesses have no separate administration department. Instead, administration tasks are carried out by people based in each department or team, e.g. secretaries, sales assistants.

Administration employees perform routine tasks so that managers or more skilled employees have more time to concentrate on running the business and focus on achieving the aims and objectives of the business.

Did you know?

Administration employees have many different job titles, such as secretary, personal assistant (PA), clerk and receptionist.

Key tasks of administration employees
Collecting, distributing and dispatching the mail
Storing and retrieving paper and electronic records
Organising meetings and preparing documents
Preparing documents using word processing, spreadsheet and presentation **software**
Sending and receiving messages by telephone, fax and email
Making arrangements for visitors
Making travel arrangements
Making arrangements for events, such as staff parties, client entertainment

Information and communication technology (ICT)

People working in the ICT department are responsible for looking after the computer equipment used in the business. Computers play a very important role in many tasks performed by businesses. For example:

▶ Specialist programs are used to automate some key tasks, such as raising invoices and customer orders, paying bills, raising customer orders, designing new products and services, and monitoring production activities and stock levels.

▶ Storing and recording data on customers, products, employees and financial transactions, e.g. computerised tills in shops record sales by product, customer, staff and store.

▶ Email communication between employees, departments and customers.

▶ Software programs such as Microsoft Word, Excel, PowerPoint and Publisher are used to prepare reports and promotional material.

ICT employees are computer experts who are responsible for maintaining the **computer hardware** and software used by the business. Their job is to make sure that the computer system serves the managers and staff, in other words, provides them with the data they need to do their jobs.

The ICT department helps a business achieve its aims and objectives by improving communication between departments and developing improved systems, which means tasks can be completed more efficiently.

Key tasks of ICT employees
Recommending new/updated systems and software to keep up to date with technological developments and the needs of the business
Buying and installing hardware and software, providing information or training to employees as appropriate
Assisting employees who have computer problems
Repairing and maintaining the computer system
Advising on obtaining/issuing computer supplies and consumables
Connecting new or additional equipment to the system
Finding and sorting data stored on the system for other functional areas such as sales or marketing
Operating a back-up system for critical data
Installing a security system which limits access to authorised users and protects against hackers and viruses

Research and development (R&D)

People working in the research and development department are responsible for developing new products and services or improving existing products and services. The type of research performed varies depending on the purpose of the business. For example:

▶ Nike would be trying to design new trainers which are fashionable and attractive to its customers.

▶ Computer games developers would be trying to think up new ideas for games.

▶ Car manufacturers would be trying to improve the performance and look of their vehicles.

Activity

The R&D department at PepsiCola Co spent money from its budget to develop 'Sunseed' oil. This allowed Walkers crisps to be made with up to 80% less saturated fat. Do an internet search for 'PepsiCo R&D Centre Leicester' and write exactly (yes, exactly!) 100 words explaining what the centre does.

R&D employees help a business achieve its aims and objectives by developing products and services which meet or exceed the needs and expectations of customers and which are better than those of its competitors. A good example is the iPod, which made Apple the market leader in the mobile MP3 market.

Key tasks of R&D employees
Researching new technological developments and understanding implications for new products or how they can improve current products
Liaising with other functional areas, such as sales and production, to come up with new ideas for products and/or services
Performing market research on new product ideas
Preparing new designs for new products
Making prototypes to test new ideas

Links between functional areas in organisations

For a business to achieve its goals, all the people it employs need to be working towards the same aims and objectives. Therefore, functional areas need to be in constant communication with each other, exchanging information about customers, problems, costs and sales; preparing plans and budgets; and working together to make and deliver the product and/or services the business sells to customers.

In order to understand how functional areas link in different businesses you need to consider two things:

▶ The flow of goods and/or services through the business. A typical flow is shown in Figure 2.5.

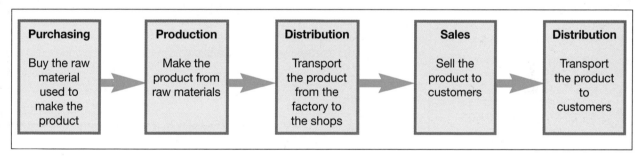

Figure 2.5 The flow of goods and/or services through the business

▶ The information that needs to be shared between the functional areas to ensure the business meets its aims and objectives. What information is needed to ensure that the business makes money... to develop new products... to deal with customer complaints?

Finance is a key functional area for sharing information as it is responsible for collecting information on sales and costs and communicating which functional areas are on or below their objectives. ICT is also important because it is responsible for the majority of the equipment (computers, specialist computer programs, shared networks) functional areas use to communicate with each other.

Some of the key reasons for links between functional areas are shown in Figure 2.6.

Figure 2.6 Reasons for links between functional areas

Functional areas	Flow of information between functional areas
Sales and Finance	• Finance need to keep track of the amount of money collected from sales (e.g. the selling price of each product and/or service and the level of discounts offered to customers). • Finance need customer details to send invoices to the correct people and check the credit rating of customers.
Finance, Purchasing and Production	• Finance need to keep track of the cost of purchasing and/or making the product to ensure that the business is making a profit when the product is sold, and that any changes in cost are reflected in the selling price of the product. • Finance need purchase price information and supplier details to ensure the invoices received from suppliers are correct.
Sales, Marketing and Customer service	• Customer information (e.g. age, gender, likes and dislikes, complaints) should be passed between the sales, customer service and marketing departments so that marketing initiatives meet customer needs and expectations and any service problems can be addressed.
Sales, Production and Purchasing	• Production need to know how many and which products are being sold so that they can plan which products need to be produced in the future. • Production must tell sales about problems that will affect delivery dates to customers. • Production need to tell purchasing what they are planning to produce so that they buy enough raw materials for the products to be made.
Sales, Production and Distribution	• Sales must know production plans and agree delivery dates of orders with production so that they can tell customers how long they will have to wait for the product to be available. • Production need to liaise with distribution to ensure that finished products are delivered to shops. • Sales need to liaise with distribution to ensure that products are delivered to customers on time.
Sales, R&D and Production	• Sales need to inform R&D of customer needs and expectations so that products can be developed which customers like. • R&D need to liaise with production over new product developments and methods of production.
HR	• HR is responsible for hiring new employees, training courses, job promotions etc. for all functional areas.
Finance and HR	• HR need to communicate changes in personnel and salary to finance so that they can update the payroll.

Assessment activity 2.2 (P4, P5, M2)

1. For the two businesses you chose in Assessment activity 2.1, describe the key tasks, and therefore functional areas, that will have to be performed in order for its aims and objectives to be met.

2. For the two businesses you chose in Assessment activity 2.1, explain how the functional areas link. Which will be the key functional areas responsible for achieving the aims and objectives of the business, and how will these functional areas work together?

Topic check

1 Which business function is responsible for turning a new product idea into a real product?
2 Which business function has to decide on the image the business wishes to create for a product?
3 PepsiCo's R&D Centre is in Leicester, many miles from its marketing department. Why might this be important?
4 Give two reasons why a firm's marketing department might need to talk to the finance department.
5 a) Identify two key tasks of administrative employees.
   b) Briefly explain the possible effect on the business if these staff fail to turn up for work.
6 Why may 'induction of employees' be an important part of the role of an HR manager?

Assessment summary

The overall grade you achieve for this unit depends on how well you meet the grading criteria set out at the start of the chapter (see page 23). You must complete:

- all of the P criteria to achieve a **pass** grade
- all of the P and the M criteria to achieve a **merit** grade
- all of the P, M and D criteria to achieve a **distinction** grade.

Your tutor will assess the assessment activities that you complete for this unit. The work you produce should provide evidence which demonstrates that you have achieved each of the assessment criteria. The table below identifies what you need to demonstrate to meet each of the pass, merit and distinction criteria for this unit. You should always check and self-assess your work before you submit your assignments for marking.

Remember that you MUST provide evidence for all of the P criteria to pass the unit.

Grading criteria	You need to demonstrate that you can:	Do you have the evidence?
P1	Define aims and objectives	
P2	Describe the purpose for a business in setting aims and objectives	
P3	Write aims and objectives for a selected business	
P4	Describe the functional areas in two contrasting business organisations	
P5	Explain how these functional areas link in one of these organisations	
M1	Compare the aims and objectives of different businesses	
M2	Compare the interaction of functional areas and how they relate to each other in two selected businesses to support the business objectives	
D1	Assess whether a selected organisation meets its aims and objectives	

Always ask your tutor to explain any assignment tasks or assessment criteria that you don't understand fully. Being clear about the task before you begin gives you the best chance of succeeding. Good luck with your Unit 2 assessment work!

3 Financial forecasting for business

Unit outline

An Abba song says that 'money makes the world go round'. Comedian Woody Allen thinks that 'money is better than poverty, if only for financial reasons'. Either way, a business without good cash flow (money available when it needs it) will not last long. And the reason most businesses exist is to make money. The key to this is good financial management.

Grading guide

To achieve a **pass**, you must show you can:	To achieve a **merit**, you must show you can:	To achieve a **distinction**, you must show you can:
P1 Identify the difference between start-up and operating costs, variable and fixed costs	**M1** Explain the importance of costs, revenue and profit for a business organisation	**D1** Evaluate the importance of cash flow and break even for the effective management of business finance
P2 Identify the different types of revenue		
P3 Outline the differences between gross and net profit		
P4 Calculate break even using given data to show the level at which income equals expenditure		
P5 Present the break even as an annotated graph showing break even	**M2** Demonstrate the impact of changing cost and revenue data on the break-even point of a selected business	
P6 Prepare an annual cash flow using monthly data	**M3** Analyse the implications of regular and irregular cash inflows and outflows for a business organisation	

Costs, revenue and profit in a business organisation

Getting started

Without profit, no business can survive for long. Profit provides the funds to help the business grow. Profit is achieved when revenue is higher than costs.

When you have completed this topic, you should:
- be able to calculate costs, revenue and profit
- understand the implications of changing levels of costs, revenue or profit.

Key terms

Costs: these are what a business spends its money on, such as wages or materials

Profit: this occurs when revenues are higher than costs

Revenue: this is the value of sales made within a period of time, such as a year

Business costs

A business has many **costs**. Some of these are spent to get the business off the ground, known as start-up costs. Some have to be paid throughout the business's life, known as operating costs.

If you were planning to set up a coffee shop, what would your start-up costs and operating costs be? These are set out in Figure 3.1.

Figure 3.1 Business costs for a coffee shop

Start-up costs	Operating costs
Furniture	Rent/mortgage on the premises
Equipment (such as coffee machine)	Wages for staff
Initial staff training	Electricity
Publicity for the opening	Regular advertisements in the local paper
Lease on the premises	Business rates
	Stock (coffee, milk, cakes, etc.)

Activity

What would be the likely start-up and operating costs for a hairdresser?

Start-up costs are faced once only, so they are not too much of a problem. Operating costs, however, are faced every week for the lifetime of the business. If times are difficult and sales are bad, the operating costs can force a firm to go out of business.

There are two types of operating costs:

1. *Fixed costs* do not change if output/sales change. Even if the coffee shop has no customers in January, the rent has to be paid, plus the wages of permanent staff, plus the cost of heating and lighting the place. A full list of fixed costs would be: rent, business rates, salaries, telephone, loan repayments and the weekly advert in the local paper. Fixed costs can also be called indirect costs.

2. *Variable costs* vary as output/sales vary. The more customers come, the more coffee and food must be bought by the business. If the coffee shop has no customers one day then the owner will have no variable costs to pay. For cafés, the variable costs are quite low (tea only costs 2p per bag, but it might be sold for £1.20 per cup!). This makes it easier for cafés to afford the high rent (fixed) costs at prime high street locations. Variable costs are also known as direct costs because they are linked directly to the activities of the business.

 **Activity**

What would be the fixed (indirect) and variable (direct) costs for a hairdresser?

Business managers worry most about total costs. These are all the costs added together. In effect they are the total operating costs for the business. They are calculated by adding together the fixed costs and the variable costs. A slight complication is that variable costs are usually quoted per item, e.g. £2 per unit. So, to work out total costs you have to know how many items are being made and sold. To work out total costs, you:

▶ multiply the variable cost per unit by the number made/sold

▶ add that total to the fixed costs.

For example, if a cake shop sold 200 cakes a week with £2 variable costs per cake and £300 of fixed costs, the total costs would be:

▶ 200 × £2 = £400

▶ £400 + £300 = £700.

 Activity

1. Calculate the total costs if the cake shop in the example enjoyed a doubling of sales to 400 cakes.
2. Explain why total costs didn't double when sales doubled.

? Did you know?

A quarter of new businesses fail in the first year – largely due to poor financial management.

Revenue

All businesses need **revenue**. This is the income a business receives from its activities. This is needed to make sure all costs are covered and in order to make a **profit**.

In our cake shop, the revenue would come from the sales of coffees, teas, sandwiches, cakes etc. However, the business could also have other sources of revenue, such as rent received from a flat above the shop.

Calculating total revenue is done using this formula:

> Unit sales price × number of units sold

If the shop sells 60 coffees at £2.20 each, what would the total revenue be?

£2.20 × 60

= £132.00

Activity

1. Calculate the revenue from a business that sells 4,000 units a month at £3.50 per unit.
2. Explain why revenue is not the same as profit.

Calculating gross and net profit

All businesses need to make a profit. Even social enterprises, such as One Water, need profit to be able to invest in their charitable causes. Only some public sector businesses, like libraries and the NHS, can survive operating at a loss.

There are two types of profit: gross profit and net profit. Gross profit is calculated by subtracting the costs of sales from the sales revenue.

> Gross profit = sales revenue – cost of sales (variable costs)

In the earlier example we identified the sales revenue for selling 60 cups of coffee at £2.20 each. If the variable cost of sales (coffee and milk) came to 70p a cup, our gross profit would be:

£132 – (60 × 70p = £42)

= £90

This may look profitable, but don't be fooled! It costs a lot more than 70p for coffee and milk to make the drinks. What about hire of the coffee machine, wages for staff, rent for the premises, electricity?

Net profit is the profit we have left after we have paid all of our operating costs. To calculate this we use the formula:

> Net profit = gross profit – expenses (fixed costs)

If the shop had fixed costs of £80 (rent, electricity, salaries and so on) then our net profit would be:

> Net profit = gross profit – expenses (fixed costs)

$$£90 - £80$$

$$= £10$$

Not quite so impressive, is it? Do you still fancy owning a coffee shop? There is worse news to come – we haven't paid tax yet!

With this in mind, how is Starbucks a global empire with a net profit of $217 million in the 13-week period ending 28 June 2009? Quite simply, they maximise profits by increasing their revenue – an average Starbucks will sell approx 100 cups of coffee an hour. Staff are trained to always ask a customer if they would like a large cup, increasing sales revenue further, and by offering hot and cold snacks they again maximise their sales and their profits.

Case study

Sunil started a limo business in Leeds in 2008. He bought two stretch limos and equipped them with TV, Blu-Ray and a drinks cabinet. The rental price for an evening is £400. The variable costs (of labour, drink and cleaning) come to £160. The business has fixed costs of £4,800 per month. Before he started Leeds Limo, Sunil expected to get 30 bookings a month. In the last 6 months the figure has been closer to 15.

1. How much revenue would Leeds Limo get per month if there were 30 bookings?

2. How much profit would Leeds Limo get per month if there were 30 bookings?

3. What has been the firm's actual monthly profit over the last 6 months?

Assessment activity 3.1 (P1, P2, P3, M1)

1. Research the costs involved in starting a business of your own choice. This could be a franchise, the purchase of an existing business or an idea for a business of your own. Give a presentation to the class showing what the start-up costs and operating costs will be. Identify which of your costs are fixed and which are variable. Include an explanation about the differences between gross and net profit, using examples.

2. Produce a table to show what the different types of revenue will be for your business.

3. What are the differences between gross and net profit? Explain, using examples, what the key differences between them are.

4. Write a short report explaining how costs, revenue and profit are important to a business.

Getting started

When a business's outgoings are exactly equal to its revenues it is said to 'break even'. Neither a profit nor a loss is being made. It is important for a business to know whether it is breaking even. When you have completed this topic, you should:

- understand how break-even charts are drawn up
- understand how to interpret a break-even chart
- see the value of break-even analysis to businesses.

Key terms

Break-even point: this is the sales level at which revenue and costs are equal

Margin of safety: the comfort zone between the actual sales and the break-even point

Balancing costs with revenues

If a business's expenditure (costs) is greater than its income (revenue) it will operate at a loss. How will the owner pay the bills and the wages? How will the business survive? Ideally the revenue should be *greater* than the costs so the business is operating at a profit, but at the very least it needs to break even.

To calculate the number of sales needed to break even, this formula is used:

$$\text{Break-even point} = \frac{\text{fixed costs}}{(\text{selling price} - \text{variable costs per unit})}$$

So, in our coffee shop, if the fixed costs are £300 a week and the variable costs per cup of coffee are 70p, the **break-even point** will be:

$$\frac{£300}{(£2.20 - £0.70)}$$

$$= 200 \text{ cups of coffee}$$

(Yes – the figures do seem a bit silly when Starbucks sells 100 cups an hour, but this is only an example!)

> The point about paying the wages is very real at the time of writing. In January 2010, for the fourth time this season, the players at Portsmouth FC went unpaid on payday. The club – making heavy losses – simply didn't have the cash. In their latest published accounts (07/08) the club paid out £55 million in wages but only received £15 million in income from customers! TV income, of course, was a valuable help, but the club still made a loss of £17 million. And that was in the year they won the FA Cup!

Break-even graphs

A graph is a useful way of showing the break-even point and looking at profit and losses made for different levels of output.

Step 1

We need to calculate the fixed and variable costs at different sales levels, as shown in Figure 3.2.

Figure 3.2

Weekly sales (of cups of coffee)	0	100	200	300
Variable costs (£0.70 per cup)	0	£70	£140	£210
Fixed costs	£300	£300	£300	£300
Total costs	£300	£370	£440	£510

Step 2

We need to calculate the sales revenue at each level of sales, as shown in Figure 3.3.

Figure 3.3

Weekly sales (of cups of coffee)	0	100	200	300
Sales revenue (£2.20 a cup)	0	£220	£440	£660

Step 3

On a graph we need first to draw the fixed costs line.

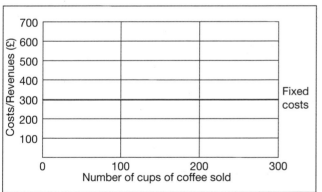

Figure 3.4 Finding the break-even point – Step 3

Step 4

We then add the total costs.

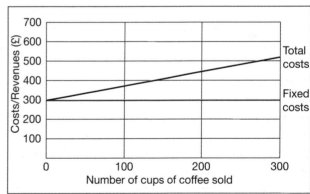

Figure 3.5 Finding the break-even point – Step 4

? Did you know?

In 2001 Amazon failed to break even, making a loss of $94 million.

Step 5

We then add the sales revenue line.

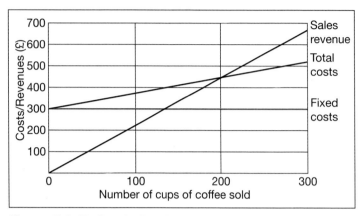

Figure 3.6 Finding the break-even point – Step 5

Step 6

The point where the sales revenue line crosses the total costs line is the break-even point. By drawing a vertical line to the x-axis we can identify the quantity sold in order to break even.

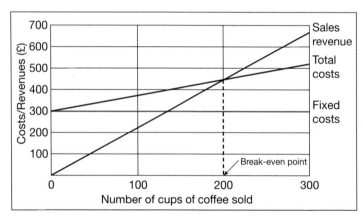

Figure 3.7 Finding the break-even point – Step 6

By analysing our graph we can identify levels of profit and loss at differing levels of output.

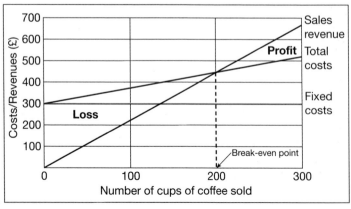

Figure 3.8 Identify levels of profit and loss

Margin of safety

The break-even point can also identify the level of risk. If the maximum output for our coffee shop is 300 cups of coffee and the break-even point is 200 cups, then the margin of safety is:

Current level of output – break-even level of output

In our case:

300 – 200

= 100

So our **margin of safety** is 100 cups of coffee, which allows for any unexpected increase in our costs so our level of risk is quite low. If our margin of safety was only 10 cups then we would be in trouble if we had an unexpected rise in costs.

Assessment activity 3.2 (P4, P5, M2)

Due to demand from the student body at your school, the canteen is hoping to offer meals sourced only from Fairtrade products.

1. Working with the school canteen manager, you are to calculate the fixed and variable costs for the new menu and then calculate the break-even point.

2. You should present your findings in a graph and include a report analysing the impact that

changing costs and revenues will have on the break-even point.

3. In your report, identify the margin of safety for the school's canteen.

If your canteen manager is unable to help you with this, then ask your teacher for list of Fairtrade products and prices.

Topic check

1 Why is it important for a manager to know the break-even point of the business?

2 Carla is opening a hairdresser's. Should she want her break-even point to be high or low? Briefly explain your answer.

3 In the first month Carla has 200 customers paying £25 each, giving her a revenue of £5,000. Her break-even number of customers is 120.

a) What is her margin of safety?

b) What monthly revenue would she be producing at her break-even point?

4 Briefly explain why a manager might be worried because the margin of safety is quite small.

Creating a cash flow forecast

Businesses crash when they cannot find the cash to pay the bills. So it is vital to manage the flows of cash into – and out of – a firm's bank account.

When you have completed this topic, you should:
- understand the purpose of a cash flow forecast
- be able to construct a cash flow forecast from data provided
- be able to interpret the figures in a cash flow forecast.

Cash flow forecasting

Very few business people have a crystal ball, and predicting the future is not easy (let's face it – if it was we would predict the lottery numbers rather than be run off our feet all day in a coffee shop...). This makes financial forecasting very important. A cash flow forecast tries to predict the inflows, outflows and balances a business will have over a 12-month period. In effect, it forecasts what the bank statement will look like over the coming months. This will allow us to identify if the business is viable and if there are times when we may need additional finance such as an overdraft.

Cash inflows

A business may have a number of sources of cash inflows:
▶ *Capital* – this is the one-off injection of cash that comes from the owners' investment into the business. When starting a new business this may be spent to buy the premises, fixtures, fittings etc.

▶ *Sales* – revenue from selling goods and services is the best form of cash as it is likely to keep coming (unlike capital and loans, which are one-offs).

▶ *Loans* – when business owners take a loan from the bank, the initial sum borrowed will be an inflow (e.g. if they borrow £5,000 then £5,000 will appear as an inflow – it will then have to be paid back, causing regular payments or outflows).

▶ *Regular and irregular inflows* – some inflows of cash into the business, such as weekly sales, will be regular whereas others, like the one-off sale of old business equipment, could be irregular.

In addition to the sums of money coming in, a business has to pay attention to the timing of the cash inflows. Knowing that cash will flow in next summer is little use to an ice cream business struggling to survive the winter. It is also very important to make sure that customers pay on time; if they delay they are starving your business of cash.

Cash outflows

A business will also have a number of cash outflows:

▶ *Purchases* – stock will have to be purchased regularly.

▶ *Loan repayments* – these will have to be made regularly (and remember, a loan has to be repaid with interest).

▶ *Wages and bills* – wages will have to be paid to staff and to yourself, along with many other bills such as electricity, water, gas, phones etc.

▶ *Regular and irregular outflows* – while the bank may insist that your loan is paid on the 1st of every month, and suppliers may insist on being paid within 30 days, other payments may be irregular, e.g. inclusion in a business directory, replacement of equipment, repairs to premises. However, irregular payments should be planned for to avoid a cash flow crisis.

Businesses also have to pay attention to the timing of their cash outflows. If a big bill has to be paid next month, the business should do all it can to delay paying out cash this month. If that means delaying supplier payments, just give them some warning so that they can prepare.

Over to you!

Which of the following are outflows or inflows for a landscape gardening business?

- purchase of plants
- monthly loan repayments for a van
- business start-up grant from The Prince's Trust
- wages
- payment from customers
- business rates
- tax
- VAT
- tax rebate

Cash balances (and constructing a cash flow forecast)

Vicky Dalton is planning to open a beauty salon and holistic therapy centre in Manchester. Vicky has found an existing beauty salon for sale for £185,000. It has a two-bedroom flat above the shop that she would rent out for additional revenue. She has savings of £50,000 and needs to borrow £140,000 from the bank. Before the bank will consider her loan application she must produce a 12-month cash flow forecast. We will work through the first 6 months.

Step 1

Identify Vicky's cash inflows. She is buying an existing business – the current owner has weekly takings of £1,500 but is only open 5 days a week. Vicky hopes that by opening 6 days a week she can increase this to £1,700. She estimates that each customer will spend approximately £25, which means she will need 68 customers a week to hit this level of sales. She intends to rent out the two-bedroom flat, and a local estate agent has agreed to market this for her at £450 a month.

Vicky's inflows are shown in Figure 3.9.

Figure 3.9 Vicky's inflows in £s

	Month 1	Month 2	Month 3	Month 4	Month 5	Month 6
Owner's capital	50,000	0	0	0	0	0
Loan	140,000	0	0	0	0	0
Sales revenue	1,700	1,700	1,700	1,700	1,700	1,700
Rental income	450	450	450	450	450	450
Total inflows	192,150	2,150	2,150	2,150	2,150	2,150

Over to you!

Complete the table showing months 7 to 12.

Step 2

Vicky must now identify her outgoings.

- ▶ In the first month she must purchase the business premises (£185,000).
- ▶ She estimates that she will need one full-time beauty therapist who will be paid an annual salary of £15,000, making her monthly wage bill £1,250.
- ▶ Her purchases each month (for beauty products and refreshments for clients) will be £100.
- ▶ Her loan repayments (she has taken out a 10-year loan of £140,000) will be £1,500.
- ▶ She will have a regular advert in the local paper for £50 a month.
- ▶ Other regular bills include utilities at £100 a month, business rates at £150 a month and telephone at £20 a month.
- ▶ In month 4 she hopes to have her own website, which will cost £500 in the first month and £30 a month every month afterwards.
- ▶ She has to pay the estate agent £50 a month to manage the let of the flat above the shop.

Excluding, for now, the purchase of premises, her outflows are shown in Figure 3.10.

Figure 3.10 Vicky's outflows in £s

	Month 1	Month 2	Month 3	Month 4	Month 5	Month 6
Wages	1,250	1,250	1,250	1,250	1,250	1,250
Purchases	100	100	100	100	100	100
Loan repayment	1,500	1,500	1,500	1,500	1,500	1,500
Advert	50	50	50	50	50	50
Utility bills	100	100	100	100	100	100
Business rates	150	150	150	150	150	150
Telephone	20	20	20	20	20	20
Website	0	0	0	500	30	30
Agency fees	50	50	50	50	50	50
Total outflows	3,228	3,228	3,228	3,728	3,258	3,258

Over to you!

Complete the outflows for Vicky showing months 7 to 12.

Step 3

Vicky needs to know how her outgoings compare with her incomings, and how much cash she has available to her each month. She needs to calculate her net cash flow each month (see Figure 3.11).

▶ In the first month she must purchase the business premises (£185,000).

Net cash flow = total inflows – total outflows

▶ And her closing balance each month:

Closing bank balance = opening bank balance + net cash flow

Over to you!

Complete the table for months 7 to 12.

Figure 3.11 Vicky's monthly cash flow

	Month 1 (£)	Month 2 (£)	Month 3 (£)	Month 4 (£)	Month 5 (£)	Month 6 (£)
Opening balance	0	3,922	2,844	1,766	188	–920
INCOME PER PERIOD:						
Owner's capital	50,000	0	0	0	0	0
Loan	140,000	0	0	0	0	0
Sales revenue	1,700	1,700	1,700	1,700	1,700	1,700
Rental income	450	450	450	450	450	450
Total inflows	192,150	2,150	2,150	2,150	2,150	2,150
EXPENDITURE PER PERIOD:						
Purchase of premises	185,000					
Wages	1,250	1,250	1,250	1,250	1,250	1,250
Purchases	100	100	100	100	100	100
Loan repayment	1,500	1,500	1,500	1,500	1,500	1,500
Advert	50	50	50	50	50	50
Utility bills	100	100	100	100	100	100
Business rates	150	150	150	150	150	150
Telephone	20	20	20	20	20	20
Website	0	0	0	500	30	30
Agency fees	50	50	50	50	50	50
Total outflows	188,228	3,228	3,228	3,728	3,258	3,258
NET CASH FLOW (TOTAL INFLOW – TOTAL OUTFLOW)	3,922	–1,078	–1,078	–1,578	–1,108	–1,108
Closing bank balance (opening bank balance + net cash flow)	3,922	2,844	1,766	188	–920	–2,028

Conclusion and evaluation

Good financial management begins with thorough research into the costs involved in setting up the business and ensuring that there are sufficient inflows to cover outflows. By calculating the break-even point, a business can assess if an idea is viable before going ahead, and the margin of safety can act like a safety net to protect against unexpected cost increases. A business needs to plan for unexpected costs and ensure that it has sufficient funds to cover unexpected costs such as repairs. Nothing is ever guaranteed in business, but one thing is for sure and that is, fail to plan a business's finances and you will plan to fail.

Over to you!

Based on the cash flow forecast, would you lend Vicky the money she needs to get started? Why? What advice would you give her to improve her position before she approaches the bank?

Did you know?

In 2008, 4,000 small businesses collapsed due to late payments impacting their cash flow. In many cases the bank would not extend their overdraft, forcing them to close.

Case study

Sian started 'Shaking Stevens' in the depths of the 2009 recession. The first few months were tough, as customers were not interested in £3 milkshakes. Three months' in, she had only enjoyed one week above her break-even point. Then sales began to pick up. After 8 months the business was making a profit of £3,000 to £5,000 a month and the future looked secure. Then her bank demanded the first repayment on the firm's bank loan. She hadn't noticed that this sum of £10,000 was coming up, and didn't have the cash. When the bill was not paid, the bank withdrew her overdraft! 'Shaking Stevens' only survived because her parents paid the bank the £10,000 plus £2,000 of extra bank charges.

1. Sian learnt the hard way the importance of good cash flow. Why is cash flow important for business survival?

2. Why may it take time for new businesses like Sian's to reach their break-even point?

Assessment activity 3.3 (P6, M3)

Margaret and Simon Concannon hope to quit the rat race and operate a ski chalet in France hosting small groups during the winter ski season. In the summer months they will rest and holiday. They have asked you to produce a 12-month cash flow forecast. Produce a report highlighting any irregular cash inflows and outflows and give recommendations about how these can be managed.

Assessment activity 3.4 (D1)

Produce a leaflet for small business owners explaining the importance of cash flow and break even for the effective management of business finance.

Topic check

1 Direct costs are so called

  a) because the business has to pay these directly to their suppliers.

  b) because they have a direct impact on profitability.

  c) because they have a direct link to the firms products and services.

  d) because they are very important unlike indirect costs.

2 Why are fixed costs so called?

  a) Because they are fixed for 2 to 3 years.

  b) Because they have a fixed rate of interest with the bank.

  c) Because they do not change according to how many sales are made.

3 True or false?

  a) Tax is paid on gross profit.

  b) The margin of safety must be at least 200.

  c) The bank will expect a new firm to break even in the first month of trading.

  d) A bank will often want to see a year's cash flow forecast before agreeing to a loan.

Assessment summary

The overall grade you achieve for this unit depends on how well you meet the grading criteria set out at the start of the chapter (see page 49). You must complete:

- all of the P criteria to achieve a **pass** grade
- all of the P and the M criteria to achieve a **merit** grade
- all of the P, M and D criteria to achieve a **distinction** grade.

Your tutor will assess the assessment activities that you complete for this unit. The work you produce should provide evidence which demonstrates that you have achieved each of the assessment criteria. The table below identifies what you need to demonstrate to meet each of the pass, merit and distinction criteria for this unit. You should always check and self-assess your work before you submit your assignments for marking.

Remember that you MUST provide evidence for all of the P criteria to pass the unit.

Grading criteria	You need to demonstrate that you can:	Do you have the evidence?
P1	Identify the difference between start-up and operating costs, variable and fixed costs	
P2	Identify the different types of revenue	
P3	Outline the differences between gross and net profit	
P4	Calculate break even using given data to show the level at which income equals expenditure	
P5	Present the break even as an annotated graph showing break even	
P6	Prepare an annual cash flow using monthly data	
M1	Explain the importance of costs, revenue and profit for a business organisation	
M2	Demonstrate the impact of changing cost and revenue data on the break-even point of a selected business	
M3	Analyse the implications of regular and irregular cash inflows and outflows for a business organisation	
D1	Evaluate the importance of cash flow and break even for the effective management of business finance	

Always ask your tutor to explain any assignment tasks or assessment criteria that you don't understand fully. Being clear about the task before you begin gives you the best chance of succeeding. Good luck with your Unit 3 assessment work!

4 People in organisations

Unit outline

Having the right staff in the right place doing the right thing at the right time can make or break a business. There are so many different roles and functions within a business that the people in charge need to have some way of ensuring that they hire the people with the skills and attributes that the business needs. Equally important though, is that you don't end up doing a job that you don't like or are not suited for. Understanding the job roles and functions within a business will help you decide what you might want to do in the future.

Learning outcomes

1 **Know about job roles and their functions in organisations.**
2 **Be able to produce documentation for specific job roles.**
3 **Be able to prepare for employment and plan career development.**

Grading guide

To achieve a **pass**, you must show you can:	To achieve a **merit**, you must show you can:	To achieve a **distinction**, you must show you can:
P1 Describe the main job roles and functions in an organisation	**M1** Compare the main job roles and functions in two organisations and explain how they may differ in different organisational structures	**D1** Analyse the relationship between job roles, functions and an organisation's structure, using appropriate illustrative examples
P2 Identify different organisational structures used within business organisations		
P3 Produce a basic job description and person specification for a specific job	**M2** Produce a detailed and relevant job description and person specification for a specific job	**D2** Analyse how effective recruitment contributes to an organisation's success
P4 Complete an application and interview for a specific job		
P5 Match current knowledge and skills to possible job opportunities using appropriate sources of information and advice		
P6 Produce a personal career development plan		

Job roles and functions in organisations

Getting started

Organisations such as Tesco plc are complex, employing hundreds of thousands of staff. There is a huge range of job roles in each of the many different business functions. In companies such as this, job roles are tightly defined, such as Market Research Manager and Clubcard Insight Manager.

When you have completed this topic, you should:

- understand the meaning and importance of job roles
- see how job roles exist within different business functions.

Key terms

Hierarchy: the layers of management within an organisation; it is often drawn as a chart that looks like a pyramid, with the boss on the top

Job function: the tasks involved in the job

Job title: the name given to a particular job role, e.g. store manager

Job roles and functions

Everyone who works will have a particular job to do, and this will be reflected in their **job title**. However, if you ask someone who works for a small business what job role they have they will probably be able to give you a list as long as your arm! People who work for small businesses are expected to perform lots of different tasks, as and when necessary. This could even include doing the vacuuming at the end of the day. By contrast, someone who works for a large business such as Tesco will have a clear and quite limited role within the organisation.

If we take the example of a supermarket, there are clearly defined roles. Take a look at http://www.tesco-careers.com/home/you and you will be amazed at the variety of different job roles available (Tesco has more than 250,000 employees!). Each job is different from the others, usually in relation to the tasks carried out or the level of responsibility the person has (where they are in the **hierarchy**).

There is a great variety of job roles available in a supermarket.

The tasks carried out

Tesco distinguishes between job functions in terms of what staff actually do. For example, within a store, there may be a Fresh Food Supervisor, a Tills Supervisor, a Customer Services Assistant and so on. The **job function** is the task itself, such as working on the fish counter.

The level of responsibility

Tesco distinguishes job roles in terms of seniority. You can be promoted to a more challenging and senior job role. The main job roles are described below.

▶ *Directors* are responsible for the medium- to long-term aims, objectives and plans for the business as a whole. They can be held to account by the shareholders if things go wrong. The Board of Directors must, together, decide on key policies, such as whether to put more cash into developing Tesco China or Tesco USA. They then approve strategies (plans) put forward to achieve the goals they have set.

▶ *Managers* are responsible for:

- setting targets for junior staff, and for achieving the targets the directors have set for them

- making sure they have enough staff and money to achieve the targets the directors have set

- making sure that suitable staff are recruited and trained (and, occasionally, dismissed)

- making sure that work is allocated effectively to staff, so no one is overworking while others are sitting around

- motivating staff to give their best to the business

- making decisions when needed and planning ahead for how the decisions are to be put into practice

- solving day-to-day problems

- ensuring that the right information is communicated to the right people.

> **? Did you know?**
>
> A manager at Tesco can earn between £25,000 and £95,000 per year!

▶ *Supervisors/team leaders* are the staff directed by the managers to make sure that shop floor staff are working effectively. They are likely to check that staff know their work rota (the timing of their next shift) and make enquiries about any absentees (people who don't turn up for work). If staff are sick or on holiday, the supervisor will re-allocate work so that all the jobs get done. Effective supervisors will build a strong relationship with their 'team'. This will motivate the team members while they are at work and is likely to reduce the amount of absenteeism.

▶ *Operatives* carry out key functions but have no responsibility for other staff. Their jobs might be critical (such as a train driver) or be important yet a little dull, such as a supermarket checkout operator.

▶ *Support staff* are employed to provide administrative and clerical support to others. Such staff may be crucial to the smooth running of the business, such as the receptionist at a doctor's surgery who makes all the appointments.

Case study

On Christmas Day 2009 a terrorist nearly blew up a plane as it was about to land at Detroit airport. Within a day or two it emerged that the terrorist had been on an 'At risk' list in America and Britain – and that the man's father had contacted the American embassy to warn that his son had developed an extreme anti-Americanism. The CIA (the US intelligence service) was informed, but even though the man boarded a plane for America under his real name, he was not stopped. Poor communication meant that the right people were unaware of the father's warning. Luckily, only the terrorist was injured when the explosives failed.

1. Comment on the quality of management within the CIA.

2. Why may communication be difficult in large organisations?

Summary

A person's job function is what they do every day, such as planning the firm's marketing and advertising. The job role gives an idea of the person's seniority within the organisation, such as the Marketing Manager.

Organisational structures

Supermarket chain Morrisons has 125,000 staff in the UK. Imagine how difficult it must be to know who's to blame if a serious mistake is made, or who to praise if there's a great success. An organisational chart can help, as it:

▶ shows who is responsible for what and to whom throughout the business

▶ identifies people's different job roles – who does what job and who is in charge

▶ shows the line of responsibility that goes from the top of the business to the bottom, in every single department.

Small businesses are unlikely to need an organisational chart as they tend to have the boss at the top and everybody else underneath. Also, all of the staff may be working in the same room, so they can make sure that everyone knows what's going on.

Although every large business has an organisational chart to show its organisational structure, there are different types of structure that can be used.

? Did you know?

Britain's Top 5 employers are:

NHS	1,300,000
Ministry of Defence	400,000
HSBC	253,000
Tesco	250,000
Sainsbury's	150,000

Source: www.PersonnelToday.com

Hierarchical structures

The term 'hierarchy' literally means the way people are ranked one above another. A hierarchical organisation structure means that the further up the hierarchy somebody is, the more important they are, with more responsibility and power (and pay!). An example of a hierarchical structure in a production company is shown in Figure 4.1.

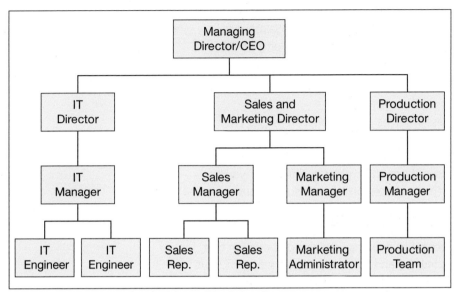

Figure 4.1 An example of a hierarchical structure

Flat structures

An organisation that does not have many layers to its hierarchy is called a 'flat structure'. Small businesses do not have many levels to their hierarchy. As they expand, it becomes necessary to take on managers to organise the increasing workforce, so a new layer appears in the hierarchy. If more and more layers are added, it becomes a 'tall structure'.

Advantages of a flat structure	Disadvantages of a flat structure
• Fewer managers are needed, which saves money. • Managers have to give more responsibility to the workers, which leads to more job satisfaction for the workers. • Communication between staff and management is faster and more efficient because there are fewer layers. • Fewer management layers usually leads to faster decision-making.	• Each manager is responsible for more people. • Managers have to rely on their subordinate staff much more to work efficiently and safely. • Managers may lose control of subordinates if there is too wide a span of control for each manager. • It can lead to overwork and stress. • There are fewer opportunities for promotion.

Matrix structures

A matrix structure is used when there are lots of project teams working within one organisation. Matrix structures establish project groups that are drawn from various sections of the business. As the focus is on the task in hand, the worker's position in the hierarchy becomes less important. For example, if Sainsbury's plans to open shops in China, a checkout operator who speaks Chinese and knows Beijing may become more important than any other checkout operator. A potential problem with matrix structures is that people may end up with more than one boss. For example, the checkout operator will still work at the local Sainsbury's 4 days a week, but may become more involved with and make a priority of the China project, which will naturally make the local store manager unhappy.

Other structures

▶ It is possible to organise a business in terms of functional areas (see Chapter 2, Topic 2.2), giving it a *functional structure*. There are some functional areas that are common to most business (e.g. finance, administration and marketing), while others will be specific to the type of business (e.g. your school or college will have departments based on subjects such as Business Studies, English and Maths).

▶ Organisations may have a *divisional structure* if they are organised into separate divisions. For example, British Telecom has divisions within its organisation that deal with private customers (you and me) and business customers.

Summary

Big organisations are so complicated that it is helpful to have a diagram that sets out who is responsible to whom. However, each business does things differently, so the key is to find out exactly how a specific company is organised and why, and to ask whether the existing structure really works.

 Assessment activity 4.1 (P1, P2, M1, D1)

Choose a small- to medium-sized business and a large business that you are interested in.

1. Produce an organisation chart for each business to show the way the different functions or departments are organised.

2. Produce a set of notes or diagrams for a new member of staff to explain the way one of the businesses is organised.

3. It may be useful to a new member of staff to understand why the business has been organised in particular way. You are to provide a written explanation to the new employee of why the structure is good for that particular business, and how working for that business would be different from working for the other.

4. Write a diary of a typical day for two employees at each of your chosen businesses. Explain the different tasks that each person performs. Analyse the function for each of the employees, and compare and contrast what they do. Explain why each task is important to the way the business is run.

Topic check

1 If there are many layers in a hierarchy, the organisation is known as:

   a) tall

   b) flat.

2 Redrow (the building firm) is building many housing developments all around the UK. Which organisational structure would be best for Redrow?

   a) matrix

   b) hierarchical

   c) divisional

3 The person within an organisation who reports to the shareholders is:

   a) an operative

   b) a director

   c) a manager

   d) support staff.

Producing documentation for specific job roles

Getting started

Every employee is entitled to a contract of employment that sets out what is expected from the person, and what they must give in return. The contract will be based on the job description, which is therefore an important document.

When you have completed this topic, you should:

- know the contents of a person specification and a job description
- understand the importance of writing these documents with care.

Key terms

Body language: the impressions given to others by the way you use your body, e.g. bored or respectful or angry (or sexy)

Covering letter: sent to an employer with a CV, the covering letter provides a brief, polite introduction ('this is me')

Curriculum vitae (CV): a document setting out an individual's achievements and hopes

Job description: a detailed breakdown of what the job consists of

Letter of application: similar to a covering letter, but usually longer, as it may not be accompanied by a CV

Person specification: the qualifications, experience and qualities required from the job applicant

Proof read: thoroughly check a document through for accuracy, spelling etc.

Shortlist: the names of the job applicants who have passed the initial selection process

Drawing up a job description

Once a business has organised how it is to be structured and knows what job roles need filling, it needs to plan each job in detail. Although not a legal requirement, most large firms produce **job descriptions** which summarise all the facts about a job and its functions. This needs to be done when a job vacancy has arisen and before the job is advertised, so that potential candidates have all the information they need about the job. It normally includes details of the job title, hours of work, salary and the precise duties involved. Job descriptions are helpful because they:

- ▶ make expectations clear to a potential employee
- ▶ give candidates a clear description of the role
- ▶ provide a structure and discipline for the company to understand where one job ends and another begins
- ▶ allow wages and salaries to be structured fairly and logically
- ▶ provide important reference points for training and development.

There are no defined methods by which a business will draw up a job description. It is almost impossible to write a job description that includes every task that a person might have to do throughout the course of their employment, so it normally includes a phrase at the end implying, 'and anything else we may ask you to do'!

There are certain steps a business can take that will help to make the job description as accurate as possible. Existing job holders may be asked to provide a description of the job they do. In larger organisations the Human Resources department may be asked to set out what the job *should* involve.

Contents of a job description

There are common elements that are contained in all job descriptions:

- ▶ job title
- ▶ location
- ▶ a description of the organisation's business
- ▶ purpose of the job
- ▶ main tasks
- ▶ standards required
- ▶ pay and benefits
- ▶ promotion prospects
- ▶ lines of reporting, i.e. who the employee is answerable to.

NCO Retail Ltd

Job description

Business:	NCO is a mail order company based in Preston. Approximately 350 staff are employed at the Head Office.
Department:	Customer Service Office, Preston
Job title:	Query Handler
Hours of work:	37.5 per week, 9 a.m. – 5.30 p.m. Monday to Friday
Holidays:	25 days per year plus Bank Holidays
Salary scale:	£8,500–£10,500
Benefits:	10% discount on any NCO products
Responsible to:	Customer Service Supervisor
Responsible for:	N/A
Job Purpose:	To deal with customer queries and complaints. To respond by telephone and email to any online queries raised and find solutions. To be available to handle queries passed on by Customer Service Clerks. Liaise with depot to arrange collection and re-order of faulty products.

Duties and responsibilities

1. Receive telephone calls, deal with queries and take messages for other team members as necessary.
2. Make telephone calls to customers and offer sensible solutions to queries raised.
3. Organise the collection of faulty products and distribution of replacements.
4. Monitor query database and be proactive in dealing with queries.
5. Ensure all customer email enquires receive prompt responses, referring these to a more senior member of staff if a solution cannot be found.
6. Attend any training course or team events that may be considered appropriate by the Customer Service Supervisor.
7. General correspondence and administration duties as required.
8. Maintain confidentiality about queries and customer information at all times and be aware that breach of this could lead to instant dismissal.

Figure 4.2 Sample job description

Summary

Job descriptions give full details about what the job involves. They can look scary because employers pack so much detail into them. It is worth asking the people who work there (or your interviewer, if you apply for the job) which features of the job description are the key ones.

Drawing up a person specification

A job description describes what the job is. A **person specification** describes who would be the perfect person for the job. It is an extension of the job description. The person specification lists the *essential* and *desirable* qualities of the ideal employee, such as qualifications, aptitudes (e.g. numeracy), interests (e.g. social activities), personal qualities (e.g. leadership qualities), circumstances (e.g. whether the person is able to move to different locations) and competency profiles (e.g. what the candidate should be able to do).

Person specifications have to be written carefully to ensure that the criteria stated do not break discrimination laws. For example, many employers might want to advertise for: 'young, good-looking staff' but that would contravene the Equality and Human Rights Act.

Writing a person specification is good for businesses for a variety of reasons:

▶ It helps them focus on the type of person they really want for the job.

▶ It makes it easier to **shortlist** potential interview candidates, as there are criteria by which to measure the applicants.

NCO Retail Ltd

Person specification

Department:	Customer Service Office, Preston	
Job title:	Query Handler	
Vacancy no:	342	

	Essential	**Desirable**
Qualifications	5 GCSEs grade C or above, including English and Maths	ICT-related qualification
Experience	Experience of office work and dealing with customers and customer service	Previous experience of office administration
Skills	Excellent verbal communication Word Processing (35 wpm)	Use of Microsoft Office
Personal attributes	Self-motivated Independent thinker Professional appearance	Friendly and personable Team worker

Figure 4.3 Sample person specification

Summary

The person specification can be a bit of a wish list. Take seriously what the business says is 'essential' from the applicant. Be less worried by what the employer calls 'desirable'. If the job is about dealing with people and you have a great personality, most employers will overlook items that are lacking from your CV.

Getting the job you want

Applying for a job for the first time is a daunting experience. There will probably be more steps if you are applying for a job in a large firm such as Virgin than if you are applying for a job in your local bookshop.

When you are looking for a job, the job description and person specification are the documents that *you* receive to help you decide whether you want the job. They also help you prepare for the interview. If you are asked to attend an interview, you will be asked questions to see how well you fit in with the requirements of the job description and person specification.

> **? Did you know?**
>
> Your CV is your chance to showcase your skills and experience to potential employers.

Curriculum vitae (CV)

So you have seen a job you want. What next? Some jobs in smaller firms will ask you to send in your **curriculum vitae (CV)**. This can be loosely translated as 'course of life' and is a document that outlines your work experience, achievements and qualifications. Firms will use this to assess your experience against that outlined in the person specification. It is important that you always tell the truth in your CV as if your new employer finds out that you have not, you could lose your job! A CV should look professional – it should be word processed and divided into clear sections. The careers advice service (http://careersadvice.direct.gov.uk/helpwithyourcareer/writecv/cvadvice.htm) recommends that you include the following in your CV.

Your personal details

You should include your name, address and contact details. It's up to you whether you include your age, marital status and nationality – recruiters should be able to make a decision about your skills and abilities without this information.

Your personal profile

This should summarise your:

▶ skills and qualities

▶ work background and achievements

▶ career aims.

It should only be a few lines and must grab the reader's attention. For example, if the job involves working with people, you could say you're a good team worker and an effective communicator. Be brief – you can highlight examples of your skills in later sections.

Employment history and work experience

If you've been working for a while, you could put your employment history first; if you're younger and don't have much work experience, you might like to highlight your education and training. In this section you should start with your present or most recent job and work backwards. You should include employer details, the dates you worked for them, job title and your main duties. Provide more detail on the relevant jobs you've had and give examples of the skills you used and what you achieved. Use bullet-pointed lists. Try to relate your skills and experience to the job description or what you think the employer is looking for. Also include any relevant temporary work and volunteering experience. Avoid unexplained gaps in your employment history. If you had time out travelling, job seeking, volunteering or caring for a relative, include this along with details of what you've learnt.

Education and training

Start with your most recent qualifications and work back to the ones you got at school. Using bullet points or a table, include:

▶ the university, college or school you went to

▶ the dates the qualifications were awarded and any grades

▶ any work-related courses, if they're relevant.

Interests and achievements

You can include hobbies, interests and achievements that are relevant to the job. For example, if you're involved in any clubs or societies this can show that you enjoy meeting new people. Try to avoid putting activities like cooking or reading, as these activities are too general and widespread to be of interest to an employer. Make them specific and interesting!

Climbing is an interesting activity that would be worth including on your CV.

Additional information

You can include this section if you need to add anything else that's relevant, such as explaining that a gap in your employment history was due to travel or family reasons. You could also include other relevant skills here, such as if you have a driving licence or can speak any foreign languages.

References

At least one referee should be work-related or, if you haven't worked for a while, some other responsible person who has known you for quite a while. You can list the contact details of your referees on your CV or just put 'references available on request'. If you decide to include their details you could also state the relationship of each referee to you, for example 'John Turner, Line Manager'.

Covering letters and letters of application

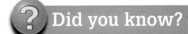

When sending in a CV it is normal to send in a **covering letter** or **letter of application**. These should be word processed and you should use standard professional business letter layout. Make sure you use the spell checker, and then **proof read** your letter carefully to check that everything is correct.

> **? Did you know?**
> Your covering letter is not your autobiography! The main bulk of your experience and skills should be listed in your CV.

A covering letter explains briefly why you are sending your CV. A letter of application is a letter that justifies your application. It is an opportunity for you to sell yourself and highlight why you would be the best candidate for the job. If you see the phrase 'apply in writing' in a job advert then the business is asking you to write a letter of application and, if requested, to attach your CV.

You should keep your letter of application short – no more than two sides of A4. You should tailor your letter to suit the job description and person specification of each job you apply for – don't assume one letter will suit every job application. Here are some tips on how to structure your letter.

▶ *Paragraph 1* should say what job you are applying for and state where you saw the job advertised.

▶ *Paragraph 2* should start with an introduction about you and your background, and should state here whether you have enclosed your CV. If you have not then you must go into more detail about your skills, qualifications and any relevant work experience.

▶ *Paragraph 3* should explain why you want the job and why you are the best person for the job. You should talk about why you want to work for that particular organisation and what you can offer them. Use the person specification to find out what the essential and desirable criteria are; highlight how you meet these criteria.

▶ *Paragraph 4* is your closing paragraph. Thank the employer for considering your application and state that you are looking forward to having the chance to tell them more about you at interview!

Some businesses will not want you to send in your CV, but it is a good idea to have one prepared as it will help you if you are asked to complete an application form. It is quite common now for companies to ask applicants to complete application forms online. If so, type your responses in a word processing package first, so you can use the spell check. Check your answers carefully before you submit the application form.

If it is a paper application form, use black ink and block capitals. Make sure that you read and follow the instructions correctly. Take your time and complete the form carefully. It is a good idea to take a photocopy of the form and practise filling it in before completing the final version.

1. PERSONAL DETAILS (Please use capital letters)	
Title: Address: Date of birth: Email: National Insurance No:	Postcode: Home telephone no: Daytime contact no:

2. CURRENT EMPLOYMENT

Employer name and address	Job title and salary	Reasons for leaving

3. WORK EXPERIENCE

Dates	Employer name and address	Job title and responsibilities	Reasons for leaving

4. EDUCATION, TRAINING AND DEVELOPMENT

College, university, or training establishment attended	Qualification or course details	Date

5. PERSONAL STATEMENT – Continue on additional sheets if necessary

Please provide details of your experience, including any unpaid work and outside interests that are relevant to the job. Give examples where appropiate. Attach additional sheets securely and ensure they are marked clearly with your name and details of the posts for which you have applied.

6. MEDICAL DETAILS – Details of any sickness absence in the last two years

Do you have or have you had any illness or medical condition which may prevent you from attending work regularly in future?　　　　　　　　　　Yes　　　　No

If you have answered 'yes' please provide details here:

Number of working days lost in the past two years:

7. REFERENCES – one must be your current or most recent employer

Name: Address: Email: Telephone No: Relationship to Applicant:	Name: Address: Email: Telephone No: Relationship to Applicant:

8. CRIMINAL CONVICTIONS

The Rehabiliation of Offenders Act 1974 requires applicants to give details of any convictions that are not spent. Failure to disclose such convictions could result in disciplinary action or dismissal.

Do you have any previous convictions?

If yes, please detail offence(s) including date(s) and sentence(s)

If you have previously applied for a Criminal Records Bureau Disclosure please state the date of issue of your Disclosure certificate.

9. DECLARATION

I certify that the information contained on this application form is accurate and true. I give my consent to the processing, transfer and disclosure of all information submitted by me during the recruitment process and throughout any subsequent periods of employment for pre-employment checks, equal opportunities monitoring payroll operations and training. (Data Protection Act 1986)

Signed:　　　　　　　　　　　　　　　　Date:

Figure 4.4 Sample application form

Over to you!

Choose two reasons why an application form can be a better way to ask candidates to apply for a job than with a letter of application.

1. Because the business can make an easy comparison between applicants.

2. Because it is quicker than reading lots of letters.

3. Because the application form is easier to read.

4. Because a letter of application may be hand written.

The interview

If you are invited to an interview you will probably find this the most challenging part of the application process – there's no doubt that most people find them nerve racking. If possible, ask your Careers Department to give you a mock interview beforehand. There are different ways that interviews can be carried out, depending on the size of the organisation and the job applied for. It could be conducted by:

- ▶ a member of the Human Resource department
- ▶ the manager of the department or business in which you will be working (if it is a small firm)
- ▶ the Human Resource department first, and then another interview with a manager or director.
- ▶ a panel (a group of people).

The interview is a chance for the employer to meet you and decide whether you would be suitable for the job, and whether the information you gave on the application form was correct.

Preparing for interview

Let's look at the example of Ravinder, who applied for a job at his local electrical superstore. He was called for interview and now he had to prepare.

Research

Ravinder's interview was with a national firm, so he went on the internet and found out as much as he could about:

- ▶ its general organisational structure
- ▶ its history
- ▶ career paths
- ▶ the current state of industry
- ▶ the location of the interview
- ▶ the size of the organisation
- ▶ the number of employees
- ▶ how long the company has been operating
- ▶ who are the major competitors of this company.

Having this information ensured that Ravinder knew as much about the business as possible, so he could have a better insight into it.

Question preparation/anticipation

At the end of an interview a candidate will have a chance to ask questions about the job and the business. As he had done his research, Ravinder was able to prepare some questions in advance. The research also meant he was better prepared for any questions they might ask him at the interview. Ravinder used the job description and person specification to make sure he had examples of when and where he had illustrated the qualities they were looking for.

Don't be late!

Arriving on time for an interview is essential. Included in the criteria for Ravinder's job were good organisational skills and punctuality. He knew that arriving late would show that he didn't have these attributes. He found out how long it would take him to get to the interview and added an extra half hour to this to make sure that he arrived in plenty of time.

What to wear

Ravinder noticed that on the job description it stated that he would have to look smart and professional, so he wore a suit and made sure that he looked well groomed and clean. Ravinder knew that things like chewing gum and smelling of cigarettes would not be looked upon favourably by interviewers so, although he likes to chew gum, he made sure that didn't in the interview.

 Did you know?

Getting your appearance right is very important in making a good impression. Fifty per cent of another person's perception of you is based on your appearance. It is recommended that you make sure you are wearing clean shoes – a person can tell a lot about you by looking at your shoes!

Be confident

Even though you might not feel it, looking confident is a must. Ravinder was very conscious of his **body language** and voice. He knew he had to give a good impression of himself the minute he walked into the room and had heard the saying, 'You never get a second chance to make a first impression!' Part of Ravinder's interview preparations involved brushing up on his knowledge and application of body language.

How to appear confident and succeed in an interview

1. Walk confidently, with your head up and shoulders back.

2. Have a pleasant facial expression.

3. Hold direct, steady eye contact, but remember that it is not a staring competition!

4. Have a firm handshake.

5. Sit comfortably and calmly in the chair, with your shoulders upright and your upper body relaxed (don't tap you fingers or bounce your knee!).

6. Rest your hands on the arms of the chair or in your lap.

7. Add emphasis to important answers by leaning forward slightly.

8. Speak clearly and take your time to answer questions calmly.

9. Remember to be polite and not to use slang words.

10. Turn off your mobile phone!

Ravinder was lucky enough to be offered the job, but whether you get a job offer or not, remember to thank the interviewers for their time and the opportunity. You never know, if another job comes up they may remember you and invite you back.

Summary

Getting a job requires a huge amount of preparation and effort. The time to start is right away. Do more; watch less. Playing sport, getting involved in the school play, going on the school trip to China – all of these will demonstrate that you are a person who wants to be involved in life, rather than just sitting back.

Assessment activity 4.2 (P3, P4, M2, D2)

1. Conduct some research and find a job advertisement from any source.

2. Prepare a job description for your chosen job.

3. Identify the essential and desirable criteria you believe will be required for the job.

4. Prepare a person specification for the job.

5. Design an application form for the job, and then complete it.

6. Write or update your CV and attach it to the application form.

7. Write a covering letter applying for the position. Make sure you give clear reasons why you would be good at the job and why you should be invited to an interview.

8. Prepare answers to some of the questions that you may be asked at interview

9. Take part in an interview. Your teacher will complete a witness statement of what happened and will give you written feedback on how well you did.

Topic check

1 The document that is used by businesses that outlines what a job entails is called a:

   a) job specification   b) job description.

2 June, the local newsagent, needs a counter assistant. What documents does she need to prepare?

   a) person specification   c) job description

   b) job title   d) personal attribute

3 Which of the following is an example of a personal attribute?

   a) persistent   c) 2 years' work experience

   b) maths GCSE   d) happy

4 When applying for a job, which characteristics are the more important?

   a) essential   b) desirable

5 What does CV stand for?

   a) character vita   c) cover of life

   b) curriculum vitae

6 Identify the three *most* important features of a letter of application.

   a) It should be short.   c) It should contain no spelling mistakes.

   b) It should be word processed.   d) It should sell you.

7 Identify two indications of confidence through body language.

   a) fidgeting   c) firm handshake

   b) direct eye contact   d) slouching

Preparing for employment

▶ Getting started

Within a year or two you will get your first full-time job. What do you need to know to be prepared for employment?

When you have completed this topic, you should:

- understand in more detail some of the issues that affect people at work
- understand the role of workplace induction and training.

Key terms

Flexible working: jobs that are not permanent and full time, e.g. sharing a job 50/50 with another person

Job security: a feeling of confidence that the income received from your job today will continue for the foreseeable future

Personal audit: checking that your skills and qualifications match what employers want

Personal audit

Some people apply for lots of jobs and can't understand why they are not successful. One way to improve your chances of success is to plan your job search carefully. Being self-aware will help to ensure that any career decisions you make are the right ones for you.

To increase your understanding of yourself you can complete a **personal audit**. This is a way of checking whether you have what employers want. Completing a personal audit will help you identify the skills and qualifications you have that employers may be looking for. You can use the results of your audit to plan how to improve your employability. For example, volunteering to join your school's Young Enterprise Programme could provide you with 'Evidence of working in teams'. Completing an audit will help you see whether you meet the criteria outlined in person specifications. It will also help you complete your CV and allow you to spot job opportunities for yourself.

Over to you!

Why is completing a personal audit of benefit to somebody already in a job?

1. Because in order to progress in their career they need to self-reflect.
2. Because they can see what they know.
3. Because it provides them with opportunities they can pursue.

What type of job to go for

There are many different types of employment. For example, Sophie works part time as a waitress, one night during the week and on Friday and Saturday nights. In the school holidays she works extra hours covering for staff who are on holiday. Richelle works on a seasonal basis at Pleasure Beach Blackpool. The job lasts from Easter to September. Both of these are examples of flexible employment. Businesses offer **flexible working** because it allows them to employ more or fewer staff to match the number of customers. In this way businesses can lower their overall wage bills.

Organisations such as Pleasure Beach Blackpool offer a range of types of employment, including:

▶ *Permanent staff* – these are staff who are employed to work from a given start date over 52 weeks a year (with holidays, of course!). These staff can continue to work for the business until they retire, so they have **job security**. They will also benefit from 4–6 weeks of paid holiday each year, they will be paid if they are off sick and may be able to join a company pension scheme.

▶ *Seasonal staff* – these are staff who are employed at particular times of the year, e.g. for the summer season.

▶ *Full-time staff* – full-time workers are generally considered to be people who are employed for between 35 and 42 hours per week. An employee may be full time but seasonal, e.g. receiving a full-time income, but only for 6 months of the year.

▶ *Part-time staff* – the general definition of a part-time worker is someone who is employed for up to 20 hours each week. Businesses may employ part-time staff working a range of different hours, e.g. some work 20 hours and some work 10. Some part-timers may see it as a stepping-stone to getting a full-time post; others, such as young parents, may enjoy the flexibility of part-time work.

Personal Audit

Qualifications	**Grade**
GCSE Maths	
GCSE English Language	
GCSE English Literature	
GCSE Science	
GCSE	
GCSE	

Skills

Oral communication

Give examples of when you have communicated orally. e.g. presentations, student council, work experience

IT skills

Which programs can you use on the computer?

Organisational skills

How organised are you? Give examples of when you have been organised.

Problem solving

How good are you are solving problems? Give an example.

Time management

Can you meet a deadline? Give an example.

Work independently

Can you work on your own? Give an example.

Working in a team

Give examples of when you have worked in a team.

For each skill listed above, score yourself from 1 to 5:

1. I am very good at this skill.

2. I am good but I could improve.

3. I need to improve this skill.

4. Developing this skill would mean hard work.

5. I have no experience of ever using this skill.

Figure 4.5 Personal audit

▶ *Paid work* – this refers to work that pays employees a regular salary, as will have been outlined in their contract of employment.

▶ *Voluntary work* – this is work that people do for no wages. They will be giving their time for free. This is quite common for charity shop workers, for example, or someone helping in a church. At the height of the summer, staff from the St John's Ambulance brigade come to help at Blackpool Pleasure Beach. They are voluntary workers.

Case study

For the last two years Graham has been in job heaven. In the winter he works as a skiing instructor in the French Alps. In the summer he teaches water skiing in Thailand. Neither job pays particularly well, but he gets free accommodation and free meals! So he is able to save while 'working' at things he loves doing. For as long as he is young and single he hopes to carry on with these two seasonal jobs.

1. Some people would say that their goal from working is to make as much money as possible. Why is Graham apparently uninterested in making money?

2. Name one job that you think you may be able to do in future. Is it only money that makes you like the idea of that job?

Getting the right advice and information

There is a huge number of different jobs and careers out there to choose from. Knowing which direction to go in requires the right help and support. Getting the right information and advice could point you in a direction that you had never even thought about. Some key things to consider include:

▶ Are there features of the job that match my own interests?

▶ What are the promotion prospects?

▶ Is the business generous at spending on staff training?

▶ Will I fit in with the people who work there? For instance, are there young people on the staff?

Case study

Jon left school with 6 GCSEs but struggled to find a good job. Two months working for a distribution company was followed by 6 hateful months working at a betting shop. Luckily his sister noticed a job advertised at a private job agency: a trainee at Mannheim, a huge motor auction business. Jon loved cars, so this wasn't a bad idea. He got the job because he sounded so enthusiastic at interview. Within 2 years he had passed the exams needed to qualify as a motor auctioneer. Now he has his own company car and mobile phone, and auctions 2 days a week in Wimbledon, 2 in Northampton and 1 in Leeds. He loves it.

Figure 4.6 shows the places where you get relevant information and Figure 4.7 where you can get careers advice. You will have a careers programme at school or college, but do you know who your careers adviser is? A good careers adviser can help you find the information you need for a successful future!

Figure 4.6 Sources of information

Source of information	Description
Advertisements	There are many websites and newspapers that advertise jobs. Local radio stations often advertise jobs. Most newspapers publish their job advertisements on particular days, as well as advertising them online.
Word of mouth	Someone you know may tell you about a job that has become available.
Employment/government agencies	Check online to find your local agency. For a small charge they will also help you complete your CV or applications.

Figure 4.7 Sources of advice

Source of advice	Description
Employment/government agencies	Local recruitment agencies will provide career advice and tell you what jobs you are most likely to get.
Careers advisers/tutors	If you are under 19 (or under 25 if you have learning difficulties or disabilities), the government's 'Connexions' will provide you with careers advice. Your tutors in school or college will be able to help you make sensible career choices.
Existing and previous employers	These can provide you with information about careers in a certain area and indicate what training you may need to be successful in that field.
Careers fairs	These are an excellent source of information because many employers have stalls manned by someone who can give you all the information you need about their industry or business.
Friends and family	This is the most common and most used source of advice. Don't forget to use them!

Career development

If you want to have a successful career then you have to be prepared to put yourself forward for training and development opportunities whenever you can.

In education

You need to make sure that you are following courses that will qualify you for any further or higher education course you want to study. You will need to find out how long the courses are. While you are at school or college, make sure you get any practical experience you will need to enable you to meet any entry requirements for future course. Find out what you will need to do to get onto any professional training courses. Have no doubt, though, that *every* employer wants to see that you have English and Maths GCSEs.

Did you know?

It takes 7 years of study at university to qualify as an architect!

Activity

Do some research into one or two courses you think you might be interested in taking after school or college. Find out what qualifications you will need and how long the course will last. Also find out what job opportunities the course will lead to.

Making the right career choices can set you on a path to doing what you want to do. The person armed with the skills and qualities regularly sought by employers will be the person who succeeds. The earlier you start to plan your career, collect evidence of your experiences and talents, the earlier in life you'll begin to reap the rewards. Maybe you don't know what to do with the rest of your life, but every employer wants students who have self-discipline, work well with others and show evidence of being willing to work hard. That is where qualifications come in.

When writing assignments on people in organisations, make sure you learn fully about the individual you are writing about. Distinctions come to those who show that they fully understand how that individual contributes to the success of the business.

In the workplace

Once you have landed yourself your dream job, it doesn't end there. When you first start a job you will be given induction training. This will provide you with an introduction to the workplace. You will find out who's who, the health and safety procedures and practical information such as where the canteen is. You should have a regular meeting with your boss, who will look at your training needs. From this your boss should establish plans for how you can develop. These plans will feed into performance targets. Each year (or 6 months) you should review your targets and development plan. In order to progress, you may have to be prepared to be flexible in your working hours. You may be expected to work shifts to enable you to attend a course at a certain time.

Over to you!

Choose the best definition of induction training.

1. An introduction to the staff in their new job.
2. Initial training to make newcomers feel comfortable in their new job.
3. Training that takes place on the job.
4. A type of training that involves everyone who is new to a job.

Sometimes at work you will receive un-certificated training, for example you may be taught how to use the telephone system. However, sometimes you may be sent on a course on, for example, health and safety where you receive certification. This is called certified training and you can keep the certificate in your personal development file. This sort of training provides a worker with progression opportunities. The more experience and training you have the more likely you are to move up the career ladder. Never forget that you will probably be working for the next 40 years – so you want to make this experience as enjoyable and successful as possible.

Take control

Managing yourself and your career is very important. Today many employers expect their staff to take control of their own personal and professional development. Your employer should provide you with all the help and support that you need, but it is up to you to seek out opportunities that you want. A career development plan requires that you identify what you require for your career. For example, if you want to be the boss of Microsoft, your technical skills won't get you there. Your career development plan will need to focus on developing leadership, presentation, financial and people skills, for example.

Case study

Arsenal's long-serving manager Arsene Wenger took control of his career. After getting a degree and a Master's Degree in Economics, Wenger became a professional footballer at 28. He only played 12 games in 3 years for Strasbourg. Yet during that time he persuaded Strasbourg to send him to a series of courses on football coaching and football management. At 31 he was appointed Youth Team Manager for Strasbourg. Three years later he became manager of Nancy FC. To become a football manager at 34 after such a short career as a professional footballer was a tribute to Wenger's ability to take control of his working life.

A career development plan

A career development plan should be an action plan for the future. It should specify particular areas for development over the next few months and identify how you will achieve your goals, e.g. what training courses to attend. It should lInclude:

▶ your name

▶ your job title/role

▶ the date

▶ your career aspirations (short term and long term)

▶ your strengths

▶ your weaknesses

▶ your areas for development and target dates

▶ where you expect to be by your next review.

Activity

Write your own career development plan.

Case study

Uzma and Talha are setting up a Winter Sports Travel Agency in Manchester. They're aiming at 25- to 30-year-old adults who have enough money to spend between £1,500 and £3,000 on a winter break. They need to recruit two staff as Customer Service Advisers selling directly to customers.

1. Advise Uzma and Talha on the steps they should take to find their new staff.

2. Explain why Uzma and Talha should look carefully at the personal attributes of any potential new staff.

Assessment activity 4.3 (P5)

1. Collect *three* examples of job adverts from at least *two* different sources.

2. For each of the three jobs you have chosen, match your current knowledge and skills to it.

a. Do you have the qualifications mentioned in the job advert?

b. Do you have the skills and qualities mentioned in the job advert?

Assessment activity 4.4 (P6)

You will review your own performance. Record the following information:

1. How well are you performing at school/college? Are you achieving good grades, completing work, meeting deadlines, gaining good effort grades?

2. Arrange a formal tutor performance review – your tutor will give their opinion on how well you are doing.

3. Ask your friends how well they think you are doing at school/college. Ask them to give reasons for their opinions.

The next step is to complete a career development plan.

Topic check

1 Why may induction training be especially useful for young people getting their first job?

2 Why may temporary jobs be unattractive to those with families to support?

3 Should employees carry out their own job audit? Or should the audit be carried out by a separate manager?

4 Explain why self-discipline might be important to workers carrying out one of these jobs:

   a) a professional footballer

   b) a supermarket store manager

   c) an air steward/stewardess

Assessment summary

The overall grade you achieve for this unit depends on how well you meet the grading criteria set out at the start of the chapter (see page 65). You must complete:

- all of the P criteria to achieve a **pass** grade
- all of the P and the M criteria to achieve a **merit** grade
- all of the P, M and D criteria to achieve a **distinction** grade.

Your tutor will assess the assessment activities that you complete for this unit. The work you produce should provide evidence which demonstrates that you have achieved each of the assessment criteria. The table below identifies what you need to demonstrate to meet each of the pass, merit and distinction criteria for this unit. You should always check and self-assess your work before you submit your assignments for marking.

Remember that you MUST provide evidence for all of the P criteria to pass the unit.

Grading criteria	You need to demonstrate that you can:	Do you have the evidence?
P1	Describe the main job roles and functions in an organisation	
P2	Identify different organisational structures used within business organisations	
P3	Produce a basic job description and person specification for a specific job.	
P4	Complete an application and interview for a specific job	
P5	Match current knowledge and skills to possible job opportunities using appropriate sources of information and advice	
P6	Produce a personal career development plan	
M1	Compare the main job roles and functions in two organisations and explain how they may differ in different organisational structures	
M2	Produce a detailed and relevant job description and person specification for a specific job	
D1	Analyse the relationship between job roles, functions and an organisation's structure, using appropriate illustrative examples	
D2	Analyse how effective recruitment contributes to an organisation's success	

Always ask your tutor to explain any assignment tasks or assessment criteria that you don't understand fully. Being clear about the task before you begin gives you the best chance of succeeding. Good luck with your Unit 4 assessment work!

5 Using office equipment

Unit outline

There is a range of functions that need to be carried out in all businesses to support their successful operation. Large organisations may have staff whose full-time job is to manage day-to-day functions such as filing, printing and diary management. In smaller organisations, people may do these things for themselves. This unit introduces you to the purpose of business support, to both large and small organisations. You will investigate the use and purpose of a range of office equipment, and how to use it safely.

You will develop your skills in providing support for a range of tasks, such as dealing with visitors at reception, taking accurate messages and filing. You will also learn the procedures used to process, retrieve and archive information, including different types of filing systems and associated issues such as confidentiality.

Learning outcomes

1 **Know the purpose of office equipment and systems.**
2 **Be able to process, retrieve and archive information.**
3 **Be able to use office equipment and systems safely.**

Grading guide

To achieve a **pass**, you must show that you can:	To achieve a **merit**, you must show you can:	To achieve a **distinction**, you must show you can:
P1 Outline different office equipment and systems	**M1** Explain procedures for using office equipment and systems	**D1** Assess the importance of having procedures for using office equipment and systems when providing business and administration support
P2 Describe the function of different office equipment		
P3 Demonstrate the procedures needed to process, retrieve and archive information		
P4 Operate an electronic diary system for business purposes	**M2** Compare and contrast paper and electronic diary systems	
P5 Safely carry out administrative tasks using office equipment		

The purpose of office equipment and systems

Getting started

When you check in to a posh hotel, there is no sign of office equipment – only a polished wood counter. Yet the reception staff have hidden computer terminals, probably linked to a global hotel booking system. The computer may prompt the receptionist to say 'Welcome back' to a regular guest – and the customer can warm to the personal service. This is the ideal model of office equipment and systems – improving efficiency and customer service.

When you have completed this topic, you should:

- know the main types of equipment used in offices
- understand the value of office equipment and systems in the workplace.

The purpose of office equipment

Successful businesses need to be run efficiently and be seen – by customers – to be efficient. Office equipment and systems have become crucial in helping businesses of all sizes to achieve success. Without the technology that has been developed such as computers, telephones and other electronic devices, businesses would be limited to working with fewer customers, in fewer countries, therefore limiting their potential.

Did you know?

The average computer user blinks 7 times a minute, less than half the normal rate of 20.

Activity

Note down as many electronic devices as possible where you are at the moment (e.g. your room, your classroom, the learning resource centre).

Types of office equipment

There is a huge array of office equipment available to help with the day-to-day running of a business.

Computers

The computer has become the most common of all business tools. The purpose of a computer is to perform calculations, store information, retrieve data from other places, process the information in the chosen way and assist with communication (e.g. letter writing, emailing, searching the internet).

Over to you!

In pairs, try to come up with as many uses for a computer as you can. Think about which tasks can be done on your class computers.

Did you know?

By the year 2012 there will be approximately 17 billion devices connected to the internet.

Computers are used for day-to-day activities such as:

▶ producing documents such as letters and contracts

▶ monitoring finances using Excel or other programs

▶ sending emails to other staff, companies or countries

▶ designing products using Computer-Aided-Design (CAD) software

▶ maintaining the office diary, booking meetings and setting reminders.

Overall, the introduction of computers on a global scale has made the running of a business easier in many ways.

 Did you know?

MySpace reports having over 110 million registered users. Were it a country, it would be the tenth largest, just behind Mexico.

Printers, photocopiers and scanners

A printer allows documents, images, receipts and other information generated on a computer to be produced as a hard copy on paper. Documents can be printed off in many different forms, with different options for things like the size and colour of the paper, and the colour of the ink. Printers, in conjunction with the computers they are attached to, enable people in a businesses to communicate with each other (e.g. by letter or memo) as well as with customers (e.g. via newsletters, leaflets, flyers).

A printer

A photocopier is a machine that makes paper copies of paper documents. These might contain text, images or graphics. It is a very quick and cheap process and can save businesses a lot of time. Documents can be copied in large numbers, in different sizes and in colour. So, for example, you can make a copy of a receipt to include in an expenses claim, or you can make lots of copies of a standard letter that will be sent out to customers. It can be cheaper and faster to photocopy multiple numbers of the same document rather than printing it out many times.

A scanner allows businesses to store documents electronically on computer. It works like a photocopier, reading the print and images on the page but, rather than transferring them to paper, it sends them in an electronic format to the computer it is attached to. The image will come up on screen and the user can save this electronic version onto the computer to be stored and used when necessary. This process means that businesses do not have to store lots of paper copies of documents, and that they can send electronic versions of a document as an email attachment to another person, rather than posting a hard copy.

A scanner

Fax machines and telephones

A fax machine sends the information in a document through a telephone line to a printer connected to a phone the other end. The fax machine then prints out the document so that it looks exactly the same as the original, effectively 'posting' a document electronically. The fax machine was first developed in 1843 by a Scottish inventor called Alexander Bain. It took over 100 years to finally produce a fax machine which could be used internationally, but by the 1960s it was being used on a global scale by businesses – they could now send documents to arrive in minutes with their customers or suppliers.

Over to you!

Describe a situation where you might use a fax machine instead of a phone or email.

Did you know?

There are over 50 million fax machines being used worldwide by businesses.

The telephone is an essential piece of office equipment. Most companies conduct a huge amount of their business over the phone. It allows direct two-way communication between the business and its customers, partners, suppliers and stakeholders. A weakness of phone calls is that the information is not recorded. Therefore, unlike an email, text or fax, there is scope for disagreement later about who said or promised what. Telephone conversations are an important part of business life, but it is often a good idea to follow a phone call with a letter or email to confirm any agreements that have been made or decisions that have been taken.

Case study

In November 2009, Orange finally announced the new prices of the iPhone. The phone had originally only been available from its competitor O2, but O2's contract with Apple had run out. It was now time for Orange to benefit from the iPhone's interactive and dynamic features. The phone received plenty of interest, with potential customers ringing the Orange customer service line, some having to wait over 15 minutes to speak to an adviser.

1. How did most of the potential customers contact Orange about the iPhone?

2. How important is the use of the telephone to Orange as a business?

Other equipment

A small yet important item of office equipment is the calculator. This everyday piece of technology allows people in business to carry out numerical calculations quickly and easily. Some businesses and job roles, such as accountants, use calculators on a very regular basis.

Another useful piece of equipment it the data projector. This takes a signal from a computer, TV or video/DVD and uses light to display a large image on a screen or a whiteboard. Most schools have interactive whiteboards that project the teacher's computer screen onto the board. The projector allows information to be shown to a large audience, making it possible for everyone to view the same information at the same time.

A data projector

A piece of electronic office equipment that helps to save time when sending letters is the franking machine, which automatically prints a stamp on a letter. At the start of *The X Factor*, producers write letters to the lucky few who make it through to 'Boot camp'. Imagine if they had to lick all the stamps! The machine can be loaded up with piles of letters which it will individually stamp within seconds. This makes sending mail easier and cheaper for businesses – the cost of postage is less when a letter is franked than when a stamp is used.

There is also a wide range of non-electronic equipment used in offices, such as hole punches, binders, staplers and guillotines (used to trim paper or cut it into smaller pieces). They each play an important part within the business, helping to make documents look professional, preparing them for storage or presentation, and speeding up certain tasks.

A franking machine

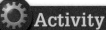
Activity

Match the following descriptions with the piece of office equipment which would be best suited to solving the problem.

a)

b)

c)

d)

A book needs to be held together...

A report needs to be put into a folder for storage...

A quote needs to be attached to some photographs...

A new poster is slightly too big...

The purpose of office systems

Within the office, there are many systems that enable employees to complete tasks in the same way.

Electronic diary systems

For a business to be efficient and reliable, the office diary has to be kept up to date in a way that all employees can understand. This can be done on paper or electronically.

Most businesses have a diary so that they can keep up to date with all their activities and arrangements. The diary can often be the focal point for staff to find out about appointments with their customers and suppliers, as well as dates and times of internal meetings.

These days most businesses keep electronic diaries, so that everyone in the office has access to the same diary – they can see what is happening when, and can alter and add things as necessary.

Over to you!

E-Studies Ltd has chosen to scrap its paper diary for a new computer version.

Explain the benefits and possible limitations of this for the business.

Telephone systems

The telephone system is important in all businesses, as it is such a common tool for communication. Every business has its own system or 'way' of doing things which all employees must be aware of.

Making calls out of the office may require the user to press a number first to get an outside line before they dial the telephone number. The call may also have to be logged or recorded so that it can be used as evidence in the future. For example, if BT were ringing up customers regarding their bill, they would need to keep a log of how many times they have rung.

The process of receiving calls is also very important. Some businesses use the telephone to sell products, so impressing the customer is crucial. Think of your phone network provider. Imagine if you rang them and they didn't answer the phone because nobody knew who was supposed to answer it. Or they answered it with a 'Wazzup?' Many businesses have a standard answer which all employees must use when answering the phone.

Not only must employees answer the phone correctly but they must also be able to deal with the situation appropriately. Forwarding calls to others and taking an accurate message show the customer that the business is efficient, caring and experienced.

Electronic mail systems

Emailing has become an integral part of business communication. Businesses around the world email each other with orders, feedback and updates. Businesses communicating in this way must make sure that their employees use the correct systems and processes. Many of us use emails as a fun, informal way to communicate with friends and family. In the business world, emails have to be written in the correct way to provide a positive image.

It is essential to have a hands-free headset if you need to use the computer while you are on the phone.

Did you know?

The average 21 year old has spent 5,000 hours playing video games, has exchanged 250,000 emails, instant and text messages and has spent 10,000 hours on their mobile phone.

Over to you!

You need to invite all your friends to your 18th birthday party.

Explain why email is the best method for this task.

Here are some dos and don'ts for sending business emails.

Dos	Don'ts
• Reply on time and in a positive manner. • Use templates to speed up your reply (signature and contact details at the end of each email). • Re-read the email before you send it. • Be concise and to the point. • Answer all the questions/queries.	• Don't swear! • Don't send unnecessary attachments. • Don't use slang in the email. • Don't forward chain emails to business customers or partners. • Don't write in capitals or add in smiley faces!

Did you know?

In August 2008, it was estimated that around 210 billion emails were sent every day. That is 2 million emails every second!

Source: Radicati Group

Emails have fast become the best way to send a lot of information to someone. You can attach documents, files and images which the other person can download and view within minutes. This is a great way to show off products in an interactive way. Emails have also become a great way to contact a large number of customers quickly and cheaply.

However, there are some risks and security issues with sending emails. There have been various viruses sent via email since its emergence, which have damaged business computer systems. This has meant that rigorous checks on emails are needed. Most businesses (and schools and colleges) have software that stops email coming in or going out if it thinks it may contain some harmful viruses. Businesses are also very careful with the information they send and who they send it to, as this stops potential fraudsters using the information.

Over to you!

Write an email to a friend explaining the benefits and drawbacks of using emails.

Topic check

1 You are the receptionist at the O2 Arena. For what tasks could you use:

   a) a stapler?   c) a guillotine?

   b) a hole punch?   d) a binder?

2 Which of the following would you use to send an important message to another business?

   a) an email   c) a letter

   b) a fax   d) a text message

3 Which machine would you use to pay for the postage on a letter?

   a) a guillotine   c) a hole punch

   b) a franking machine   d) a stapler

4 List and describe three machines which may be used in an office.

5 Explain the benefits and drawbacks of using a paper diary in the workplace.

Processing, retrieving and archiving information

▶ Getting started

Bedrooms can easily turn into chaos. Offices can be worse still – unless there is a sense of order they can become buried under paper. So the choice must be made: create an effective filing system or scan everything into computers, so that every piece of information can easily be processed, archived and retrieved.

When you have completed this topic, you should:

- understand why information needs to be processed
- understand the systems used to archive and retrieve information.

Key terms

Archiving: storing information that is not needed currently; this should be done in such a way that the information can be found easily when needed

Processing information: putting information into categories, such as 'confidential'

and 'non-confidential', then deciding how to store it and who has access to it

Retrieving information: finding information, either from a stack of papers, or from an archive

? Did you know?

Google is attempting to scan every book that has ever been written, so that every scrap of past information can be retrieved with ease.

Processing information

Businesses usually have strict guidelines in relation to **processing information**. These help to maintain the confidentiality of documents and the security of the company. It is vital to protect confidential or secret information and prevent competitors from accessing it. Confidentiality within the business is also important, so employees should not be able to access information they are not allowed to see. For example, in the Human Resources department, passwords are used on documents which store employee pay and benefits information. This information is confidential and should only be read by those who have permission to see it.

Electronic documents can also be logged and tracked. This means that each document has a history of who has read it and when, which can be very useful in finding out who is accessing information.

? Did you know?

While it took the radio 38 years, and the television 13 years, it took the World Wide Web (internet) only 4 years to reach 50 million users.

Businesses need to be aware of any potential hazards (e.g. viruses, worms and spyware) that could damage their information processing system. These can all attack the computer systems that businesses use. If an employee is unsure about whether a document, email or attachment is legitimate, then it is very important that they seek help rather than continue to process it anyway.

Retrieving information

A successful business will be swamped with past information, such as old orders, emails, receipts or letters. However, it is vitally important to be able to retrieve these when necessary. Employees should know the procedure for finding the correct information quickly and efficiently.

Imagine you have been asked to find an order from Malik Mechanics for new tyres in September 2009. The information may have been organised in different ways, for example:

▶ *alphabetically*: in order from A–Z

▶ *numerically*: in order using a number system – this is useful when each order has an order number, e.g. 'order 01' is the oldest, with the most recent order having the highest number, e.g. 'order 2098'

▶ *chronologically*: in date order, with the oldest first.

This makes **retrieving information** easier, if you know which method has been used. Once the information is found, it is important to put it in the correct format so that it is accurate and useful. The process shouldn't take very long if employees understand the system in place. Timescales should always be agreed so that there is enough time to find and sort the information required.

Over to you!

Which method of organising data do you think would have been best for the Malik Mechanics example? Why?

Archiving information

Archiving is collecting up documents, either paper or electronic copies, which are then packed together for storage or backed up. Archives may be stored in a different location, e.g. in an office cupboard or computer system elsewhere. This may be done for safekeeping or to free up some space in the office or on the computer hard drive.

In business it is important that the correct information is archived. It may be necessary for all information to be confirmed or checked by a senior manager before it is taken. This limits the possibility that the information will be needed again any time soon. Normally, the information is chosen and sorted by date rather than topic. For example, if there were over 300 orders, an employee could be asked to archive any orders more than one year old. This would be very easy to work out and should limit the mistakes and make the job quicker to do. The details of any information that is archived needs to be recorded in a safe place. This may include a list of what has been archived as well as details for how to access and find the information in the future.

Archiving may happen every year as part of an office 'clean up' which reduces paperwork or documents slowing down the computer system. However, there should also be a timescale for keeping the archived information, so it can be thrown away when it is no longer needed.

Using office equipment and systems safely

 Getting started

When scanners were first used in supermarkets, checkout staff started to suffer with back problems. The speed of the process meant that they were lifting as much as half a ton of groceries a day! With more staff missing work, supermarkets began to look at the design of the checkout operator's chair. Only when this was redesigned was the new system safe to use.

When you have completed this topic, you should:

- understand the need for employers to provide safe working conditions
- explain how to ensure that staff use office equipment safely.

Using equipment

When setting up office equipment it is vital to follow the instructions carefully and in the correct order. It is common to attempt to set up computers and phones at home without reading the instructions properly, as many people feel they manage without them. However, within a business it is important that all equipment is working at 100% capacity as quickly as possible and then all of the time once it has been set up. Much equipment comes with instruction manuals that contain lots of information about setting up, using and maintaining it. However, there can be times where you need more information and this can usually be found on the manufacturer's website.

Despite the importance of careful set up, there is room for using some initiative in the workplace when problems arise. For example, if you are setting up or using a new office computer, there may be an instruction in the manual that you do not understand. You could check the website for guidance, but you could also use your initiative if it's a problem you feel you can solve yourself.

New equipment often comes in a lot of packaging. Make sure that you dispose of this sensibly. Much of it can be recycled, minimising waste.

 Did you know?

Most companies now have a 'Frequently asked questions' (FAQ) area on their website. This can be used to help solve problems when setting up equipment.

Did you know?

12.5 million tonnes of paper and cardboard are used annually in the UK.

On average, every person in the UK throws away their own body weight in rubbish every seven weeks.

Source: http://www.uk-energy-saving.com

Support tasks

Within businesses of all sizes, there will be a number of support staff who perform tasks to help the business improve its efficiency and productivity. These are called support tasks. A good example of an employee in a support role is the receptionist, who is key in any company as they are the first point of contact. It is important that reception duties are carried out with enthusiasm and accuracy, for example phones calls must be directed to the most appropriate person without keeping customers on hold for too long.

A receptionist may also have to dispatch and distribute the mail for the staff. This involves making sure the post is sent on time, as well as making sure employees get their post each morning. Letters from customers, for example, must be dealt with quickly. Large businesses may have a post room that is responsible for internal and external deliveries of post.

Another support task is completing forms and filing them (e.g. someone's job application) so that they can be found easily. Some businesses employ assistants who are solely responsible for filing. In effect they are doing the task Google is proud to boast that it does: 'Organising information'.

Health and Safety

In the business environment it is very important to maintain the safety and wellbeing of the staff. Health and safety procedures are not just needed in factories and on building sites, but in offices as well. For example, offices must have procedures in place in case of a fire, and equipment such as fire extinguishers must be easily accessible. Staff must know what these procedures are and how to use the equipment.

 Did you know?

Back pain is the most common cause of days off work. An estimated 500,000 workers a year take time off for back injuries.

Employees who work in an office throughout the day must also think about the way they sit. Although it seems a trivial point, many office workers suffer injuries (e.g. back injuries, repetitive strain injuries) because of the way they sit at their desks or use their keyboards.

 Over to you!

How many threats to your health and safety do you face at school?

Within the workplace there are plenty of other potential hazards, such as lifting heavy boxes, and electrical and fire hazards. There may also be hazardous materials and chemicals on the premises, which must be clearly labelled and stored properly. If it is necessary to dispose of them this must be done in the most appropriate and safe way.

It is important that a business can identify these hazards so that staff can be warned and measures put in place to ensure their safety. Staff must also know how to use electronic equipment such as computers, photocopiers and scanners properly and safely.

A range of hazard warning symbols.

 Case study

An RAF typist has won £484,000 in compensation and legal costs after developing repetitive strain injury (RSI).

Working as a data entry clerk, the woman developed 'de Quervain's tenosynovitis', the symptoms of which are pain and tenderness at the side of the wrist and at the base of the thumb. The condition was thought to be related to her job as it occurred at the same time as an increase in her work rate.

Bringing an action against the Ministry of Defence (MOD), she claimed that the condition was permanent and caused her to become depressed. Medical experts judged that she is unlikely to be able to return to work.

Employers have a duty to assess the risks involved in all jobs that may cause harm.

1. Why may an employer be blamed if a member of staff has been unable to 'safely carry out administrative tasks using office equipment'?

2. To what extent should the employee share the blame in a case such as this?

Assessment activity 5.1 (P1, P2, P3, P4, P5 M1, M2, D1)

Since its arrival in 1998, Google has grown to become the world's largest search engine. Competitors like Yahoo have struggled to keep up with Google's consistent development.

Over the last few years, Google has become famous for the layout of its offices. The offices, situated all over the world, can boast the best free employee meals, as well as games areas and recycled Google logos! However, the office continues to operate using the same technology and systems that businesses all over the world use. The senior mangers all use electronic as well as paper diaries, so that they are always organised.

Over the years, Google has created thousands of pieces of paper, folders and files which have needed to be archived for future use.

1. Using follow-up research, outline the different office equipment and systems used by Google in its offices.

2. Describe the functions of different office equipment.

3. Using Google offices as an example, demonstrate the procedures needed to process, retrieve and archive information.

4. Having identified the equipment and systems used by Google, explain the procedures that may be in place for using these.

5. Assess the importance of Google having procedures for using office equipment and systems when providing business and administration support.

6. Google uses both paper and electronic diary systems. Compare and contrast these.

7. A successful business depends on all employees being able to carry out administrative procedures. Follow your teacher's instructions and carry out a range of administrative tasks using office equipment.

Topic check

1 Why is it important to archive old documents and information?

2 What potential hazards could employees face in the workplace?

3 Assess the importance of having procedures for using office equipment and systems when providing business and administration support.

Assessment summary

The overall grade you achieve for this unit depends on how well you meet the grading criteria set out at the start of the chapter (see page 91). You must complete:

- all of the P criteria to achieve a **pass** grade
- all of the P and the M criteria to achieve a **merit** grade
- all of the P, M and D criteria to achieve a **distinction** grade.

Your tutor will assess the assessment activities that you complete for this unit. The work you produce should provide evidence which demonstrates that you have achieved each of the assessment criteria. The table below identifies what you need to demonstrate to meet each of the pass, merit and distinction criteria for this unit. You should always check and self-assess your work before you submit your assignments for marking.

Remember that you MUST provide evidence for all of the P criteria to pass the unit.

Grading criteria	You need to demonstrate that you can:	Do you have the evidence?
P1	Outline different office equipment and systems	
P2	Describe the function of different office equipment	
P3	Demonstrate the procedures needed to process, retrieve and archive information	
P4	Operate an electronic diary system for business purposes	
P5	Safely carry out administrative tasks using office equipment	
M1	Explain procedures for using office equipment and systems	
M2	Compare and contrast paper and electronic diary systems	
D1	Assess the importance of having procedures for using office equipment and systems when providing business and administration support	

Always ask your tutor to explain any assignment tasks or assessment criteria that you don't understand fully. Being clear about the task before you begin gives you the best chance of succeeding. Good luck with your Unit 5 assessment work!

6 Providing business support

Unit outline

The administrative support necessary for a business to be successful comes in different forms, depending on the size of the business. In large firms, an administrative function would be responsible for diary management, printing, filing etc. In smaller organisations one secretary may undertake all of these tasks.

This unit explores the range of business support that organisations need in order to be successful, irrespective of their size. It investigates a range of office equipment and duties and looks at their purpose and how to use or undertake them safely.

You will develop your organisation skills and learn about business support tasks such as arranging meetings and carrying out diary management under time constraints. You will learn from several practical tasks, including booking venues and equipment, sending information to attendees and organising resources.

Learning outcomes

1 **Understand the purpose of providing business support.**
2 **Be able to carry out office work safely.**
3 **Be able to organise and provide support for meetings.**

Grading guide

To achieve a **pass**, you must show you can:	To achieve a **merit**, you must show you can:	To achieve a **distinction**, you must show you can:
P1 Explain the types and purposes of business support	**M1** Explain the appropriate uses of office equipment types, features and functions to suit different business purposes	**D1** Analyse the contribution that office equipment makes to the provision of business support
P2 Describe the use of office equipment to meet different business requirements		
P3 Demonstrate using office equipment safely in accordance with health and safety legislation		
P4 Draw up a checklist for a meeting	**M2** Produce all post-meeting documentation	
P5 Produce documents needed for a meeting	**M3** Explain the organisation and support provided for meetings	**D2** Analyse the organisation and documents and materials provided for a meeting, making recommendations for any improvements

Understanding the purpose of providing business support

Getting started

In many businesses, the big opportunities are to be found in high-growth China or India. A key executive may be in Beijing for 3 weeks. Meanwhile, back at home, plans have to be developed and appointments made. So the executive's PA (personal assistant) may have a key role, and may have to take significant decisions.

When you have completed this topic, you should:

- understand that business support is a key factor in turning ideas into action
- understand that business support helps the business to operate consistently and efficiently.

The purpose of providing business support

All businesses need to ensure that their administration tasks are completed effectively and efficiently. Regardless of the size of the organisation, business support is usually carried out by secretaries. Secretaries have a whole host of jobs that they have to do in order to keep the organisation running on a daily basis. They are responsible for:

- dealing with visitors
- arranging and organising meetings
- ordering supplies
- any other task needed to make the office operate smoothly.

Due to the wide-ranging responsibilities, the pay isn't bad either – in London, secretarial and administrators' wages range from £18,000 per year to £33,500 per year!

 Did you know?

The majority of organisations agree that keeping administrative staff happy is critical to the effectiveness of their organisation, 'They will know from first-hand experience what the problems are and may be able to identify solutions or highlight potential difficulties in any reorganisation.'

Source: www.timeshighereducation.co.uk/

Over to you!

Check out specific secretarial surveys for yourself at http://www.morganspencer.co.uk/shell/salary-survey.aspx or type 'secretary salary surveys' into a search engine such as Google.

Did you know?

Secretaries are often referred to as the 'gatekeepers' of organisations. This means that they are trained not to put everyone through to a manager who asks to speak to one on the phone. There are websites dedicated to how to get past the gatekeepers! Check out sites such as:

http://www.jobx.com.au/-2121/getting-through-gatekeepers and
http://www.sideroad.com/Sales_Techniques/get-past-gatekeeper.html

The importance of business support

So, why is providing business support so important? There are several reasons, including:

To ensure consistency

All office procedures need to be carried out in the same way, no matter who does the job. If this did not happen, mistakes might be made, and customers might notice inconsistencies.

To make effective use of time

In any job, managing your time is one of the most important skills you have to acquire. Tasks have to be prioritised, otherwise important jobs that need to be done straight away may not be done until too late. Therefore, if the secretaries do not plan their time and prioritise their jobs, deadlines will be missed and the business will fail to meet its objectives.

To provide support for managers, teams, colleagues and departmental processes

▶ Managers' time is very precious and they cannot waste it worrying about administrative jobs. They need to be able to rely on their secretarial staff to carry out all tasks on time and in the agreed way.

▶ Teams of staff may also be assigned a secretary to carry out jobs on behalf of everybody in the team. The purpose of this is to enable the team members to concentrate on doing their job, while the secretary can ensure that all of their administrative needs are carried out consistently.

▶ It is also important that administrative staff provide support for other secretaries that they are working with, as well as for managers and teams. The job can be very demanding, and time management is essential, so it is vital to support each other in important jobs that are time pressured.

▶ Administrative staff can also be assigned to whole departments, such as marketing. In this role, they have to ensure that meetings between staff are organised appropriately and that communication is effective between all colleagues. Some jobs will be specific to those departments, such as checking promotional budgets in the marketing department.

To provide effective service to internal and external customers

▶ *Internal customers* are colleagues who need your assistance in order to fulfil their job roles. Providing effective service to internal customers is important, as they will be able to do a far better job if they can rely upon support staff for the assistance they need.

Activity

Steven and Henry own and run a music business called Lonely Records. They have to work away in Slovenia launching a new album for one of their artists.

Suggest the benefits that Steven and Henry could gain by employing an administrator, and the type of jobs that this person could do for Lonely Records.

▶ *External customers* are the people who visit an organisation because it can provide something they need. If the secretarial staff do not do their part, for example answering the phone, the customer will leave dissatisfied with that organisation. Secretaries play a very important role, as they are often the first point of contact for external customers.

Case study

Derren, a Library Services Assistant, has a wide range of jobs. He starts by tidying up after last week's Pirate Story half-term event for under-8s. He then writes a short report on the event to be emailed to the 12 Council members. They like to know about successful events. Later he sorts out 'the bin', which has 200 books sent by other libraries locally. He enters them onto the library electronic catalogue, then phones to query why some of the books have been sent. Towards the end of the day he works on the desk – greeting library users and checking books in and out. Two new users have to be registered with the library. He completes their details and puts a photocopy in a file. It's been a relaxed, varied day.

Types of business support

Several types of support jobs have to be carried out in all types of organisations, no matter what the sector, age or size of the organisation, as shown in Figure 6.1.

Figure 6.1 Types of business support

Types of support	What does it mean?
Dealing with visitors	Greeting visitors, signing the visitors in and out, contacting the necessary people within the organisation and directing the visitors to the right place.
Organising travel and accommodation	Assisting with the organisation of events such as conferences and VIP visits, making hotel reservations and booking train/aeroplane tickets.
Managing diaries	Arranging and entering appointments and meetings into managers' diaries, either electronically or manually.
Using telephone systems to make, receive and transfer calls	Making telephone calls to external businesses, answering the telephone and using the internal telephone system to transfer the caller to the appropriate person within the business.
Organising and supporting meetings	Preparing meeting documents such as agendas, booking and preparing the rooms, booking catering and typing up minutes.
Producing documents	Writing letters, emails, reports, using word processing and spreadsheet packages and writing up presentations.
Processing and storing information both manually and electronically	Researching, finding, recording and storing information such as expenses into manual and computerised systems.

Summary

The purpose of business support is to make it easier for managers to spend their time on big decisions and big issues. Neither Alan Sugar nor David Cameron want to spend time sorting out meeting dates or figuring out how a new phone system works. Effective business support helps in making an organisation work more effectively.

Over to you!

You have all come into contact with administration staff every day when you are at school or college.

- Over the next week, try to take notes of all of the different activities that you see them do. Make a list of all of the activities that they do on a daily basis.
- For each point, explain how this helps your school or college to run effectively. Explain what would happen if they did not do each of these jobs.

Assessment activity 6.1 (P1)

Look at the job advert for an administrator at Walford High School below:

Job title: Junior Administrator

Pay: £16,000–£18,000

Enquiries to: Mr Yao email: yao@WalfordHighSchool.com

A well-spoken vibrant person is needed to work in a busy school office. The role will involve customer-facing roles, so good communication skills are essential. There will be times when you will need to supervise others in order to ensure the smooth running of the office. Literacy skills are essential, as well as good typing skills. Excellent IT skills are a must, especially the use of Excel. Ideally, we would like a person who has had previous experience at problem solving in an office environment, handling mail and organising diaries and schedules. You will be reporting to the administrating coordinator.

1. Explain the different jobs that the junior administrator would have to undertake.
2. What skills would the junior administrator need in order for them to do their job?
3. Find two administrative job adverts. Explain the types of activities that the job holder would have to undertake.
4. Explain why administrative support is needed by organisations.

Topic check

1. Why may 'consistency' be important to a business?
2. Identify one way in which a member of support staff could 'support a meeting'.
3. What is meant by the term 'an internal customer'?
4. You are asked to schedule next week's appointments for your boss. Identify two mistakes you should take care to avoid.

Getting started

A wide range of equipment is used in offices in order to undertake all of the administrative tasks quickly and easily. All of the administration staff will need training in order to be confident in using the equipment appropriately and safely.

When you have completed this topic, you should:

- understand the main types of equipment used in an office
- understand the risks that may be involved in operating this equipment.

Office equipment

Administrative staff may be trained in different ways to use the range of office equipment available. They may be shown by an experienced member of staff or given instruction manuals. Instructions on how to use the equipment may be displayed next to it as a reminder, to ensure that it is used correctly.

The features and functions of the equipment will vary depending on the type and quantity of work that needs to be carried out. The types of office equipment outlined below are used to help with the smooth and efficient running of a business, such as getting documents to the right people at the right time.

▶ *Printers* are used to make hard (paper) copies of documents that are produced on computers. Many copies can be printed and then distributed to the appropriate people. Many documents need to be signed, so have to be printed out. For example, a letter would be printed out, signed and then posted.

▶ *Scanners* are used to duplicate images and text into a digital format, so that important documents can be stored as electronic copies. For example, a secretary may scan a receipt in order to keep a copy to support an expense claim.

▶ *Photocopiers* are used to make copies of documents. They can make documents double sided in order to save paper and can make documents smaller or bigger, e.g. enlarged from A4 to A3. For example, a photocopier could be used to make copies of an agenda to be given to all the attendees of a meeting.

 Did you know?

Nowadays, many businesses have multifunctional devices that photocopy, scan, fax and print all from the same machine.

▶ *Emails* are used for communicating messages and documents to people within and outside the organisation. They are often used to send detailed information to people and are useful because records of email 'conversations' can be kept easily.

▶ *Telephone systems* are used for quick communication with people within and outside the organisation. They are used when a record of the conversation does not need to be taken. In most large firms, a designated person will operate a switchboard, which is the first point of contact for callers. Most advanced telephones used in businesses have several functions, as outlined in Figure 6.2.

Figure 6.2 Telephone functions

Telephone feature	What it enables the admin staff to do
Call back	Calls back an extension number when the line becomes free.
Caller display	Shows the caller's number.
Conference calls	Allows you to speak to several people at once.
Divert or call forwarding	Calls can be redirected from an extension to another phone.
Hands free	The handset can be replaced and you can talk through the speaker.
Last number redial	Automatically redials the last number called.
On hold/caller waiting	Enables incoming calls to be held while the correct person is found to take the call.
Transfer/redirect	Enables the caller to be transferred to the correct extension number.
Secrecy button	This is used if you do not want the caller to hear you, perhaps when you are talking to another colleague.
Speed dialling	You can store a certain number of phone numbers on the phone, so that you only have to press one button to dial the number. You would usually only store numbers that are called regularly.
Voicemail	This is the equivalent of an answer phone and enables you to replay, store and delete messages left by callers.

⚙ Activity

Make a list of all the different types of office equipment that exist in your school or college. Describe the features of each machine and why they are used, giving examples.

What contribution does all of this equipment make to the effective running of your school? How does it help the admin staff do their jobs effectively?

Report your findings back to the class.

Working safely

It is important that staff know how to use office equipment safely and comply with the organisation's health and safety regulations. European regulations exist to protect the health and safety of employees who use computers for a considerable part of their working day, and who may have to lift equipment. This covers:

▶ *Seating* – chairs with adjustable height and back rest are recommended. Thighs and lower arms should be in a roughly horizontal position when working at the keyboard.

▶ *Screens* – all new screens should be fitted with tilt and swivel stands. Sufficient room is needed for the screen to be moved backwards and forwards. Ideally, the top of the screen should be at eye level.

▶ *Mouse and keyboard* – the distance between the worker and the keyboard and mouse must be sufficient to allow the lower arm to be placed horizontally on the desk in a comfortable position.

▶ *Safe lifting techniques* – when lifting equipment it is important that steps are taken to avoid the lifter suffering an injury, especially to their back. The heavier the equipment to be lifted, the more important it is to ensure that it is lifted correctly. The key is to bend the knees and used the legs to do the lifting, rather than the back (see the activity below).

Health and safety at work is an important 'duty of care' for managers. In reality, many will expect support staff to take care of this area themselves, as it has no direct bearing on the success of the business. However, poorly handled health and safety can cause severe problems to a business – both in terms of staff morale and bad publicity.

Figure 6.3 It is important to maintain a good posture when working at a computer.

 Did you know?

More that half a million British workers suffer from repetitive strain injury (RSI), largely due to working on computers.

 Activity

It is important to be able to follow instructions safely in an organisation, to comply with health and safety regulations. Follow the instructions below:

1. Place a textbook on the floor and follow the instructions in order to lift it safely.

2. Stand close to the textbook and centre yourself over it with your feet shoulder-width apart.

3. Tighten your stomach muscles.

4. Keep your back straight, bend your knees and squat to the floor.

5. Grasp the textbook with both hands.

6. Keep the textbook close to your body and use your leg muscles to stand up, lifting the textbook off the floor.

7. Your back should remain straight throughout the lifting, using only the muscles in the legs to lift the load.

8. Do not twist your body when lifting the textbook. If you do need to move, take small steps with your feet until you are in the correct position.

9. Using your knees to bend, place the textbook on a surface in front of you.

Assessment activity 6.2 (P2, P3, M1, D1)

You have applied for the job advertised in Assessment activity 6.1 and you have been successful! One of your first tasks is to use Microsoft Outlook (a computer diary system) to book the Head's appointments and meetings. You also need to make bookings for the teachers who want to use the laptops, ICT rooms and the hall.

In addition to the computer, there is a range of other equipment that you will need to use. The fax machine is used to track any students who are absent without a reason, by faxing their names and student numbers to an external agency.

The telephones are used to ring parents and for parents to ring the school for various reasons, such as to explain why their child is absent. You are expected to answer the phone, take messages for other members of staff, and then email these to them and let them know if they are expected to ring back the caller.

The administrating coordinator also shows you how to transfer calls to the Head's office and how to use the photocopier to make copies of worksheets for teachers. When new students start at the school, you have to scan their passports or birth certificates so that an electronic copy of their identity can be stored.

You attend a training session to ensure that you know how to use all of the office equipment correctly, including how to sit safely so that you do not injure yourself while working on the computer.

1. Describe how the different office equipment is used to enable the effective running of the school.

2. Demonstrate your knowledge from your training session on how to use office equipment safely, in accordance with health and safety legislation. Your tutor will observe you and complete a witness statement.

3. Explain how the school uses different office equipment to meet different business purposes.

4. Analyse the contribution that office equipment makes to the provision of effective support to the workings of the school.

Organise and provide support for meetings

This topic introduces you to the ways in which organisations organise meetings, ensure that they are run appropriately and that all measures are in place for them to be successful. When you have completed this topic, you should:

- know the different types of meetings
- understand how meetings are organised
- understand the support that is provided for meetings
- know the documents used in meetings.

Different types of meeting

Meetings are a regular and important part of business life because they improve communication in an organisation, generate ideas and solve problems. In order to be effective, meetings need to be properly organised and details communicated to all of the necessary people.

Meetings are held for different reasons and can have different formats. Some are very formal, with specific rules and procedures; others are informal and do not necessarily feel like a meeting. Some are held regularly, at the same time and place every week; others are held only once or a few times for a particular reason. Some meetings will involve many people; others will involve only a few. Some meetings will only include attendees who work for the company, whereas others will have guests from external companies. Types of meeting include:

▶ *Confidential meetings* – whatever is discussed in a confidential meeting is private and should not be discussed outside of the meeting. This may involve matters such as disciplinary procedures (i.e. somebody has done something that has breached company policy), or company strategy. If it is a strategy meeting, managers will discuss what the company intends to do in the future, and will not want this information to be made public yet as they will not want their competitors to find out!

▶ *Team meetings* – these are meetings between people who usually work together within a particular department in a firm, or who have been put into a team to do a specific task or job. They may hold a meeting to discuss the plans for the task in hand, delegate jobs and feed back to the other group members.

▶ *Training meetings* – staff often need to be trained in new skills or to update previously learnt skills. This can be achieved through meetings at which attendees learn new skills or techniques, e.g. using a new computer program.

▶ *Publicity meetings* – these are meetings used to publicise an event, for example, to let staff know about new types of publicity the organisation is investing in (e.g. a new advert that is going to be televised), or about the Christmas party.

▶ *Update meetings* – these are meetings to update the attendees on matters that have occurred since their previous meeting, such as issues involving a long-term project. Update meetings are held to update attendees on others' and their own progress towards achieving the task. The meeting might also be about new legislation that affects working conditions. For example, in July 2007, the UK government made it illegal to smoke in public places. A meeting might have been held to update staff about this legislation and what the company intended to do keep the employees that smoke happy!

Did you know?

It is a legal requirement for the minutes of meetings to be signed by all present in order for a business decision to be approved.

Organising meetings

Administration employees have to do a lot of preparation and organisation before a meeting takes place. Below is a checklist of all of the points that have to be considered in order for the meeting to be a success.

Checklist for organising meetings

▶ *Meeting brief and agenda* – sending notice of the meeting to attendees, distributing the agenda, preparing and photocopying documents for circulation, including the agenda.

▶ *Checking dates and times* – confirming the date and time of the meeting with the chairperson and the attendees.

▶ *Confirming the budget* – confirm how much is to be spent on preparing the meeting, e.g. catering costs, photocopying costs etc.

▶ *Choosing and booking the venue* – deciding on and booking appropriate meeting rooms; checking the required furniture and layout. This will need to be done again shortly before the meeting.

▶ *Arranging catering* – ordering and checking refreshments required, confirming the exact number required the day before the meeting.

▶ *Organising equipment and resources* – checking what equipment and resources are required (e.g. flipcharts, projectors, paper and pens) and that these are available. You will also need to ensure that there are extra copies of documentation (in case people have forgotten or lost them) and extra paper and pens in case they are needed.

▶ *Inviting people to attend* – this includes sending an email to the attendees confirming the date and time of the meeting, the venue address and, if necessary, including a map and details of transport links and local accommodation (accommodation may also need to be booked and confirmed).

▶ *Confirming attendance* of attendees and keeping a record of this – this can be done via telephone or email. A record of the attendees is usually kept in a spreadsheet so that the correct amount of catering and resources can be ordered. You will need to also make a list of apologies, i.e. the people who cannot attend the meeting.

▶ *Special requirements* – it is important to find out if the attendees have any special requirements, such as if they are vegetarian or they have mobility impairments (e.g. they are in a wheelchair). If this is the case, admin staff will need to ensure that these requirements are met and are checked a day before the meeting.

Providing support for meetings

A good referee is the one you don't notice. Similarly, good administrative support for a meeting may hardly be noticed. Yet it is crucial. A badly run meeting – with tea and coffee clattering in early, in the middle of the boss's main presentation – will affect the outcome. Effective support requires good training and an understanding that:

▶ Meetings can be critical (e.g. in ensuring that a major client keeps their business with you), so the meeting must be supported efficiently.

▶ Managers might have put in months' of work (and spent large sums, e.g. on market research) preparing for a meeting; the least they expect is that it should run efficiently.

▶ People can leave meetings with different views on what has been said and agreed, so keeping an accurate record of the meeting is vital.

Case study

Claire learnt to type and take shorthand before going to university. In her first summer holiday she worked for the Metropolitan Police (in London). Just 10 days into her temporary job she was taking shorthand at a Murder Squad meeting. She took the notes then typed them up afterwards. She was sworn to silence, but admitted that 'it was amazing'. The following summer she was assigned to the Vice Squad. Again, she loved it.

Explain why Claire loved her job providing business support.

The administration staff also have a lot of work to do to support the meeting just before it begins or while it is taking place – see the checklist below:

Checklist for supporting meetings

▶ *Checking that the room is set out correctly* – it is important that the room is checked just before the meeting to ensure that it is laid out in the best way for the meeting to be effective. This may mean, for example, having the correct number of chairs around a circular table, or having the chairs facing a screen.

▶ *Checking that equipment is working* – it is important that equipment is checked just before the meeting. For example, it is essential to check that projectors and laptops work.

▶ *Documentation for attendees* – it is important to ensure that all necessary documentation is in place in the room ready for attendees. This includes copies of the agenda and other documents necessary for the meeting. It is always a good idea to have extra copies in case anyone has forgotten or mislaid theirs.

▶ *Attendance list* – it is important to know who is going to attend the meeting so that all documents and refreshments can be ordered in the right quantities and to meet the requirements of the attendees.

▶ *Taking accurate records of meetings* – this is essential. Important discussions often take place and decisions are made during meetings. Particular jobs and tasks may be allocated to certain people to carry out after the meeting, with deadlines for their completion. It is important that these are all recorded so that the attendees have a written record of what was said, what action is to be taken and what tasks they have to complete by when.

▶ *Serving refreshments* – it is important that refreshments are served to the attendees on time, that there has been enough ordered for the number of attendees and that any dietary requirements have been taken into consideration.

Activity

Find out when your teachers have their weekly staff meetings. Interview one of the teachers, asking the following questions:

1. What procedures are in place to organise the meeting?
2. What happens during the meeting?
3. What happens after the meeting has taken place?

Follow-up activities

A successful meeting is usually followed by actions of some sort. The minutes of the meeting are therefore very important as they will serve as a written record of what actions are to be taken. Once the minutes have been written up, the attendees must agree that they are a fair record of what happened at the meeting. This means that the person taking the minutes has to be alert in the meeting and accurate afterwards. It is best to type up the minutes as soon as possible after the event.

Checklist for following up after the meeting

▶ *Clearing the venue* – the venue must be left as it was found so that it can be used for the next appointment without causing unnecessary work. This includes putting the layout of the room back to its original state and disposing of all litter.

▶ *Compiling an accurate list of those present* – it is important to make a list of all the people who were present at the meeting so that any follow-up documentation, such as minutes, can be sent to them.

▶ *Apologies for absence* – it is important to know who was invited to the meeting but could not attend, so that they too can be sent any documentation. You also need to know if anyone else who did not attend the meeting needs to be sent the documentation.

▶ *Agreeing minutes of last meeting, if appropriate* – sometimes the minutes of the last meeting need to be discussed and agreed at the present meeting, to ensure that there are no discrepancies in the records.

▶ *Writing minutes* – minutes are a written record of what was said, including any action points and deadlines decided at the meeting. They are an important legal document that needs to be written at any meeting. Some minutes, for example if they relate to financial information, should be signed off by attendees to confirm what was discussed and actioned in the meeting.

▶ *Action points* – action points that must be completed before the next meeting must be agreed on and noted in the minutes. This is an effective way of monitoring progress from one meeting to the next.

▶ *Circulating records to attendees within agreed timescales* – minutes and other documentation related to the meeting should be circulated to all attendees within an agreed time. This is so that everybody has written evidence of what was discussed and what, if any, tasks they need to complete before the next meeting.

Meeting documentation

Several documents are needed for meetings to run efficiently and successfully. Administration staff need to prepare and circulate this documentation before, during and after the meeting. The documentation includes:

Notice and agenda for a meeting

The notice of a meeting is used to inform all attendees when and where the next meeting is to be held, the purpose of the meeting and the refreshments that will be provided. This is distributed before the meeting and used during the meeting. The purpose of this document is to notify people of the meeting and the topics proposed for discussion. It is also to establish who can attend – it will usually include a contact number for people to call if they are unable to attend the meeting.

The notice will include the agenda of the meeting. This is an important part of the notice and is usually a bullet list of all the items that are going to be discussed in the meeting. The last item on the agenda is usually called 'AOB' or 'Any other business', which is a time when people can raise any points they want to discuss that have not already been addressed.

Clearview College

Notice of meeting

15 September 2010

The next meeting of the College's school council will be held in the main lecture theatre at 1 p.m. on Tuesday 3 October. Tea, coffee and biscuits will be provided.

Please contact Sarah Reed on extension 5678 if you are unable to attend.

Agenda

1. **Apologies for absence** (*a list of those who cannot attend*)
2. **Minutes of the previous meeting** (*gives people the chance to correct mistakes from the previous minutes*)
3. **Matters arising** (*enables people to give updates or report on action taken from the last meeting*)
4. **Report on the students' fundraising activities and money raised** (*main business of the meeting*)
5. **Proposed student interviews for new teaching staff** (*main business of the meeting*)
6. **AOB** (*Any Other Business – minor issues that people want to raise*)
7. **Date and time of next meeting**

Sarah Reed

Student Council Secretary

Figure 6.4 Example of a notice and agenda of a meeting

Minutes or the record of meeting

It is essential that there is a record of what was said in the meeting. Minutes are written during the meeting, typed up after the meeting and then circulated to all attendees. Having an agenda often makes taking minutes easier as you can make notes under each agenda heading. Writing minutes ensures that the important points that were discussed are recorded and circulated to those who need the information as soon as possible, so that the minutes can be agreed at the next meeting, and to remind people what they have to do following the meeting.

 Activity

In groups, you are going to hold your own meeting about what activities you think should be held in your school and why. You must:

1. Create a notice and agenda for your meeting.
2. Decide on a chairperson for the meeting.

3. Hold your meeting, ensuring that someone is taking minutes.
4. Distribute the minutes to everyone who attended the meeting.

Clearview College

Minutes of meeting

A meeting of the student council was held in the main lecture theatre at 1 p.m. on 3 October.

Present: Frank Middleton (Chairperson), Charles Smith, Henry Begley, Steven Bunn, Elizabeth Kennedy, Sarah Reed.

1. Apologies for absence

Apologies were received from Jill Folley.

2. Minutes of the previous meeting

These were agreed as a true reflection and record and signed by the chairperson.

3. Matters arising

Henry Begley said that the upcoming parents evening would mean that all student council representatives would be needed from 4 p.m. until 8 p.m. on 10 October.

4. Students' fundraising activities and money raised

Steven Bunn has now raised £400 for Save the Children by doing a sponsored silence.

More proposed events were outlined by Elizabeth Kennedy and included a readathon, a teachers' cross-country event and car washing. **EK**

5. Proposed student interviews for new teaching staff

New teacher interviews will be happening on 12 October. Charles Smith, Elizabeth Kennedy and Henry Begley have agreed to be a part of the interviews. **CS/EK/HB**

6. AOB

Frank Middleton asked for two volunteers to attend the parent governors meeting on 15 October to update them on the work of the student council. It was agreed that Steven Bunn and Henry Begley would be present. **SB/HB**

7. Date and time of next meeting

The next meeting will be held at 1 p.m. on 4 November.

Signed: _____ (chairperson)   Date: _____

Figure 6.5 Example of minutes of a meeting

Other documentation

Other documentation may be produced before and after the meeting, but this will depend on the type of meeting it is. For example, if a presentation is being given during the meeting, the presenter may want hard copies of the presentation to be distributed before, during or after it. The administration staff need to ensure that this is done within the given time frame.

Summary

Many meetings are internal and quite informal. But some are vital meetings with key customers – or perhaps with important people from Head Office. A well-prepared, well-run and effectively followed-up meeting will give a good impression and help the business to run efficiently. A poorly supported meeting might undermine the managers' attempts to make the business look good.

 Assessment activity 6.3 (P4, P5, M2, M3, D2)

You have now been at work for one week and the Head has asked you to prepare the documents she needs for a meeting. The meeting is with the deputy heads at 3 p.m. next Thursday. She would like the meeting to be in the boardroom, next to her office. She would like tea, coffee and biscuits (at a cost of £3 per head). The main subject of the meeting is exam results, and the head wants to discuss a few particular areas in more detail. These include: the achievements of all girls in the school in comparison with their target grades, the achievement of all of the white and Asian boys in the school compared with their target grades, and the possibility of the deputy heads giving a presentation to all of the staff to present the GCSE results to them.

1. Create a checklist of what you have to do in order to prepare for the meeting.

2. Produce all of the documents needed for the meeting.

3. Create all of the documentation needed following the meeting.

4. Explain what organisation and support is needed for the meeting to be a success.

5. Analyse the organisation of the meeting and documents and materials provided for it, making recommendations for any improvements.

Assessment summary

The overall grade you achieve for this unit depends on how well you meet the grading criteria set out at the start of the chapter (see page 105). You must complete:

- all of the P criteria to achieve a **pass** grade
- all of the P and the M criteria to achieve a **merit** grade
- all of the P, M and D criteria to achieve a **distinction** grade.

Your tutor will assess the assessment activities that you complete for this unit. The work you produce should provide evidence which demonstrates that you have achieved each of the assessment criteria. The table below identifies what you need to demonstrate to meet each of the pass, merit and distinction criteria for this unit. You should always check and self-assess your work before you submit your assignments for marking.

Remember that you MUST provide evidence for all of the P criteria to pass the unit.

Grading criteria	You need to demonstrate that you can:	Do you have the evidence?
P1	Explain the types and purposes of business support	
P2	Describe the use of office equipment to meet different business requirements	
P3	Demonstrate using office equipment safely in accordance with health and safety legislation	
P4	Draw up a checklist for a meeting	
P5	Produce documents needed for a meeting	
M1	Explain the appropriate uses of office equipment types, features and functions to suit different business purposes	
M2	Produce all post-meeting documentation	
M3	Explain the organisation and support provided for meetings	
D1	Analyse the contribution that office equipment makes to the provision of business support	
D2	Analyse the organisation and documents and materials provided for a meeting, making recommendations for any improvements	

Always ask your tutor to explain any assignment tasks or assessment criteria that you don't understand fully. Being clear about the task before you begin gives you the best chance of succeeding. Good luck with your Unit 6 assessment work!

7 Verbal and non-verbal communication in business contexts

Unit outline

Good communication is essential for the success of any business, large or small:

▶ staff must be able to understand tasks that they have been set

▶ and managers must understand any problems that staff are facing.

It is not only through spoken communication that a workforce communicates; there are also non-verbal forms of communication, such as a shrug of the shoulders.

In this unit you will learn how to use non-verbal communication skills and to understand the purpose of verbal communication in business contexts. Furthermore you will be able to use verbal communication in business contexts.

Learning outcomes

1 **Be able to use non-verbal communication skills.**
2 **Understand the purpose of verbal communication in business contexts.**
3 **Be able to use verbal communication in business contexts.**

Grading guide

To achieve a **pass**, you must show you can:	To achieve a **merit**, you must show you can:	To achieve a **distinction**, you must show you can:
P1 Demonstrate interpersonal interactions in a business context	**M1** Explain how interpersonal interaction skills are used to support business communication	**D1** Assess the importance of effective interpersonal interaction skills in a given business situation
P2 Explain, using examples, the purpose of verbal business communications in four different business contexts	**M2** Discuss how verbal communications can be used effectively in business situations	
P3 Demonstrate speaking and listening skills in a one-to-one business context		
P4 Demonstrate speaking and listening skills in a business group context	**M3** Carry out a review of their speaking and listening skills in both a one-to-one, and group context, identifying their strengths and weaknesses	**D2** Assess the effectiveness of speaking and listening skills in supporting business operations in a given business context

Using non-verbal communication skills

 Getting started

Have you ever seen someone and known what they were thinking without them saying? Do you know when your parents are unhappy with you without them having to tell you? This is non-verbal communication. It could be the scowl on your parents' face, or that they are standing with their hands on their hips – these are body language clues that are sending a message of dissatisfaction to you! Non-verbal communication is like talking without saying a word.

When you have completed this topic, you should:

- understand different forms of non-verbal communication
- understand its importance in the workplace.

 Key terms

Body language: messages you send that others pick up from the way you look and stand

Communication channel: a route for passing messages, e.g. Clubcard gives Tesco an email communication channel to its regular customers (as Clubcard users are asked for their email addresses)

Dress code: formal or informal rules about 'proper' clothing at work, e.g. jacket and tie

Non-verbal communication: messages given without words, e.g. a thumbs-up sign

Conveying a professional image

Everybody sends and receives messages using a variety of **non-verbal communication** methods, including:

▶ dress

▶ **body language**

▶ eye contact

▶ time management.

Research shows that clues in the non-verbal **communication channels** (*how* something is said) are often more important than words alone (*what* is said). Non-verbal communication is important to business because it creates or destroys the image of the business. Non-verbal communication can affect the reputation of business, both in a good and a bad way.

 Did you know?

Verbal communication uses words, either written or spoken. Non-verbal communication is all other forms of communication.

Appropriate dress and personal hygiene

Do you have a part-time job? Some of you may have jobs in supermarkets or in restaurants. Do you wear a uniform? Take a look around next time you are at work, or think about your school uniform. Why do businesses and schools like uniforms? The obvious answer is to identify those wearing the uniform as part of that organisation. Virgin Atlantic uses the bright red uniforms of its cabin crew to create an image for the airline as bright, young and flirty. Uniforms also make sure that staff (e.g. in a bank) or pupils look smart and businesslike.

Case study

Hola! is a tapas restaurant in Preston. Sophie has worked there for a year. Sophie is expected to wear a white shirt and a black skirt or trousers and has to stick to the **dress code**. Sophie is also expected to have a positive attitude, always look busy and never allow customers to be kept waiting. This is a major part of the business success of Hola! It has high service standards and there is attention to every detail. Presentation of the food is crucial, but Andrea (the owner of Hola!) places the same emphasis on the presentation of staff. She thinks it's essential that staff be clean and well presented, particularly as they are dealing with food. If staff looked scruffy, customers might think that food hygiene is not a priority.

Shabnam works in the kitchen at Hola! and she has to wear a particular uniform, have her hair tightly tied back and wear a hat or hairnet when preparing food. If hair is not tied back or covered, it is more likely to fall into food. This is not Andrea's demand, it is dictated by food and hygiene laws. In other words, it is a government regulation.

Andrea insists that kitchen staff wear clean aprons over their work clothes and that they get changed into their work clothes at work. Andrea insists that all staff should wear clean clothes when working with food. Clothes can bring dirt and bacteria into food preparation areas.

1. Explain why Andrea has a dress code for her staff.

2. What might be the effects of a government decision to abolish regulation governing business activity in the food industry?

Personal hygiene is vital in the restaurant industry, as the last thing a restaurant owner wants is to make a customer ill due to poor hygiene practices in their establishment. There are also legal requirements that have to be fulfilled, including:

▶ Work clothes should be long-sleeved, with no external pockets. This prevents skin from touching food and helps to stop hairs, fibres and the contents of pockets (which can carry bacteria) getting into food.

▶ Work clothes should be light coloured (to show any dirt).

Activity

1. Food hygiene regulations state that all businesses that sell food must send staff on a hygiene course. Is it fair to force businesses to spend their money in this way?

2. In July 2007 Cadbury was fined £1 million for food hygiene errors that caused a salmonella food poisoning outbreak. Apart from the £1 million, in what other ways would this incident have cost Cadbury money?

Dealing with staff and customers professionally

It is easy to identify unprofessional behaviour, such as chewing gum, using foul language and running down corridors! So what type of behaviour is professional and businesslike? Conveying a professional image is all about:

▶ dressing appropriately for your workplace

▶ being aware of your facial expressions and gestures

▶ being polite and courteous.

Case study

Staff at Hola! have to be polite and courteous to customers at all times, this is an essential part of running a successful restaurant. Andrea insists that staff make themselves look busy at all times; if a member of staff is standing around slouching and not doing any work, this can send negative messages to customers. Customers could think that they will receive poor service because the staff are lazy. This could result in Hola! losing potential customers.

Furthermore, Andrea insists that all staff are aware of their gestures and keep smiling at all times.

Smiling is a powerful cue that makes both customers and colleagues feel welcome and relaxed. It signals:

▶ happiness

▶ friendliness

▶ warmth

▶ liking

▶ affiliation

Thus, if you smile frequently you will be perceived as more likable, friendly, warm and approachable. Smiling is often contagious and customers and colleagues will usually react favourably to someone who is smiling.

It can sometimes be hard to deal calmly with an angry or unpleasant customer. This can be especially tough for a young member of staff. It is therefore important that junior staff are trained to know when to say, politely: 'Excuse me a moment. I'll just get my supervisor, who may be in a better position to help'.

Did you know?

Expressions and gestures are not the same around the world. For example, the 'thumbs-up', which is a positive gesture in many Western countries is a rude insult in other countries, such as Nigeria and Thailand.

Organisational skills and time management

Time management is a key skill needed in any business. Turning up late to a business meeting is like saying: 'You're not important to me'. The more the latecomer gives excuses for why they're late, the more the message is converted from, 'I don't care' to, 'I'm inefficient'. When going to a meeting or a job interview, it's sensible to be half an hour early, check where the entrance is, then find a café in which to wait until it is time for the meeting.

If you want to convey a professional image you must become a good time manager. Deadlines must be met and work priorities must be set. Effective staff are the ones who get the most important tasks completed first. Some people have naturally organised minds, but others may need to write a list of what they have to do today. The important thing is to show customers and colleagues that you care about doing a great job.

Assessment activity 7.1 (P1, M1, D1)

During your work experience placement you will carry out some assessment activities. You will have the opportunity to communicate with a range of different people and use a range of methods. Choose a small to medium-sized business and a large business that you are interested in.

1. List the main non-verbal skills that a new member of staff at your chosen organisation would be expected to have.

2. In relation to the business you have chosen, explain how the non-verbal skills shown by staff can have an impact on one of the following groups:
   a) customers face-to-face with staff
   b) customers ordering by phone
   c) suppliers.

3. Assess the importance of non-verbal skills to one specific member of staff within your chosen business.

Topic check

Tick the correct answer(s) in the questions below.

1 Identify two methods of non-verbal communication:
   a) holding a meeting
   b) body language
   c) time management
   d) a telephone call

2 Which form of communication is not non-verbal?
   a) smiling
   b) waving
   c) staring
   d) texting

3 'Wow!' clothing store insists that all staff wear the clothes that are currently in stock. Identify the reason for this:
   a) Staff look smart.
   b) Staff are clean.
   c) Staff are fashionable.

4 Identify the three main skills required to convey a professional image.
   a) to be enthusiastic
   b) to be able to manage their time
   c) to be polite
   d) to have a professional appearance
   e) to understand financial controls

The purpose of verbal communication in business contexts

Getting started

Verbal communication is needed to ensure that everyone understands what has been ordered or agreed.

When you have completed this topic, you should:

- understand the role of verbal communication
- understand the limitations of verbal communication.

Key terms

Feedback: receiving a response to your communication (e.g. 'Yes, sir')

Informal communication: communicating outside official channels, such as a boss giving a verbal instruction to a member of staff

The purpose of verbal communication

Verbal communication, both spoken and written, occurs constantly in any organisation – words are the main way people communicate with each other. Some of the most common reasons for verbal communication are shown in Figure 7.1.

In organisations, communication takes place both within the organisation (internally) and with groups outside the organisation (externally). For example, verbal communication methods are used in with:

- supervisors
- colleagues
- customers
- dealing with complaints
- giving verbal presentations.

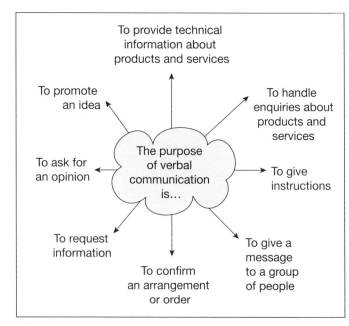

Figure 7.1 The purposes of verbal communication

The business context

When communicating with the different groups listed on page 128, people may choose different verbal methods and will adjust the 'tone' and type of language used. Messages to colleagues are likely to be much less formal than those to supervisors or customers. It is always best to avoid using slang, partly because it may mean different things in different places, but also because it can seem informal and unprofessional.

The key thing about verbal communication is that it provides relatively little scope for misunderstanding – especially if it is in writing. It is always important to remember the purpose of the communication. If you want to confirm an order, having it in writing (such as an email) will be helpful. It is proof that the order has been received and it may be helpful to refer back to it (Did they order three items or four?). On the other hand, if you plan to have a friendly chat with a customer, a phone call or a lunchtime meeting may be more suitable.

 Did you know?

In 2009, 265 million texts were sent per day in Britain. On Christmas Day the number rose to 441 million!

Formal and informal verbal communication

There are different types of verbal communication and, depending on the situation or the size of the organisation, it will be for different purposes. In big businesses, internal communication is more formal because staff may not know each other as well and there are more layers of management. If the purpose of the communication is formal then this will influence the choice of communication method.

Sometimes **informal communication** methods will be use in the workplace, for example where colleagues know each other well and work closely together they may sometimes have less formal discussions.

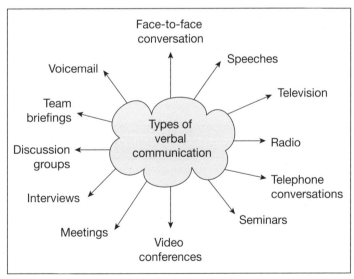

Figure 7.2 Types of verbal communication

 Did you know?

In 2009 there were 176 email messages per day per email user, of which 143 were Spam! So the average emailer wrote 33 messages.

Source: www.webuser.co.uk

Figure 7.3 Different ways in which verbal communication may take place in a business

	Type of communication	Example	Reason for use
Formal	Presentation	To explain a new product line to senior management	Allows **feedback** and questioning
	Video conference	To set up a contract with an overseas firm	Allows negotiation to take place
	Meetings	To inform middle managers of new production systems	Provides a forum for discussion minutes can be taken
	Letters and emails	Sending a customer details of product types, colours and prices	It would be impossible to remember all the details if they were given in a conversation
Informal	Telephone	To ask for an update on a job's progress	Quick response possible
	Face to face	To ask a colleague for an opinion on the design of a newspaper advert	Quick and possible to see reaction
	Emails and texts	Many people treat email informally or casually – though it can be used as legal proof	

Effective spoken communication

As you learned earlier, the way you say something can be just as important as what you say. Have you every heard the speech made by Dr Martin Luther King? His 'I Have a Dream' speech is considered to be a classic example of great verbal communication. Why? Because it contained strong images that provoked strong emotions; it was delivered with passion by someone who captured the dreams of an entire race.

Tips to improve your spoken communication skills

1. *Vary the speed* – a good speaker will talk slowly to generate anticipation or to accentuate an important point, and will talk faster to excite the listener.

2. *Vary the pitch* – lowering the tone of your voice slightly suggests you know what you are talking about. Raising the tone of your voice slightly indicates surprise or uncertainty. This is known as inflection.

3. *Control the volume* – to make an impact you need to be easily heard. If your voice is too loud it can be annoying! Aim to speak loudly enough to ensure that your message is clearly understood, but not so loudly that it sounds domineering.

4. *Articulate* – clear, crisp words suggest confidence, competence and intelligence.

5. *Pause for impact* – pauses are important because it gives the listener time to process the information you have given them.

Activity

1. Identify four situations in which it would be useful to communicate by letter.

2. Which method of communication should be used for each of these situations? Explain why.

   a) An airline has decided to cancel flights that some customers have already booked online.

   b) A boss needs to tell her 80 staff that 20 jobs have to go.

   c) A junior manager wants to make a complaint about being bullied by her boss.

Assessment activity 7.2 (P2, M2)

1. Conduct some research to find four situations in your chosen business where verbal communication takes place.

2. Explain why verbal communication takes place in these four situations.

3. Discuss how verbal communication can be used effectively in your chosen business.

Topic check

Tick the correct answer(s) in the questions below.

1 Dalbir has received a complaint from a customer. They are demanding an immediate response. Which method of communication should he use?

   a) letter   c) fax

   b) email   d) telephone

2 Peter wants to propose changes to the working day to all the staff. Which method of communication would be best?

   a) staff meeting   c) report

   b) telephone   d) email

3 One example of internal communication is with a:

   a) supervisor   c) supplier

   b) shareholder   d) customer

Using verbal communication in business contexts

Getting started

Effective communication requires a loop to be completed. This involves sending a message and getting a reply. If the communication is complex, it may require a whole conversation, with messages going back and forth. For this to happen there needs to be effort from both the sender of the message and the receiver. Successful communication requires the participants to have both speaking and listening skills.

When you have completed this topic, you should:

- know how to be a good listener
- know how to be a good speaker
- be able to take part in one-to-one and group discussions.

Listening skills

How well do you listen? Do you always hear what people are really saying? Or do you stop listening when you think you have heard what they have said and then fill in the blanks from your own assumptions? Being a good listener is one of the most important skills you can have. How well you listen has a major impact on how well you will do at school, in the world of work and in personal relationships. By becoming a better listener, you will improve your productivity, as well as your ability to influence, persuade and negotiate. Furthermore, you will be able to avoid conflict and misunderstandings – all necessary for workplace success. Sometimes, misunderstandings are

unavoidable if someone is in a hurry or they use jargon or technical terms. If you do not listen well then you are likely to make mistakes – something which can be very costly in business.

The way to become a better listener is to practise 'active listening'. This is when you make a conscious effort to hear not only the words that another person is saying but, more importantly, to try and understand the total message being sent.

Tips to becoming an active listener

1. *Pay attention* – stop what you are doing and give the speaker your complete attention.

2. *Show that you are listening* – nod occasionally and add verbal comments like 'yes'.

3. *Provide feedback* – this gives you the chance to make sure you understand the message. Reflect by saying thinks like, 'What it sounds like you are saying is…'. Ask questions to clarify points: 'Is this what you mean?' Summarise what the speaker has been saying.

4. *Defer judgement* – it is bad mannered to interrupt. Always allow the speaker to finish before you comment. If you want to disagree, wait for them to finish!

5. *Respond appropriately and think about what the person is saying* – be open and honest in your response, but be respectful in giving your opinions. Treat the other person as you would want to be treated – don't just think about your own reaction.

Over to you!

Choose two reasons why it is important to listen carefully.
a) To fully understand the full message.
b) To make assumptions about what you are being told.
c) To be able to seek clarification.
d) Because it is rude not to listen.

The ability to understand verbal instructions is a necessary requirement in most workplaces across all industries. Using the active listening skills outlined above will help you to understand any instructions that you are given and to be successful in completing tasks correctly.

Sometimes instructions can be brief and given quickly; sometimes they can be more complicated. In order to make sure that you understand, remember follow this useful tips:

1. *Make notes* – write down all the key points you have been told. It is important that you aren't distracted when you are doing this or you will lose track! Remember to write neatly as it can be very frustrating not being able to read your own notes later.

2. *Reflect* – a great way to reflect is to say something like, 'So, what I understand is…'. This gives the speaker a chance to correct you if you have misunderstood and for you to be sure what the task is.

3. *Confirm understanding* – if the speaker is using jargon or technical language that you do not understand, let them know or they will assume that you do understand.

4. *Seek clarification where appropriate* – try to avoid misunderstandings and misinterpretations at all costs as these lead to mistakes. If you are not sure, you should ask the speaker to clarify the instruction.

5. Always make sure you know how to get in touch with the person who has set you the task. You may find that a question only arises when you start a task, and it is always better to ask than to carry on and do it wrong!

Over to you!

Why will having effective listening skills make you better at work?

a) Because you can provide good feedback.

b) Because you will understand instructions properly.

c) Because it allows you to know what to say.

One-to-one communication

Good communication is the key to managing people effectively in the workplace. Being able to make yourself and your instructions understood to others is very important. One-to-one communication involves talking to another person. This could be in a formal or informal context and could take place either face-to-face, over the telephone or using the internet (instant messaging). Informal one-to-one communication could be when you chat to a colleague; your performance review with your supervisor would be a formal communication context. One-to-one communication can also be with people from outside the business, such as customers or suppliers.

One-to-one communication methods

Face-to-face communication occurs in a wide range of business activities, including formal meetings, coffee room chats, one-to-one coaching, a quick chat on the corridor with someone, annual evaluations and job interviews. Face-to-face communication allows all participants the opportunity to hear more than just what is said. If they can see you, they can tell how much you care. Remember, it is not only what you say but how you say it that is important.

Making sure that a message is communicated well is an important skill in business, particularly in a busy office with lots of distractions. Interruptions often occur in a busy workplace, which is why organisations schedule formal meetings and pre-arrange any interviews, so that participants will not be interrupted. It is also important to use your listening skills to receive messages – you could make sure you are prepared by carrying a notepad with you. Day-to-day, face-to-face communication will often take place in noisy environments and instructions may even be given in a busy corridor!

Telephone calls may be used to give and receive messages and instructions, and listening skills are essential when taking a call in a busy office environment. Sometimes you may not know the caller, and it can be hard to know what they are thinking because you can't see them. In these situations it is essential to clarify that the message has been received and understood correctly.

Did you know?

Football manager Roy Hodgson took Fulham from relegation certainty to seventh place in the Premier League. When asked what made the difference compared with the previous manager, player Chris Baird said, 'Roy talks to each of us individually every day: whether we've played well or badly.' One-to-ones work.

Use of language and expressions

When you started this course, your teacher will have spent some time explaining the many terms and phrases that were new to you, which you didn't understand. In business you should use language that will be understood by the receiver; you should avoid using terms and phrases (jargon) that are too technical and that the person you are communicating with may not understand.

Messages to suit different situations

In order for communication to be effective you need to choose the right method of communication and the right tone for the situation. For example, if you had to inform a member of staff that they were about to be made redundant, a phone call would not be appropriate. Face-to-face communication would be more sensitive. You would also want to use a sensitive and sympathetic tone. On the other hand, if you were informing someone of an upcoming promotion opportunity you could sound really pleased about it!

You should choose face-to-face communication:

▶ when you are giving somebody bad news
▶ when the matter is personal or confidential
▶ when you want somebody to do something outside of their normal duties
▶ to explain something in detail to a member of staff.

You should communicate by telephone in the following situations when:

▶ the matter is urgent and you need a quick answer
▶ it is a quick question you need a simple answer to
▶ you are at a different location and it would take a lot of time to see the person
▶ you have an important question and the person is away.

Over to you!

Choose the correct definition of one-to-one communication:
a) Where an individual communicates with a group.
b) Where one individual communicates with another.
c) Where one individual communicates with anybody.

Working in a group situation

At school you probably work in groups or teams a lot. It is the same in most businesses. Teams work together to complete projects, and in order to be effective they must be able to communicate well. This means being able to:

▶ make relevant contributions to a discussion about business tasks
▶ contribute to meetings and team briefings
▶ respond appropriately to others and move a discussion forward.

There is no point attending a meeting and not asking a question or contributing if you have something important to say. Your job role will influence how you contribute to a meeting or discussion. If you are a project manager you will be expected to lead the meeting and keep the discussion going. It is also important to listen to other viewpoints and ensure that everyone is heard. In most meetings contributions are managed through a Chairperson. If someone wants to contribute they indicate to the Chair, perhaps by raising their hand, and then the Chair will direct them to speak. In all cases, you would be expected to speak and not just to sit and 'switch off'! A badly organised and poorly run meeting is a waste of everybody's time, as is a meeting that is overshadowed by one individual who does not allow anyone else to speak, or who will not listen to others' opinions.

Formal meetings will have an agenda that is shared with those attending. This should be given in advance to all those invited to the meeting, to allow them to prepare. During the meeting a record of discussions and actions are kept and recorded in the 'minutes'.

Does your school have a team briefing with all the staff in the morning before school? In most organisations staff have to attend a briefing on a regular basis. The purpose of this is to pass on information and give updates. Briefings are used by senior managers to pass information on to staff in the lower levels of the hierarchy.

 Topic check

1. Lisa has to speak to Phil about the fact he has been missing his sales targets. Which form of communication should she use?

   a) telephone   b) email   c) meeting

2. Uzma needs to confirm the dates Imitiaz wants for his holidays. Which form of communication should she use?

   a) telephone   b) meeting   c) briefing

3. Identify the three most important rules of a meeting.

   a) issue agenda   c) listen to all viewpoints   e) keep no records

   b) have Chairperson to run it   d) managers speak first

4. Why is feedback necessary for communication to be effective?

5. Identify whether the following forms of communication are formal or informal:

   a) body language   b) team briefing   c) a business meeting

6. Why may a manager want to hold a team briefing at the start of every day's work?

7. Identify one communication strength and one communication weakness in a system of group working.

8. Identify two circumstances in which it would be better for a manager to use verbal communication rather than non-verbal communication.

Case study

Chantelle is organising a fundraising event at work, but has not yet decided what event to stage and when. She has set up a team to manage the project, which she is leading.

1. Advise Chantelle of how to go about deciding on the theme for the event. What should be her next steps?

2. Chantelle's team have decided to organise a fancy dress fun run. Chantelle wants to check that the senior management team are happy with this decision and explain her plans for the event. Describe the best method of communication to achieve this task.

Assessment activity 7.3 (P3)

During your work experience you will need to ask your supervisor to complete a witness statement to show when you have demonstrated speaking and listening skills in a one-to-one business context.

Your task is to write a brief commentary on what you learnt from this feedback from your supervisor. It should be no more than 150 words.

Assessment activity 7.4 (P4, M3, D2)

During your work experience you will need to ask your supervisor to complete a witness statement to show when you have demonstrated speaking and listening skills in a business group context.

a) You will then need to carry out a review of your speaking and listening skills in the situation in both a one-to-one and group context, identifying your strengths and weaknesses.

b) You must assess the importance of speaking and listening skills in supporting business operations at your work experience placement.

Write a report of 150–200 words for each of tasks a) and b).

Assessment summary

The overall grade you achieve for this unit depends on how well you meet the grading criteria set out at the start of the chapter (see page 123). You must complete:

- all of the P criteria to achieve a **pass** grade
- all of the P and the M criteria to achieve a **merit** grade
- all of the P, M and D criteria to achieve a **distinction** grade.

Your tutor will assess the assessment activities that you complete for this unit. The work you produce should provide evidence which demonstrates that you have achieved each of the assessment criteria. The table below identifies what you need to demonstrate to meet each of the pass, merit and distinction criteria for this unit. You should always check and self-assess your work before you submit your assignments for marking.

Remember that you MUST provide evidence for all of the P criteria to pass the unit.

Grading criteria	You need to demonstrate that you can:	Do you have the evidence?
P1	Demonstrate interpersonal interactions in a business context	
P2	Explain, using examples, the purpose of verbal business communications in four different business contexts	
P3	Demonstrate speaking and listening skills in a one-to-one business context	
P4	Demonstrate speaking and listening skills in a business group context	
M1	Explain how interpersonal interaction skills are used to support business communication	
M2	Discuss how verbal communications can be used effectively in business situations	
M3	Carry out a review of their speaking and listening skills in both a one-to-one, and group context, identifying their strengths and weaknesses	
D1	Assess the importance of effective interpersonal interaction skills in a given business situation	
D2	Assess the effectiveness of speaking and listening skills in supporting business operations in a given business context	

Always ask your tutor to explain any assignment tasks or assessment criteria that you don't understand fully. Being clear about the task before you begin gives you the best chance of succeeding. Good luck with your Unit 7 assessment work!

8 Business communication through documentation

Unit outline

Every day thousands of emails, letters, reports and memos are sent and received from businesses and within businesses for a variety of purposes. Businesses rely on staff to communicate effectively using a variety of methods that are appropriate to the context of the communication:

▶ formally, such as sending a response to a complaint from a customer, or confirming the delivery of some supplies, or

▶ informally, such as a chatty email between colleagues.

Learning outcomes

1 **Know the purpose of written communication in business contexts.**
2 **Be able to complete and use business documents for internal and external communication in an organisation.**
3 **Know the importance of using appropriate methods of written communication depending on the audience.**

Grading guide

To achieve a **pass**, you must show you can:	To achieve a **merit**, you must show you can:	To achieve a **distinction**, you must show you can:
P1 Identify, using examples, the purposes of written business communications in four different business contexts	**M1** Describe appropriate methods of written communication in different business contexts	**D1** Explain the importance of written communication in an organisation in specific business contexts
P2 Produce three documents of different types to support straightforward business tasks for internal communication in an organisation	**M2** Compare your choice of internal and external documents	**D2** Justify your choice of internal and external documents explaining why each document is appropriate for its intended audience
P3 Produce three documents of different types for external communication by an organisation		
P4 Identify appropriate methods of communication to different audiences	**M3** Describe appropriate methods of written communication to different audiences	**D3** Explain appropriate methods of written communication to different audiences

The purpose of written communications in business contexts

> ▶ **Getting started**

There are various methods of written communication used in business (e.g. handwritten, word processed, electronic). The method used will depend on the context of the communication and its purpose (e.g. formal or informal, who it's to, what it's for).

When you have completed this topic, you should:

- know the types of written communication used in business
- know the purposes of written communication
- understand which sort of written communication to use in different contexts.

Types of written communication

Written communication can take a variety of forms, depending on what it is being used to communicate and who it is to.

Figure 8.1 Examples of written communication

Type of written communication	Example
Formal report to all staff	Giving staff details of everyone's sales performance last year
Formal letter	Written confidentially to a member of staff, confirming their new role and salary
Informal notice	Details of the Christmas party
Formal email	Request sent to a manager, asking for an afternoon off to go to a school governors' meeting
Informal email	Confirming lunch arrangement with colleagues

The purposes of written communication

Written communications have a variety of purposes, including:

▶ to inform
▶ to confirm
▶ to promote
▶ to make a request
▶ to instruct.

The context of written communications

The context in which the communication takes place will affect the tone and style of communication. The layout, structure and language used within a document must be appropriate to the needs of the reader and the tone of the message.

▶ *Formal* forms of written communication are used when a professional impression needs to be made, for example, when writing a letter for a job application. Formal documents should be written using professional language, with correct spelling, punctuation and grammar, using the correct layout and a high standard of presentation.

▶ *Informal* forms of written communication are used when a more relaxed and casual style of writing is appropriate, for example, an email to a colleague or text message to a friend.

There are some dos and don'ts of formal communication, as shown in Figure 8.2.

Over to you!

Write a letter of 80–100 words asking for your money back after going to a concert where the sound system was faulty. Make sure you follow the dos and don'ts in Figure 8.2.

Figure 8.2 Dos and don'ts of formal written communication

Dos	Don'ts
When you've finished writing: • Go over it again and try to halve the length; the author/genius Mark Twain once wrote: 'Sorry it's a long letter, I didn't have time to write you a short one.' • Check that there are no spelling or grammatical mistakes. • Check that it is clear and strikes the right tone.	• Don't use slang. • Don't use exclamation marks. • Don't be 'matey' – be formal. • Don't add in social comments such as, 'How was last Friday night?'

Over to you!

Which is the correct definition of a formal document?

a) Written using a more relaxed and casual style of writing.

b) Written using business words and using correct formatting features.

c) Written using professional language, the correct layout and a high standard of presentation.

Topic check

1 Briefly explain what is meant by the term 'formal communication'.

2 Give two examples of formal communication at your school/college.

3 Why are exclamation marks rarely used in formal written communication?

4 Why may it take longer to write a short letter than a long one?

Using business documents for internal and external communication

Getting started

Successful employees know the right type of communication to use at the right time.

When you have completed this topic, you should:

- know which document to use in different circumstances
- know how to use each document.

Key terms

Conventions: standard ways of writing, e.g. formal grammar

Format: the layout used in a document, e.g. double-line spacing

Proofread: to re-read your work with great care, to check whether there are any errors

Recipient: the intended receiver of the communication

Synonym: an alternative word with the same meaning as another, e.g. a synonym for 'scared' is 'frightened'

Template: a standard format for formal communication, perhaps including a firm's logo

Types of document

There is a variety of types of written document, which are suitable for different purposes.

Figure 8.3 Types and purposes of written documents

Written method	Appropriate use
Letter	As a response to a letter of complaint from a customer
Memo	As a reminder to staff to follow procedure
Report	To report on a new production method
Email	To confirm a lunch arrangement with a colleague
Notice	To announce staff social functions
Agenda	To provide details of what is to be discussed at a meeting
Minutes	As a record of what has been discussed at a meeting
Purchase order	To request that goods are sent by a company to a supplier
Invoice	To give details of a purchase and serve as a record
Text	To confirm a meeting date

Appropriate layouts

Most documents have set layouts that have been designed so that they are:

▶ *Fit for purpose* – this means that the document exactly matches the needs of the intended readers, e.g. the style of writing, language, layout and the appropriate use of language within the document.

▶ *Appropriate to the task* and the *internal/external audience* – sometimes documents are produced that could have a similar purpose, e.g. letters and memos can both be used to inform, but a memo would be used internally and a letter sent to a customer. The layout and the content will vary according to the intended receiver.

▶ *Use of different formats and styles* – business documents all have their own layout and design. **Format** is a word used to describe the design of a document. All documentation from a business must reflect the corporate identify or brand image. This is called the 'house style'. All corporate documents should include the logo, slogan and contact details; they must have a consistent layout and colour scheme. To ensure consistency, most businesses have standard **templates** that can be used. There will be instructions about what fonts (e.g. Times New Roman) and sizes can be used, as well as any headings and images that can be used. The templates will already have set pagination (page numbering) and document headers and footers.

Examples of the most common types of business documents are given below.

Business letter

Notice that the business letter in Figure 8.1 has a house style letterhead. When writing a business letter, always use formal language. It is also important to get the layout and the format right.

All business letters must include the following:

▶ *Our Ref*: – your reference number for the letter.

▶ *Your Ref*: – the receiver's reference number for the letter (if known).

▶ Sir/Madam – use this form of address if you do not know the name of the person you are writing to.

▶ *Re*: – this introduces the subject of the letter; it is short for 'regarding'.

▶ *Yours sincerely* – use this ending if you know and have used the person's name.

▶ *Yours faithfully* – use this ending if you don't know the person's name and have started the letter 'Dear Sir' or 'Dear Madam'.

29 High Street Preston Lancashire PR6 2HT	**IHT Car Supplies** *Think IHT. Think Quality.*

Our Ref: 15/MB/09
Your Ref: UM/IH
20th January 2010

Mrs U Woods
Sales Director
Cerry's Vehicles
15 Main Road
Preston
Lancashire
PR25 9HU

Dear Mrs Woods,
Re: Purchase of cambelts

(Write the main body of your letter here)

Yours sincerely,

(Signature)
L. Wright (Mrs)
Sales Manager
IHT Car Supplies

Figure 8.4 Business letter layout

Memo

A memo should be short and straight to the point. The style of writing can be formal or informal, depending on the topic.

When producing a memo, include:

▶ *To* – name of **recipient**

▶ *From* – name of sender

▶ *CC* – stands for 'carbon copy' and indicates any one else you have sent the memo to for reference

▶ *Date* – the date the memo is sent

▶ *Re*: – the topic ('regarding').

Then write your short message

IHT Car Supplies
Think IHT. Think Quality.

Memo

To:	Miss J Farnborough
From:	Mr M Robett
CC:	Mrs S Corningham
Date:	15 September 2010
Re:	Request for meeting

(You would write your message here.)

Figure 8.5 Memo layout

Report

A business report is a formal method of communication. It is a written document designed to convey information in a concise but detailed way. A report begins with a formal section showing who the report if for, who has written it, the date it was written and the title, as on a memo.

Did you know?

Memos are rapidly disappearing in business, replaced by emails. However, reports remain widely in use.

IHT Car Supplies
Think IHT. Think Quality.

Report

To:	Mr J Jones
From:	Mr K Robson
Date:	20 January 2010
Re:	Report on Sales 2009–10

1.0 Terms of reference

This report is about the level of sales starting from the period January 2009 to January 2010. This report will investigate which products have sold well and will examine those that have not generated a high sales volume. At the end of the report, reasons why and recommendations for 2010 will be made.

2.0 Procedure

In writing this report I made a number of investigations.

2.1 I collated the sales data for each quarter from the sales department.

2.2 I interviewed customer service assistants.

3.0 Findings

As a result of my enquiry I obtained the following:

3.1 *(Findings would go here)*

4.0 Recommendations

My conclusions are as follows:

4.1 *(The conclusion is very important and should aim to bring together points raised and analysed in previous sections. A recommendation or series of recommendations should be made.)*

Figure 8.6 Report layout

All formal reports should include:

▶ *Terms of reference* – outlines what the report is about.

▶ *Procedure* – defines the methods used to find the data or information for the report.

▶ *Findings* – details the findings of the report (the data and information that was gathered).

▶ *Conclusions/Recommendations* – details any conclusions that can be drawn and makes suggestions for future action.

Email

An email should be short and straight to the point. The style of writing, like a memo, can be formal or informal, depending on the topic. Many businesses have a corporate email template that must be used for all electronic mail correspondence. The user is able to set their email to include their own name and job title as well as contact details.

Notice

Notices should be straight to the point and easy for the audience to read. The style of writing can be formal or informal, depending on the topic.

29 High Street Preston Lancashire PR6 2HT	**IHT Car Supplies** *Think IHT. Think Quality.*

Hi Joe

I was just getting in touch to check that you were still OK for our meeting tomorrow? Let me know if there are any problems.

Kind regards

Ken Hodgins

Sales Supervisor

Tel: 01772 766455 Fax: 01772 7463829

Figure 8.7 Email layout

	IHT Car Supplies *Think IHT. Think Quality.*

Notice to all staff

All staff are reminded to ensure that they sign in as they arrive at work.

J Jurior

HR Manager

Figure 8.8 Notice layout

Agenda

An agenda is a formal document outlining the details of a meeting. The agenda itemises the programme of points to be discussed in a logical and structured order. An agenda is distributed before the meeting to all people that will attend.

The first points that must be on an agenda are:

▶ Apologies for absence

▶ Minutes and matters arising from the minutes of the last meeting

The last two points on an agenda must be:

▶ Date and time of next meeting

▶ AOB (any other business)

What comes in between will depend on what the meeting is for and what is going to be discussed.

	IHT Car Supplies *Think IHT. Think Quality.*

Management Meeting Agenda

Date: 1 October 2010

Venue: Conference Room

Time: 15.00 hrs

1. Apologies for absence
2. Minutes and matters arising
4. Progress update
5. Date and time of next meeting
6. Any other business

Figure 8.9 Agenda layout

Minutes

The minutes of a meeting are usually completed by someone who attends the meeting, normally a secretary or an administrative assistant. They serve as a record of who attends, the time, date and venue, and of all discussions, action points and decisions.

After the meeting, the minutes are written up in a clear, neat format and all those who were present at the meeting receive a copy. Once it is agreed by the attendees that the minutes are correct they can be made available to other staff.

Minutes of a meeting should include:

▶ the name of the organisation at the top of the page

▶ the time, date and venue of the meeting

▶ the attendees at the meeting

▶ the points discussed and decisions made at the meeting

▶ comments made by each attendee next to the points covered.

| IHT Car Supplies |
| Think IHT. Think Quality. |

Management Meeting Minutes
Date: 1 October 2010
Venue: Conference Room
Time: 15.00 hrs
Present: JHA, CRO, JWO, UIS, LSH. Apologies: CHA.

Agenda item	Discussion	Action
Minutes and matters arising		
Progress update		
Date and time of next meeting		
Any other business		

Figure 8.10 Layout for minutes of a meeting

Purchase order

A purchase order is sent to a supplier to give an official instruction to deliver a specific number of specific goods at a specific time.

29 High Street
Preston
Lancashire
PR6 2HT

IHT Car Supplies
Think IHT. Think Quality.

Purchase Order
Date: 12 September 2010
PO Number: 2453322
To: Jane Crunch   Ship to: IHT Car Supplies

Quantity	Item	Units	Description	Unit Price	Total
10	Alternators	1	Engine part	£53.50	£535.00
				Subtotal	£535.00
				Shipping	£20
				Balance due	£555.00

Figure 8.11 Purchase order layout

Invoice

An invoice tells a customer how much they must pay as a result of making a purchase. An invoice is usually sent in response to a purchase order.

Over to you!

Choose the business document that should be used by a manager to let all the staff know that the building will close early for maintenance.

a) invoice

b) letter

c) memo

d) notice

		29 High Street Preston Lancashire PR6 2HT	**IHT Car Supplies** *Think IHT. Think Quality.*

Invoice

Date: 28 September 2010

Invoice Number: 3680983HJ

Re: Order Number 2453329

To: Kens Cars

Quantity	Item	Units	Description	Unit Price	Total
2	Alternators	1	Engine part	£75	£150.00
				Subtotal	£150.00
				Shipping	£30
				Balance due	£180.00

Please pay within 28 days of the date on invoice.

Figure 8.12 Invoice layout

Internal and external written communications

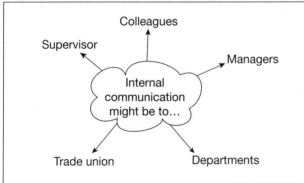

Figure 8.13 Internal communication

Figure 8.14 External communication

When writing a business document, there are certain things to bear in mind.

Use of relevant technical language

We have already looked at the importance of being careful not to use technical language or jargon if there is a possibility that the receiver of the communication may not understand it. However, sometimes it is acceptable, even advisable to use jargon. For example, when communicating with someone in the same department, it may be quicker and more accurate to describe something using technical language. The key is to know when it is appropriate to use jargon. If you can be certain that the receiver understands, then use it.

Graphical information

Sometimes it's easier to convey information by representing it using graphs and diagrams. If you are doing a presentation to staff about the rate of increase in customer numbers, this would be shown best as a line graph; the growth would be clearer to see as a graph. The key is to make sure that the audience understands how to read and interpret any graphs.

Drafting and redrafting to ensure accuracy

In order to ensure that a professional image is maintained, it is important to ensure that there are no errors in spelling, punctuation or grammar in any business document. Customers who receive a letter that is incorrectly laid out and full of spelling mistakes are going to form a negative opinion of the business. Remember, the quality of the document is also sending a message. The key is to take your time, read your work, make corrections, then read it again. This is particularly important with emails, where the temptation can be to type them in quickly and then click send before you have re-read them.

Legibility and consistency

Most communications these days are done using ICT, but there may be situations where you need to hand write – perhaps to take a telephone message for someone. In these situations you must ensure that you take the time to write neatly and clearly; an unintelligible note is no use to anyone! Another common mistake in business documents is lack of consistency. If you start writing a letter from yourself, remember to be consistent, so don't, for example, change to 'we' halfway through. Consistency also refers to the way a document is formatted; business letters must be set out in a certain way. For example, there should be a set amount of space between paragraphs, which must stay the same throughout the whole letter.

Conventions

There are certain rules you should follow when producing business documents. These include **conventions** relating to spelling, punctuation, grammar and paragraphing. Spelling of all words should be 'UK' rather than 'US' English (check the setting of your spell checker). Punctuation should be helpful and guide the reader through the document. The layout should be appropriate for the particular business document, as seen earlier.

Checking for accuracy, consistency and fitness for purpose

Checking your work for mistakes is essential when tasked with creating a business document. You must be able to **proofread** your work and measure how successful you have been in creating a quality piece of writing. Many people rely on spell checkers and the '**synonym**' facility on the computer. It is important to be aware that the spell checker will not always pick up small grammatical errors, such as the use of 'wear' instead of 'where'.

> ## ? Did you know?
>
> Recent research in America suggests that for every 10 external communications by managers there are 72 internal ones. This might suggest that people in business spend too much time talking with colleagues, but not enough time with customers.

Meeting deadlines

This is one of the most important things in business. When a deadline is set, it must be met. There is no flexibility for deadlines in business, as there may be in school or college. If a document is to be delivered by a certain time or date, then it is your responsibility to make sure that it is. If you need help then you must ask, but not when the deadline has already passed.

Recording and reporting

More often than not a record needs to be kept of conversations and communications in a business, so that there is something to refer to if anyone needs to check what has been said and any actions that have been agreed. These records need to be accurate and complete.

Different types of record are kept for different things, for example:

▶ *Meetings* – we have already discussed taking minutes in a meeting. The person taking the minutes must ensure that all actions are recorded clearly, along with the name of the person responsible for completing the task. Before any minutes are finalised they are sent to everyone who attended to the meeting to check that they are an accurate reflection of what was said and agreed in the meeting.

▶ *Internal conversations* – sometimes you may need to record conversations that you have on the phone with a colleague. If you being given instructions it is useful to jot down some notes to refer back to later.

Accurate and concise reporting within given time frames

It is vitally important, when keeping records of conversations, to make sure that the notes are accurate and that you have included all the relevant details, such as any deadlines you must meet. If you are taking a message for someone else, for example a phone message, it is essential that you take the name and phone number of the caller accurately, as well as the time and date when they called. If you are not sure what someone has said, ask them to repeat it. You should repeat any names and contact details back to the caller to make sure you have got them right.

It is also important that you work within given time frames and meet deadlines. If you take an urgent message for someone, you must make sure you get it to them as soon as possible. Similarly, if you have been asked to take the minutes of a meeting, you must make sure they are completed and distributed within a couple of days. The sooner you write them up, the fresher your memory will be. If there are any points to action, people will need the minutes to refer to. If you are asked to do something by a certain time or date then, in the world of business, you must meet that deadline.

Reporting issues as they arise to the appropriate person

If you are asked to do a task and something happens to prevent you from meeting the deadline, then you must let the relevant person know as soon as possible, and definitely before the deadline has passed. Similarly, if you are not clear about something, it is good to try to solve the problem yourself, but you must tell someone if this is going to cause delays or if you do not think you can solve the problem on your own. There is nothing wrong with admitting that you need help, and the more experienced you become at a job, the less help you should need.

Over to you!

Why might someone want to take a record of a conversation?

a) Because they want to know what you wrote.

b) Because they need to keep an accurate record of actions.

c) Because they might need it for a legal dispute.

Assessment activity 8.1 (P1, M1, D1)

Working in groups, use the internet and perhaps your work experience placement to find *four* different businesses with clear differences between them.

1. Identify the purposes of written business communications in each of those businesses, giving different and specific examples for each.

2. Describe, using examples, four different methods of written communication that each business can use.

3. Explain, giving examples, the importance of written communication to each of the businesses you have chosen.

Assessment activity 8.2 (P2, M2, D2)

Thrifty's is a small supermarket chain in Manchester. It is known as a good employer, and good communications are considered to play a key part in its success.

1. In small groups, discuss the documents that Thrifty's should have available for internal and external communications.

Peter, the Director, needs to call a meeting of all the managers to discuss the following:

- proposals about charging for carrier bags

- the new store opening in Urmston

- recruitment of new staff.

2. Write a memo to inform all the store mangers about the time, date and venue of the meeting.

3. Prepare an agenda to be given to all those who are attending the meeting.

4. Draft an email from Peter to inform the Board of Directors that he has arranged the meeting and that it is going ahead this week.

To gain a merit and distinction you need to explain the difference between the written documents you have prepared, explain why the written documents are suitable for the purpose and justify why they are appropriate for the task and the audience.

Topic check

1 Identify three features of all business documents:

   a) logo   c) name of sender

   b) contact details   d) slogan

2 A supplier needs to contact a business and ask for payment. The business document they will send is a:

   a) purchase order   c) invoice

   b) memo   d) text

3 'Re' stands for:

   a) report   c) response

   b) regarding   d) remain

4 Which business document would a business choose to record what happens in a meeting?

   a) minutes   c) memo

   b) agenda   d) report

5 Which of the following is a style of writing used in business?

   a) formal   c) polite

   b) conservative

6. When writing an agenda, what should always be the first item?

   a) AOB   c) date of next meeting

   b) minutes/matters arising

7. What does AOB stand for?

   a) anybody's business   c) anybody's objections

   b) any other business

8. Which document would you use if you wanted to confirm an order placed with a supplier?

   a) memo   c) invoice

   b) email   d) purchase order

9. You have started a letter Dear Sir/Madam. Which ending should you use?

   a) Yours sincerely   c) Kind regards

   b) Yours faithfully

Using appropriate methods of communication

Getting started

The key skill in business communication is to match your approach to the audience. Whereas adults may be able to read about the safety features of an aeroplane from a card, young children would learn more from a cartoon video.

When you have completed this topic, you should:

- be able to select the right communication method to match the target audience
- be able to use each communication method effectively, e.g. writing in clear, simple language for overseas visitors to Britain.

Key terms

Crystal Mark: an award given for exceptionally clear writing

Fog Index: a measurement of the lack of clarity of a piece of communication

Jargon: technical terms that are known only to insiders, e.g. teachers use the term INSET to mean training for teachers

Dealing with confidential matters

Often, business communication is confidential. It is understandable that businesses have secrets in their external communications. Not only is it important to keep things from competitors, but there are many things managers want to keep from their suppliers and customers. For example, Cadbury might be paying more to one sugar supplier than another. If the lower-paid supplier found out, it would demand extra payments.

Many forms of communication are not secure, i.e. it is easy for others to obtain the information. Mobile phone conversations can easily be 'hacked' into, and email or texts are equally insecure. In general, the communication of confidential matters requires thought and care. The best method is hand-delivery of a letter, especially if the recipient signs to confirm that they have received it. A good alternative is a face-to-face, one-to-one meeting.

It is less obvious, though, that there is a lot of confidential communication within an organisation, i.e. internally. All businesses want to keep staff from knowing the salaries of their fellow workers. As is clear from football players, even those with a weekly wage of £70,000 get upset with their pay, if a teammate earns £90,000. Other internal matters that should be kept confidential include:

- complaints about another employee, e.g. 'My manager is too flirty'
- new product ideas (after all, today's colleague could leave in a month and get a job with a competitor)
- personal issues, e.g. an employee tells his manager that his marriage is breaking up.

In all cases of confidentiality the keys are to:

▶ handle things with sensitivity, making sure to keep secrets secret

▶ choose the communication medium that can keep confidential items confidential, e.g. the personally delivered letter

▶ understand the law relating to data protection; you may have found an email address list for all the customers at company A, just as you're switching jobs to work for the rival company B; taking that list would be theft, and would also break the Data Protection Act.

Communicating with clarity

Good communication means finding the right way to get the right message to the target receiver. The London Underground is widely used by tourists, yet a regular message given to travellers is 'alight with care'. Tourists (and quite a few British people) must be worrying more about fire than getting off a train.

To measure the effectiveness of communication you can apply a test known as the **Fog Index**. If the words are measured at a high Fog Index, the text is unclear. This might be because of poor wording, or because the language level is too high (lots of long words or lots of **jargon**).

An opposite of the Fog Index is the **Crystal Mark**. This measurement of language gives an award for (crystal) clear English. It would be good if every exam paper had to go through this test before being used among students.

 Case study

In November last year Mandy and Dave opened a restaurant in China. It cost £110,000 to get the business up and running, and it was launched by running this small advertisement in all the main newspapers in Beijing:

'*York* is a British restaurant with a vision and mission to bring the best of Yorkshire to Beijing. The cuisine will be rooted in the Yorkshire Dales, featuring fare such as Barnsley Chops and

Yorkshire Pudding. We welcome Chinese gourmets to Yorkshire.'

1. Identify two words or phrases that might have proved especially difficult for Chinese customers to understand.

2. How well do you think this advertisement would have scored on the Fog Index and on the Crystal Mark?

Audit and evidence requirements

In certain businesses, an 'audit trail' is critical. If an aeroplane crashes because of a faulty fuel pump, it is vital to trace who supplied it, who fitted it, and who serviced it last. Therefore a detailed paperwork system is required to record exactly what happened when.

Unfortunately, other organisations (such as schools) have adopted the same paperwork system, even though nobody dies if a teacher forgets to set homework! But in an era where people are likely to rush to court for compensation, organisations want to protect themselves by keeping careful records. So if a parent attempts to sue a school for incompetence, the school likes to have detailed records of what homework was set when (and when the student failed to get the work done).

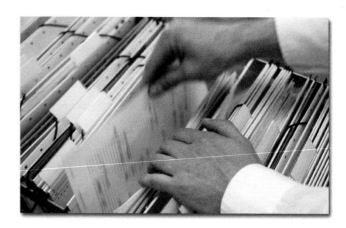

Case study

You and some friends have decided to run a small business enterprise making and selling bars of soap. You want to sell the soap at the Summer Fair at the end of the year. You need to contact some local businesses to ask them if they will supply you with the resources needed. You know you need some help from some other pupils making the soaps as well as making sure you have all the business document templates ready for when your business is established.

1. Identify who the business will need to communicate with and why.

2. Discuss the range of business documents the soap business will need; their purpose and audience.

3. Describe the problems the business might encounter.

Assessment activity 8.3 (P3, P4, M3, D3)

Future Sports is a UK-based sportswear and accessories retailer and manufacturer. Future Sports get their supplies from a range of businesses both in the UK and abroad; they sell both their own and other brands. Future Sports are expanding rapidly and are opening new stores every 6 months.

John, the manager of the new Leeds store, must inform Sandra that she has been successful following her recent interview for the post of Customer Sales Assistant.

1. Write a formal letter to Sandra to confirm her appointment and informing her of when her induction will start.

Uzair works in the Head Office of Future Sports in the Finance Department. Uzair has to prepare two documents: an invoice and a purchase order.

2. Prepare an invoice for Board Sports, who have purchased 20 Barton Skateboards to be delivered to their shop on Bridge Street, Kirkby.

3. Prepare a purchase order to confirm an order made to Raddike Sports for 100 pairs of Fuerto Board Shorts priced at £15 per pair.

4. Identify and explain which methods of written communication should be used by Uzair for the following:

   a) to inform the manager of the York store that the order for Fuerto Board Shorts will be delivered next week.

   b) to arrange a meeting with the bank manager on behalf of the Finance Director.

   c) to provide the Managing Director with information about of all Future Sports' spending last year.

Topic check

1 Identify two types of information a business might want to keep confidential from its customers.

2 Explain how a business might find it useful to use the Fog Index to check its internal documents.

3 Identify two types of information that a business might wish to keep on file for several years to come.

4 Do you think this chapter would be awarded the Crystal Mark? Briefly explain your reasoning.

Assessment summary

The overall grade you achieve for this unit depends on how well you meet the grading criteria set out at the start of the chapter (see page 139). You must complete:

■ all of the P criteria to achieve a pass grade
■ all of the P and the M criteria to achieve a merit grade
■ all of the P, M and D criteria to achieve a distinction grade.

Your tutor will assess the assessment activities that you complete for this unit. The work you produce should provide evidence which demonstrates that you have achieved each of the assessment criteria. The table below identifies what you need to demonstrate to meet each of the pass, merit and distinction criteria for this unit. You should always check and self-assess your work before you submit your assignments for marking.

Remember that you MUST provide evidence for all of the P criteria to pass the unit.

Grading criteria	You need to demonstrate that you can:	Do you have the evidence?
P1	Identify, using examples the purposes of written business communications in four different business contexts	
P2	Produce three documents of different types to support straightforward business tasks for internal communication in an organisation	
P3	Produce three documents of different types for external communication by an organisation	
P4	Identify appropriate methods of communication to different audiences	
M1	Describe appropriate methods of written communication in different business contexts	
M2	Compare your choice of internal and external documents	
M3	Describe appropriate methods of written communication to different audiences	
D1	Explain the importance of written communication in an organisation in specific business contexts	
D2	Justify your choice of internal and external documents explaining why each document is appropriate for its intended audience	
D3	Explain appropriate methods of written communication to different audiences	

Always ask your tutor to explain any assignment tasks or assessment criteria that you don't understand fully. Being clear about the task before you begin gives you the best chance of succeeding. Good luck with your Unit 8 assessment work!

9 Training and employment in business

Unit outline

At the heart of any successful business are its people. Without their creativity, drive and passion for success, a business would cease to exist. Can you imagine Apple without the designers of its iPhone, or Dyson producing the same old vacuum cleaner?

This unit focuses on the importance of people within the organisation, from the bosses down to the shop floor staff. This chapter considers the rights and responsibilities of the employer to its employees and of the employees to their employer. It looks at what motivates people, including training and performance review.

Learning outcomes

1   **Know the rights and responsibilities of the employee and employer.**
2   **Understand how employees can be motivated.**
3   **Understand the importance of training and performance review.**

Grading guide

To achieve a **pass**, you must show you can:	To achieve a **merit**, you must show you can:	To achieve a **distinction**, you must show you can:
P1 Outline the rights and responsibilities of employers in a chosen organisation	**M1** Explain the rights and responsibilities of employers and employees	**D1** Compare the rights and responsibilities of employers and employees
P2 Outline the rights and responsibilities of employees in a chosen organisation		
P3 Explain the importance of job satisfaction and teamwork in the workplace	**M2** Explain the relationship between motivation, teamwork and job satisfaction	**D2** Analyse the relationship between motivation, teamwork and job satisfaction and how they contribute to organisational success
P4 Examine how employees can be motivated in the workplace		
P5 Describe the importance of training to an organisation		
P6 Explain the benefits of performance appraisal		

Rights and responsibilities of the employee and employer

Getting started

Few employers hire you and then let you 'get on with it'. Even staff who are earning the minimum wage are a big cost to an employer, so managers want to make sure their people are well trained. This training is not only to do the job well, but also to do it safely. In law, the employee is also responsible for health and safety, so managers and staff must work together.

When you have completed this topic, you should:

■ know the rights and responsibilities of employers

■ know the rights and responsibilities of employees

■ understand how disagreements may arise between employers and employees.

Key terms

Anti-discrimination policies: policies that attempt to create greater equality in the workplace

Code of practice: an employer's rulebook, setting out what employees must and must not do, together with penalties for breaking the rules

Contract of employment: a legal agreement between the employer and the employee, setting out the responsibilities of each

Employment tribunal: an informal, local court in which an employee with a grievance can take an employer (or former employer) to court

Statutory rights: rights laid down by law, i.e. by Act of Parliament

Trade union: a group of employees who have come together to achieve common goals

Employees' rights

In the past businesses could force employees to work extra hours and could discriminate against female or non-white workers. However, over the last 30 years, new laws have given employees **statutory rights** in their workplace. These are 'required' rights, which all businesses have to grant to their employees. These may be things that we now take for granted, like being allowed paid holiday each year, but they represent a significant change in the law. Most of these rights were opposed strongly by employers and by many politicians when they were first suggested. Workers in many parts of the world envy the rights UK citizens have in the workplace.

A business must make sure it has effective **anti-discrimination policies** at every stage in the employment process. All individuals employed by the business should be treated fairly and be valued equally whatever their race, gender, disability, health, religion, nationality or age. Breaking employment laws can result in huge fines for a business. It may also give the business bad publicity, which may stop other, talented people from applying for jobs with the company.

Each business will draw up its own equal opportunities statement, which will be available for all employees to read. Laws on discrimination and equality were all brought together within the Equality Act 2006. This Act also set up the Equality and Human Rights Commission which oversees:

▶ *Equal pay* – men and women doing work of 'equal value' must receive the same pay.

▶ *Sex discrimination* – both sexes must be treated equally at work. It is illegal for businesses to discriminate against men or women within the business with regard to pay, selection, training, promotion, redundancies and benefits.

▶ *Race discrimination* – it is illegal for businesses to discriminate against employees because of their ethnic background.

▶ *Disabled people* – there should be no discrimination, and businesses should employ a quota of registered disabled people.

Despite all this valuable legislation, no one doubts that discrimination still occurs.

Activity

'Disabled student wins legal fight against Abercrombie & Fitch'

A student with an artificial arm who did not fit the 'look' of the clothes store Abercrombie & Fitch was awarded £9,000 compensation. The student was banned from the London shop floor of the clothing retailer. She was instead made to work in the store room. The student quit after 5 shifts due to unhappiness. A court ruled that Abercrombie had harassed the student over her disability, leading her to quit the job.

1. How do you think the decision against Abercrombie & Fitch could affect the business in the future?

2. Do you think the court's decision was right?

3. If the same situation happened to a small sole trader, what effect could it have on the business?

To make sure businesses are employing the new laws, employers have to issue any employee who has worked for one month or longer with a **contract of employment**. This contract will include the following details:

▶ *Job title* – e.g. Health and Safety Manager.

▶ *Working hours* – you should not work more than 48 hours per week unless you choose to.

▶ *Rate of pay* – this sets out how much you will receive per hour (wage) or per year (salary).

▶ *Holiday entitlement* – this is how much paid holiday an employee gets. It is usually 28–30 days per year, although some businesses offer more.

Did you know?

Employers have many legal responsibilities they must meet, including the minimum wage, maternity and paternity leave, and to provide a safe working environment.

▶ *Non-statutory rights* – this will include details of any schemes the businesses contributes to on behalf of the employee, such as a pension scheme or health insurance.

▶ *Notice* – this will specify how much notice the employer has to give to the employee if they dismiss them or make them redundant.

▶ *Health and safety* – this will outline the company's policy on health and safety.

▶ *Discipline* – this will outline the company's disciplinary procedure.

▶ *Trade union* – this will give details of any unions the business is a member of or that it recommends its employees to join.

Procedures to protect relationship with employers

Within most businesses, the rights of employees are protected by procedures that maintain the relationship with the employer. The principles and **code of practice** of the business should enable all members of the business to understand what procedures will be used in different situations. For example, if an employee has an unexplained absence, the code of practice will set out the procedure that should be used to deal with this (e.g. giving a warning). This ensures that all employees are treated in the same way.

Many employees become members of **trade unions** so that they can gain advice on their rights. Some unions are made up of professionals from the same industry (e.g. the National Union of Teachers), whereas others are made up of people from a variety of industries (e.g. Unison, Britain's biggest public sector trade union).

When employees need to negotiate with employers, it is much easier for them to work together as a group rather than try to negotiate on their own. This is known as collective bargaining. Trade unions also try to help their members find training opportunities that might help them develop their careers. If an employee feels mistreated, the trade union will offer legal advice and representation.

The GMB is a general union.

Some professions are represented by a professional association rather than by a trade union (e.g. the Professional Footballers Association (PFA)). A professional association aims to develop the industry that it represents, as well as protect the public interest and those who join it.

> ## Over to you!
>
> Why do you think a contract of employment is important to:
> - the employee?
> - the employer?

Activity

In September 2009, the Sheffield United goalkeeper Paddy Kenny was suspended from playing football for 9 months after failing a drugs test. He tested positive for the stimulant ephedrine, and could have been given a 2-year ban. However, ephedrine is found in some cold remedies, and the PFA said that it would support Mr Kenny with an appeal as they felt the punishment was too harsh for the crime.

1. Paddy Kenny was suspended by the Football Association. On what grounds might his employer (Sheffield United) have also decided to penalise the player?

2. How does Paddy Kenny's case illustrate the benefit to a worker of belonging to a trade union?

Employees' responsibilities

As well as having many rights within the workplace, employees have to be aware that they have responsibilities as well. Once hired, an employee must keep within the terms of the contract, uphold the policies of the business and respect the company's property. In effect, every employee must work to uphold the business's aims and objectives.

An employee must also follow the rules (e.g. regarding health and safety) as set out by the company. For example, rail repair workers must always wear a high-visibility jacket when on the tracks. Failure to follow health and safety or other rules can be grounds for dismissal.

Employers' rights

Employers also have rights and responsibilities within the workplace. In recent years, the responsibilities of employers have been in the spotlight, with treatment of employees becoming ever more important. Having said that, employers have the right to support the aims of their business. For example, they can set targets for employees that may help the business achieve success, and they have the right to expect 'a fair day's work for a fair day's pay'.

In law, employers have a legal duty to provide a safe workplace to support the health and safety of their workforce. This gives employers the right to force staff to use equipment that will help them to stay safe. For example, an employer in the construction industry can sack a worker for persistently failing to wear a hard hat. Staff are expected to make appropriate use of company equipment and company time. At the exam board Edexcel, staff have access to Facebook only between 12.30 p.m. and 1.30 p.m. each day. In effect, the company's conditions of service make it very clear that time at work is for working.

Over to you!

Discuss the following statement:

'The employers should have more rights than the employees as it is their company.'

Disciplinary and grievance procedures can play an important role in a company. Employers have the right to dismiss lazy or disruptive employees, but only if they go through specified legal procedures. Victimisation is not allowed. If an employee feels mistreated or undervalued, there must be a procedure in place that allows them to air this opinion. It is the same for employers. If they feel an employee isn't working to the terms of their contract then they can start disciplinary procedures.

Adrian Mutu

- The disciplinary procedure normally starts with a verbal warning issued by the employer to the employee. This may be, for example, because they have been late for work on a few occasions, been rude to their manager or have made several mistakes at work.

- If the employee continues this behaviour or a new incident occurs, they will be given a written warning. This will outline the details of the incident as well as offer advice and support for solving it. It will also tell the employee that if it continues they will have just one further warning before dismissal.

- The employee receives one last written warning clearly stating the next breach of contract will result in them being dismissed.

- Dismissed! The employee will have their contract terminated.

In some circumstances, the employer will not go through all four stages. For example, in October 2004 Adrian Mutu was sacked by Chelsea FC for failing a drugs test. He had breached his contract so severely that Chelsea could sack him immediately.

Employers' responsibilities

On the other hand, employers also have responsibilities to the employees of the company. They must make sure they observe the employment law and codes of practice. The law states that employers have a duty of care towards all their staff (including temps and freelance staff). The Employment Protection Act 1978 protects the employee against unfair dismissal. If they feel they have been treated unfairly, they have the right to an **employment tribunal** to have their case heard. Employers, therefore, have the responsibility to make sure they follow the correct procedures, as well as maintain fair and equal treatment of their employees.

Many employers have a range of procedures in place to protect their relationship with their employees. There may be a system allowing employees to discuss issues arising, supporting trade union membership and allocating members of staff to focus on training. A major part of an employer's responsibilities is to provide training.

Lastly, employers must make sure they provide public liability insurance. This covers the legal costs and penalties if the company is taken to court by those affected by the business. For example, customers at a leisure centre may slip, get injured and sue the company. The public liability insurance would ensure that the claimant gets paid (if they win the court case) even if the company goes into liquidation.

Assessment activity 9.1 (P1, P2, M1, D1)

The government has made it very clear that employer and employee responsibilities are both very important in the successful running of a business. The website www.direct.gov.uk allows business owners and staff to find out exactly what they are entitled to.

The volcanic eruption in Iceland in April 2010 caused thousands of people to be stranded all over the world, unable to return home to work. Some had their pay docked, with others being forced to take it as annual leave. This natural event caused many to seek legal advice to clarify their rights and responsibilities.

1. Conduct some follow-up research at www.direct.gov.uk. Using an organisation of your choice, outline the rights and responsibilities of both the employees and employer.

2. Explain the importance of each right and responsibility highlighted in your previous answer.

3. Having conducted follow-up research, compare the rights and responsibilities of employers and employees.

Topic check

1　Pick two occasions at work when discrimination is most likely to take place:

　　a) When decisions are being about promotion.

　　b) When customers are on the phone.

　　c) When the staff party is being arranged.

　　d) When recruiting new members of staff.

　　e) When writing new training programmes.

2　Identify two reasons why a business may benefit from clear policies to avoid discrimination in the workplace.

3　How might an employee benefit from knowing his/her statutory rights?

4　Explain why it can be hard to get another job after being dismissed by an employer.

5　How might an employment tribunal help an employee who feels she has been unfairly dismissed at work?

Understand how employees can be motivated

Getting started

Motivation is a huge issue in every part of life: in sport, in school and – especially – in the workplace. Two people may be equally skilled and talented, but one wins gold while the other vanishes in the pack. Therefore, all managers should recognise the importance of motivating their staff.

When you have completed this topic, you should:

- understand why motivation matters
- understand how staff motivation can be developed.

Key terms

Empower: to allow an employee to make more decisions and choices

Hierarchy of needs: a pyramid-shaped diagram showing the five stages of human needs identified by Maslow

Incentives: carrots dangled in front of workers to get them to work as hard as possible, such as the bonuses given to bankers

Innovation: putting bright new ideas into practice

Job satisfaction: the sense of reward received from doing a good job well

Theories of motivation

What motivates people to work? If you ask your friends what they want out of their job, you will probably get a variety of answers. Some may suggest basic needs such as money, whereas others may wish for enjoyment or promotions. At certain times, some people may feel job security is most important, especially in a recession.

There are many different theories of motivation. On this course, we look at just two: Maslow's hierarchy of needs and Professor Herzberg's two-factor theory.

Did you know?

The first person to run the mile in less than 4 minutes received no financial reward. In those days Olympic athletes were amateurs, i.e. they ran for the medals alone, not for money.

Maslow's hierarchy of needs

Abraham Maslow was a psychologist who developed a model of human needs to show how people are motivated. It is called the **hierarchy of needs** as it puts these needs in order. Maslow believed that everyone starts at the bottom, with basic needs such as money, food and shelter being of utmost importance. Once these have been achieved, people will then start to move up the hierarchy, looking for the next level. He believed that in order to move up to the next level, the level below must have been achieved. It is also the same if reversed, if low-level needs are not being met, the high level needs become less important. If you are hungry, food will always be the most important need.

The single most important part of this theory is the idea that once people's basic needs have been satisfied by earning a reasonable wage, money will no longer motivate them to give their best. Other needs kick in, such as social and psychological needs.

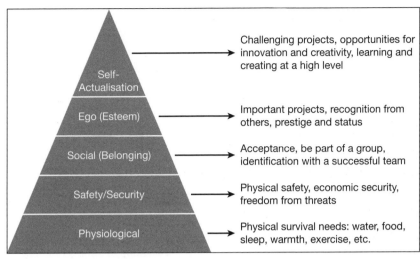

Figure 9.1 Maslow's hierarchy of needs

Frederick Herzberg's two-factor theory

Frederick Herzberg conducted research in the 1950s into factors affecting workers' job satisfaction. He carried it out on 200 accountants and engineers in the USA. He asked the employees to describe recent events or situations which had given them extreme satisfaction or dissatisfaction at work.

Herzberg found that there were five satisfying factors which stood out:

- achievement
- recognition for achievement
- meaningful, interesting work
- responsibility and growth
- advancement at work.

Activity

In early 2010, the footballer Sean Wright-Phillips seemed unhappy with his treatment by his employer, Manchester City FC. His weekly wage of £75,000 was below that of players such as Adebayor. Newspaper stories suggested that Wright-Phillips needed reassurance by City (presumably in the shape of a big pay rise).

1. Identify one of Wright-Phillips' human needs that was being met, and one which was not being met.

2. How should the management of Manchester City have dealt with this situation?

He realised that these factors focused on the job itself and didn't relate to pay or status. He called these 'the motivators'. These factors will generate job satisfaction and improve motivation.

He then researched the reasons behind dissatisfaction at work. He found five different factors for this:

- company policy and administration
- supervision
- pay
- interpersonal relations
- working conditions.

He decided that these surrounded the job but were not related to the job itself. He called these 'the hygiene factors'. Meeting these prevents dissatisfaction but does not cause job satisfaction or improve motivation.

One of Herzberg's most significant findings was that pay was a hygiene factor rather than a motivator. This meant that if the employee felt underpaid then it would lead to them being disheartened but high pay would be taken for granted.

Herzberg also decided that financial incentives could be used to improve productivity but should not be used alone. He found that bribes ('carrots') would not make people give their best – they would just do enough to achieve the bonus. He also found that by offering financial **incentives**, people would resent working hard at a task they didn't enjoy, and this would cause problems in the future for the employer.

Activity

'Money is not everything.'
Using a motivation theory, explain why this may be true.

"Mr Frimley, sir, can I have a word about the motivational artwork..."

Job satisfaction

At the heart of motivation is the idea of **job satisfaction**. This is the feeling of achievement and wellbeing gained from doing a satisfying job. Clearly, carrying out a successful heart operation would be hugely satisfying. But many people gain satisfaction from far more ordinary jobs. Ways to improve job satisfaction might include:

▶ *Design jobs to fit people* – Professor Herzberg was the first to emphasise the importance of 'job design'. Managers need to think how to divide up the work that needs to be done in ways that will be motivating to staff. People enjoy 'complete units of work', i.e. seeing a task through from the start to the finish. Dividing jobs up into small, repetitive tasks creates boredom.

▶ *Job enlargement* – this means introducing new tasks to enlarge an existing job. This involves training staff to undertake a variety of tasks, some of which may involve greater responsibility. This has become very popular in car manufacturing plants where staff used to carry out the same task each day. One disadvantage is that this method does lead to increased training costs.

▶ *Job rotation* – this is similar to job enlargement. Instead of one worker doingone job all day, workers are moved between tasks. Unlike job enlargement, though, job rotation implies giving people a range of tasks of the same level of challenge, e.g. checkout in the morning, shelf-stacking in the afternoon. Professor Herzberg doubts that this improves job satisfaction. It is helpful to the employer, though – if staff are used to doing a range of tasks, they can easily fill in for sick colleagues.

▶ *Job enrichment* – this means giving employees more responsibility and involvement in the day-to-day running of the business. This approach has been very successful in businesses such as John Lewis.

▶ *Allow employees to make their own decisions* – as Herzberg showed, responsibility is motivating. People like to have a feeling of control over their lives, and to feel valued for what they can do.

Did you know?

Nando's has been voted best place to work by its employees. The 6,300 staff voted Nando's top for: 'Strong sense of family in our teams', 'Managers care about an individual' and Managers talk openly and honestly with me'. Seventy-four per cent of staff say that managers help them fulfil their potential.

Source: Sunday Times Best 100 Companies to Work for

Case study

In 2009 the management of Royal Mail introduced new work schedules for postmen. Posties who had worked on the same round for years were put into a pool of workers – to work where they were told. Managers had used a computer system to work out the timings on different rounds. The postal workers were to go where they were told, and get the job done in the time calculated by the computer.

Postal workers complained that they knew their own rounds well enough to make sure that the letters were sorted properly, and having a regular round meant they could get to know the customers. After the changes, they would no longer have the same amount of control over their work and would not have any opportunity to make decisions.

During the whole of that autumn the UK postal service went downhill as unofficial strikes took place and temporary workers made mistakes in deliveries. Not all managements appear to understand how to motivate staff.

1. Use Maslow's hierarchy to examine how well motivated postal workers would have felt in Autumn 2009.

2. Use Herzberg's theory to explain two ways the postal workers' motivation could have been increased.

Teamwork

Being a member of a team can be motivating. If each employee is involved in decision-making within the team it will give the worker a feeling of importance. Team working has many benefits to the business. Many employees want to be part of a team, making a contribution to departmental and organisational success. By working in teams, employees feel they have contributed to the success achieved.

Dyson (who make floor cleaners and other electrical goods) is renowned for allowing employees to work together in a relaxed and informal way, developing new products. They agree objectives with each team, and targets such as to design a new way to air-dry hands quickly and cheaply. To succeed attaining team objectives, staff have to show inventiveness and the company has to encourage **innovation**. They **empower** each employee, increasing their capacity to make decisions and choices.

Working in a team will also lead to multi-skilling as employees learn new skills from their colleagues, as well as having the support to try new roles. Working in teams allows knowledge-sharing among employees. By taking ownership of decision-making, staff create synergy within the business, i.e. they produce more together than the sum of their individual efforts would produce. However, in some circumstances, working in teams can demotivate staff. For example, if the members of the team do not get on, then efficiency may drop.

Activity

In teams, create a poster outlining the benefits of teamwork. You may wish to divide up the tasks depending on the skills you have in the team.

Topic check

1 Identify three ways a business such as Marks & Spencer could benefit from a motivated workforce.

2 Place Maslow's five levels of need in order, starting with the lowest-order need and ending with the highest-order need.

3 Why might an employee be motivated by being given more responsibility?

4 a) Why may Herzberg believe that money is a hygiene factor, not a motivator?

   b) Explain why managers need to understand that money is a hygiene factor, not a motivator.

Training

Getting started

Professor Herzberg once said that: 'the more a person can do, the more you can motivate them'. Therefore, training is crucial to motivation (and so is good teaching; the better the teacher, the more motivated the student becomes towards that subject). Some firms treat training as a 'cost'. Better ones treat it as a key to business success.

When you have completed this topic, you should:

■ know why training is important
■ know how training is carried out.

Key terms

Ethical implications: these are important, because managers who think about the moral impact of decisions help staff to keep faith in the business they work for

Line manager: someone responsible for specific aspects of business performance, and in charge of specific staff

Vocational: training that is vocational focuses on the job someone does, rather than the things they would like to learn

The need for training

Training is a necessary and important part of running a business. It helps to maintain and improve the skills of the workforce so that the business can stay competitive. Can you imagine the England football team not training before the World Cup, or a hairdresser not being trained to cut your hair?

Below are some of the reasons why businesses and employees undergo training:

▶ Staff need to be able to do the job competently. For example, a paramedic without any medical training wouldn't be able to save someone's life. If staff are not trained then they will not have the skills to undertake their responsibilities.

▶ Businesses must legally train their staff in areas such as health and safety. This aims to make the workplace a safer environment.

▶ There are financial implications, for example, better employees will leave if not trained. They will feel they are not progressing professionally. By training employees, businesses are allowing them to achieve their potential, learn new skills and develop. As staff are expensive to recruit, it makes sense to make sure that they stay – so training can, in effect, pay for itself. Training can also make staff more efficient at their job, leading to savings or additional income for the business.

- **Ethical implications** should be considered. Some businesses feel it is morally correct to train people. Morrison's boasts on its website about the 1,417,000 training days completed in 2008. It includes this information in a section on 'Duties to Society'.

- Induction and initial training occurs when new employees start a job. Its purpose is to introduce the new staff to the job, so that they can work competently and safely. It also introduces them to the business in general and to their colleagues, which it is hoped will make the new member of staff feel valued and welcome at the new organisation. Induction training can vary in its duration, from a few hours to 3–4 days, depending on the company and the role being filled.

- Sometimes, training is necessary so employees can update skills they already have. This may be vital due to new technology or new health and safety laws. Or it may be needed as part of a plan to provide multi-skilling training. Head teachers love staff who can teach maths and French and games. At the time of writing, Alex Ferguson has just spoken about missing John O'Shea, a Manchester United player who can perform well in almost any position on the pitch.

Training courses

There are various courses that businesses can use to train their staff. A business that has moved to a new computer operating system will need to provide internal training on the new software to all staff. A business planning to open branches in China will need to provide language training to some of its staff – probably at a local college.

- *In-house courses* train employees within the business, either in a meeting room or by putting them with another, experienced member of staff. This form of training is usually done with apprentices. This type of training is cheap, effective and highly motivating.

- *External courses* involve training the employee away from the workplace. This could be at a college, workshop or specialist training centre. The training could be **vocational**, leading to qualifications such as NVQs, or professional, leading to accountancy or IT qualifications. External courses can be short or can run over a longer time period, allowing the employee to study or practise the skills they are being taught.

External training is more expensive and so is often delivered alongside in-house training to minimise costs. For example, an employee may do an external 2-day course on health and safety, achieving a certificate to train other staff members. This is then passed on to the other employees through on-the-job training.

Training requires a serious investment from the business as it can prove very expensive. The constant worry of training staff that then leave has to be offset against the potential benefits the business gains from new skills, motivation and efficiency.

Advantages of training	Disadvantages of training
• Increase motivation of staff • Brings in new skills to the business • Multi-skilled staff • Improves efficiency • Keeps the business competitive • Lack of investment in staff leads to shortages of skilled workers	• Costs are often high • Staff may leave and go to a competitor • The money may be better invested in new technology • There is no guarantee that the employee will use the new skills • Some training is poorly run and too general for the needs of experienced staff

Over to you!

Would you choose on- or off-the-job training for the following employees?
- a new mechanic at Kwik-Fit
- an accountant
- a police officer
- a teacher

Performance appraisal

Performance or staff appraisal is used by many businesses. It involves an interview between the employee and their manager, reviewing their performance within the workplace. The interviews allow the manager and the employee to discuss possible targets, as well as reviewing the targets set at the last meeting. These interviews are usually held every 12 months, allowing the employee time to work towards their targets. The process is outlined in Figure 9.2.

Before the interview: the employee is given time to think about possible targets as well as some answers to the questions they may be asked about their performance.

At the interview: the appraiser (usually the **line manager**) will talk about the employee's performance. This will point out areas for development as well as areas of strength. At this point, they may discuss possible training needs or promotions.
The employee will then be rated on his/her performance, normally out of 5. The employee has the right to disagree with the ratings being given and, if necessary, to discuss this with a more senior manager.
The interviewer will then set new objectives with the employee which will be assessed 12 months later. These are created together and have to be agreed by the employee.

After the interview: the employee will work towards the new objectives for the next 12 months so that they can show evidence that they have achieved them at the next appraisal.

Figure 9.2 Performance appraisal

The appraisal system allows managers and employees to build a relationship at work, giving them both a better understanding of what is expected. The time set aside for appraisals can be used both by the manager and by the employee to highlight any issues or grievances. Employees may decide they want to be trained in a certain area, as it will help them achieve one of their objectives. It may also highlight skills which the manager wasn't aware of, helping to gain the employee promotion.

It also gives the employee the opportunity to talk about future promotion opportunities and pay rises. If the employee has been hired on performance-related pay, then the appraisal system may contribute to the amount they are to be paid in that year.

In some circumstances, the objectives previously set may not have been met. This may stop the staff member from sharing in annual bonuses enjoyed by other staff.

Assessment activity 9.2 (P3, P4, P5, P6, M2, D2)

Dyson was created by James Dyson in 1993, with just six fellow Royal College of Art engineering graduates. Since then he has continued to develop a 'studenty' atmosphere within the company, with the average age only 26.

The Dyson ethos has been developed on teamwork and innovation, with employees encouraged to take risks and be creative. The company prides itself on not pressuring its staff, so they achieve job satisfaction. Each employee receives hours of training each year, paid for by Dyson. This allows employees to improve and continue their development. Dyson also use performance appraisals to help staff focus on specific weaknesses and to help reward those who are working well.

Dyson has reaped the benefits of this approach, with James Dyson reported to have a personal wealth of around £700 million. Dyson itself has now reached worldwide sales of £3 billion.

1. Explain the importance of job satisfaction and teamwork at Dyson.

2. Explain the relationship between motivation, teamwork and job satisfaction.

3. Using your own research, as well as the information above, analyse the relationship between motivation, teamwork and job satisfaction, and how they have contributed to Dyson's continued success.

4. Using follow-up research, examine how employees can be motivated in the workplace.

5. Using Dyson as an example, why is training so important if the company is to continue in its growth?

6. Explain the benefits to Dyson of performance appraisals for all employees.

Topic check

1 Why might a business such as British Airways decide to use off-the-job training for its new staff?

2 Explain why a business might want to spend money training staff who have already been working from the company for many years.

3 Give two reasons why an employee might want to receive training in order to become multi-skilled.

4 Outline two ways an employee could benefit from regular performance appraisal.

Assessment summary

The overall grade you achieve for this unit depends on how well you meet the grading criteria set out at the start of the chapter (see page 157). You must complete:

- all of the P criteria to achieve a **pass** grade
- all of the P and the M criteria to achieve a **merit** grade.
- all of the P, M and D criteria to achieve a **distinction** grade.

Your tutor will assess the assessment activities that you complete for this unit. The work you produce should provide evidence which demonstrates that you have achieved each of the assessment criteria. The table below identifies what you need to demonstrate to meet each of the pass, merit and distinction criteria for this unit. You should always check and self-assess your work before you submit your assignments for marking.

Remember that you MUST provide evidence for all of the P criteria to pass the unit.

Grading criteria	You need to demonstrate that you can:	Do you have the evidence?
P1	Outline the rights and responsibilities of employers in a chosen organisation	
P2	Outline the rights and responsibilities of employees in a chosen organisation	
P3	Explain the importance of job satisfaction and teamwork in the workplace	
P4	Examine how employees can be motivated in the workplace	
P5	Describe the importance of training to an organisation	
P6	Explain the benefits of performance appraisal	
M1	Explain the rights and responsibilities of employers and employees	
M2	Explain the relationship between motivation, teamwork and job satisfaction	
D1	Compare the rights and responsibilities of employers and employees	
D2	Analyse the relationship between motivation, teamwork and job satisfaction and how they contribute to organisational success	

Always ask your tutor to explain any assignment tasks or assessment criteria that you don't understand fully. Being clear about the task before you begin gives you the best chance of succeeding. Good luck with your Unit 9 assessment work!

10 Personal selling in business

Unit outline

Shopping on the internet is becoming increasingly popular, but many people still prefer to visit a shop and be dealt with by a sales person. Yet many businesses still manage to get staff appointments and training horribly wrong. When did you last experience rude sales staff or staff who didn't know about the products they were selling?

This chapter will help you to understand the role of sales staff. It will discuss selling skills and processes and their importance to the success of a business.

Learning outcomes

1 **Understand the role of sales staff.**
2 **Be able to demonstrate personal selling skills and processes.**

Grading guide

To achieve a **pass**, you must show you can:	To achieve a **merit**, you must show you can:	To achieve a **distinction**, you must show you can:
P1 Describe the role of sales staff	**M1** Explain the role of sales staff and the sales technique they use	
P2 Identify the techniques used when making personal sales		
P3 Describe the knowledge and skills when making personal sales		
P4 Prepare to make personal sales	**M2** Compare the selling skills and processes used in different situations	**D1** Demonstrate the confident use of personal selling skills when making sales
P5 Use selling skills and processes to make sales		**D2** Evaluate the preparation, skills and processes used in different situations

Understand the role of sales staff

Getting started

The demands put on sales staff can vary greatly. So can the rewards. Whereas many sales staff are poorly paid, some are able to earn £100,000 a year in commissions from selling high-value items such as houses, aircraft or luxury yachts.

When you have completed this topic, you should:

- understand the main skills required by sales staff
- understand the rewards sales staff can receive.

Key terms

Closing the sale: persuading an interested customer to part with his/her cash or sign the contract

Product surround: the extras that may turn an attractive product into an irresistible one, e.g. Kia's offer of a 7-year warranty on a new car, when no one else offers longer than 3 years

Staff turnover: the rate at which staff leave a business and need to be replaced

Voluntary code: an agreement between businesses on how to behave; it is not backed up by laws and therefore can be broken without fear of penalty

The role of sales staff

Retail is a very competitive business to be in. 2009 saw a number of major names close their doors for the last time, such as Woolworths, Zavvi and Borders. While these died, other retailers continued to thrive at a time of global recession. B&Q managed to increase its profits from the previous year. How? By selling its products and services successfully, through sales staff well trained enough to encourage customers to buy.

Customer requirements

Good sales staff find out what customers want, how much they're prepared to pay, and suggest a solution to the customer's problem or need. If a successful sale is made, they may then make suggestions to encourage the customer to buy add-ons, e.g. 'Do you want fries with that?'

The challenge involved in personal selling ranges from the simple (fries) to the extremely complex. In October 2009 Rolls Royce won a $720 million order from Virgin Airways for aero-engines to power ten Virgin aircraft. The Rolls Royce sales team spent 6 months working on this order, and had to fight off competition from two massive American aero-engine makers. In this case, personal selling can only be effective if the sales staff know a huge amount about aircraft engineering. In order to succeed the Rolls Royce staff had to:

- find out the customer requirements
- explain how the engines matched the customer's needs
- explain the '**product surround**', i.e. the supporting service package such as warranty (guarantee) promises, extended credit terms and after-sales care
- identify a purchase price that was acceptable to Virgin and to Rolls Royce.

Case study

Alun Davies is a sales supervisor for a car dealership. He believes that the key to personal selling is finding out exactly what the customer needs (a family car, a run-around), their budget and then finding the product that best suits both. Once Alun has made a match he informs the customer of details such as service history, miles per gallon and insurance group. He says, 'you don't often have to press customers to clinch the deal. If you've found the perfect match they can't wait to sign and pay.'

1. What does Alun mean by the term, 'the perfect match'?

2. Alun expects to sell ten cars a week at an average price of £5,000 each. He receives a 0.5% commission on his sales.

   a) What is his average weekly bonus payment?

   b) How might this affect his sales effort?

First point of contact

When you walk into a shop the sales staff are usually the first point of contact. Some customers complain if sales staff are over-eager and pounce with a smile and a 'Can I help you?' Others complain if they are ignored. Getting the balance right isn't easy. Sales staff at Next stores are given a seasonal clothing allowance and have to wear clothes from the current collection to work. Marks and Spencer staff all wear a uniform. Sales staff are representing the organisation and it is important that customers get the right message about the personality and image of the business.

Developing customer care, gathering feedback and promoting the product

Making a sale is only part of the role of sales staff. They must also provide appropriate customer care – after-sales service, repairs, replacements, refunds, follow-up – to ensure loyalty and that the customer comes back next time they want to make a purchase.

Many stores now recognise that sales is a two-way process, and that feedback from customers (good and bad) is key to improving sales. This is used to reward staff and identify training needs.

Very few products sell themselves, and it is often the job of sales staff to promote the product when dealing with customers – next time you visit a department store, count how many people try and spray you with perfume.

Knowledge and skills

Product knowledge

Two of the biggest complaints among customers are that they are mis-sold products, or that sales people do not know enough about the products they are selling. Staff have to be trained sufficiently to cope with all kinds of customer queries (e.g. 'Does this phone work in France?' 'Does this season ticket give me free travel at weekends?). The keys to good product knowledge among staff are to ensure that:

▶ they are trained well, and kept up to date by regular retraining

▶ **staff turnover** is low – if staff do not stay long in a job, product knowledge will be weak

▶ they are motivated – i.e. they want to learn and want to help customers – as this will help their product knowledge.

Sales motivation

One good way of finding out why people buy certain things is to list the benefits they are looking for. These benefits can be real (e.g. I am thirsty; I need a drink of water) or they can be perceived (e.g. water is healthier than Pepsi; if I buy water I will be more healthy and attractive). By understanding the customer's motivation, sales staff have a better chance of making a sale.

When buying, customers go through the following process. They:

▶ recognise the problem ('Oh no, I have run out of chocolate.')

▶ search for alternatives ('What have I got in the cupboard? Cornflakes? Biscuits?')

▶ evaluate the alternatives ('Would I like a biscuit or a bowl of cornflakes instead?')

▶ make a choice ('No, I want some chocolate.')

▶ BUY (go to shop and get some) or DO NOT BUY (still want some chocolate)

▶ consider post-purchase consumption ('Mmm, that was yummy, I will buy it again', or 'That was disappointing, I wish I had bought something else.').

Good sales staff will be on hand to identify the problem, offer alternative products and encourage customers to make a choice that satisfies them, yet is profitable to the business.

Closing the sale

Some sales staff are good at chatting to customers, but struggle at '**closing the sale**', i.e. getting the customer to decide to buy. Good sales people will identify the doubts the customer has and turn them into a positive:

▶ Worried about the cost? 'We can do you a buy now pay later deal.'

▶ Worried about the maintenance? 'We will throw in a reduced 3-year warranty.'

▶ Worried about getting the item home? 'We will deliver for free.'

What matters to the sales person is closing that sale.

Sales techniques

There are a number of techniques involved in personal selling. The techniques employed by sales staff will vary according to the product being sold.

▶ *Cold calling* – this is when sales people make calls to people they don't know in order to try and make a sale.

▶ *Face to face* – this is another name for personal selling and is where sales people deal personally with the customer.

▶ *Drop-in visits* – this is where a sales person will visit customers in the workplace or their home to persuade them to make a purchase.

▶ *Telemarketing* – this is using the telephone, mobile phone or internet to make contact with customers to try and make a sale.

Legislation

Retailers have to operate within the law, and there are a number of laws that they must adhere to. The importance of each of these laws depends on the type of business.

▶ *Sale of Goods Act* – this means that goods must be of satisfactory quality and therefore fit for the purpose for which they are sold (i.e. free from defects, durable and safe). If I bought a pair of Wellington boots and they leaked, I would be entitled to a refund.

▶ *Trade Descriptions Act* – goods sold must be as described, and companies have to support any statements they make about their products and show them to be 'demonstrably true'.

▶ *Consumer Credit Act (1974)* – companies offering credit must make the APR (annual percentage rate) clear to customers.

▶ *The Weights and Measures Act (1985)* – this law states that goods sold must be the weights and measurements they are labelled as – if I buy a kilo of apples then they should weigh 1 kg!

▶ *Food Hygiene Act (1990)* – anyone selling food must adhere to food safety rules, and members of staff need to be trained in food hygiene.

 Did you know?

It is estimated that 20–25% of all purchases are now online, but this means that 75–80% of all purchases still take place in retail shops.

Case study

Food at an Indian restaurant was found to be contaminated with dead flies, environmental health officers said.

Mr Kadir, the owner of the Raj Gate in Llanfrechfa, Cwmbran, was fined £19,600 for food hygiene and health and safety offences.

Visits to the premises by Environmental Health Officers led to the discovery that the premises were dirty and chefs were unable to wash their hands properly.

Speaking at the hearing, a councillor stated that it was only good luck that diners eating at the restaurant hadn't become seriously ill.

1. For what business reason may Mr Kadir have allowed his food handlers not to wash their hands properly?

2. What may the effects of this publicity be on the business?

Organisational policies

Many retailers have policies that help secure sales e.g.

▶ *Price matching* – John Lewis claims it is 'Never knowingly undersold' and will match the price charged by any other high street retailer. If Debenhams has a 'blue cross' sale, then John Lewis will also discount its products to match them.

▶ *Discounting* – Alun Davies is allowed to make discounts on the cars he sells to ensure the sale – the level of discount varies according to how easily persuaded the customer is.

▶ *Guarantees* – many stores will extend the manufacturers' warranty to ensure that consumers make a purchase. John Lewis offers a free 2-year warranty on all its electrical items; most shops give just 1 year.

▶ *After-sales service* – providing customers with a 'Help desk' like the one in the Apple store means that customers feel reassured if things go wrong.

▶ *Customer care* – a good organisation will look after customers at every stage of dealing with them. Good department stores, for example, will:

- have someone at the entrance to offer help and advice as shoppers enter
- have facilities such as a baby changing rooms, complete with free nappies
- will order an item if it is out of stock and then deliver it for free.

Reflective practice, e.g. Gibbs' cycle of reflection

One way to encourage sales people to improve is by training them in becoming reflective. In other words, to keep them self-critical – getting them to ask themselves how they could improve. One way of doing this is to teach them about Gibbs' cycle of reflection (see Figure 10.1).

By using this cycle of reflection, sales staff can look back on their experiences and make changes to the way they deal with customers. This should help improve sales.

> ## ? Did you know?
>
> A Chief Examiner for Psychology once said that 'self-critical students are the ones that keep improving'. Are you self-critical?

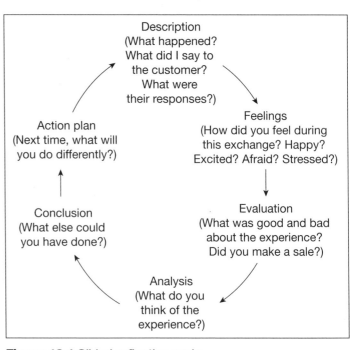

Figure 10.1 Gibbs' reflective cycle

Case study

Concerns about the practices of some door-to-door salespeople has led to an increase in legislation to protect consumers

The BBC's Inside Out programme had an undercover reporter secretly film a salesman from NPower lying to homeowners to try and persuade them to switch to NPower.

A spokesperson for NPower said that the salesman responsible had been dismissed. They apologised for his behaviour and promised to make training for all their sales staff a priority to make sure this didn't happen again.

NPower also agreed to pay compensation to anybody who was tricked into switching their energy supplier.

Last year, there were 12,000 complaints about energy salespeople and NPower was one of the worst offenders. The company has recently signed up to a new **voluntary code** of conduct and has promised to improve its practices.

1. Why may some firms ignore a voluntary code, even if they have signed up to be part of it?
2. Why may some individual sales staff act wrongly when dealing with customers?

Topic check

1 Choose two reasons why cold calling may not be an effective way of making sales.

   a) Because its intrusive and people don't like it.

   b) Because it's a cheap way of selling your product.

   c) Because its proven to be very effective for some products like kitchens.

   d) Because it is seen as unethical and people complain about it.

2 What are the correct stages in the buying process?

   a) attention, interest, desire, action (AIDA)

   b) identify need, evaluate want, make selection, purchase, consumption

   c) enter store, engage with sales team, who use persuasive techniques, make offer, sale

   d) recognise problem, search for alternatives, evaluate, choose, buy, consider post-purchase consumption

3 Why is providing good customer care seen as a good way of making sales?

   a) Because the extra staff will use your shop for their own shopping.

   b) Because it comes out of profit – toilets, carrying goods to cars and extra floor staff all are extra costs.

   c) Because if a customer has a good experience they will tell their friends.

4 Putting 'Use by' dates on food products comes under which piece of legislation?

   a) food safety   b) consumer protection

5 If a customer changes her mind about an item she has bought, the retailer has to refund their money – a credit note is unacceptable.

   a) true   b) false

6 A customer who signs a credit agreement can change his mind and cancel within 30 days.

   a) true   b) false

7 A customer who buys a TV that breaks after one week is entitled to a refund, replacement or repair under the Trades Descriptions Act.

   a) true   b) false

Demonstrating personal selling skills and processes

Personal selling requires excellent knowledge of the product you are selling, an intelligent understanding of customers and their needs, and the self-confidence to turn an opportunity into a sale.

When you have completed this topic, you should:

- understand the skills required for personal selling
- recognise whether you have the qualities required for personal selling.

 Key terms

Interest-free credit: postponing paying for an item without having to pay interest charges

Upselling: persuading a customer to buy an extra item or service, e.g. 'Would you like some leggings to match that dress?'

Personal selling skills

Selling is about communicating effectively with customers. There are six steps in this process, as shown in Figure 10.2.

To get through all of these steps successfully, the most important thing is to convince the customer that they want to buy from you and trust what you say. If your product knowledge is weak, the customer will never develop that trust. But there are also many personal issues that may help or hinder your efforts. These include:

▶ Your spoken English: it helps to be clear and, especially, concise. In other words, don't waffle on about the product. Be brief and accurate.

▶ Your non-verbal communication, e.g. body language.

▶ Your eye contact, which should be warm and friendly.

▶ Your written English, for example, a customer would be worried if the person selling an £800 handbag could not spell Versace, the producer's name.

Figure 10.2 Six steps to successful selling

Steps to successful selling	Examples
1. Greeting: making polite contact to make the customer feel welcome	'Good morning, madam.'
2. Introduction	'Hello, I'm Michelle, the sales manager. Can I help at all?'
3. Attracting customers' interest	'I'd love to show you our new collection – in this morning. Can you spare five minutes?'
4. Identifying customer needs	'What exactly are you looking for today?'
5. Presenting product information	'This coat could be just right. It's red leather with a sheepskin lining. Warm but very stylish.'
6. Closing the sale	'So, would you like to pay by cash or plastic, madam?'

It also helps enormously if you seem genuinely enthusiastic about the product they are buying. Some people are good at pretending. For most of us, it's hard. The ideal salesperson would be:

▶ smartly dressed in line with the brand image

▶ hugely positive about the products

▶ warm and friendly, yet still leaving the customer their own personal space

▶ have good manners and show courtesy (politeness)

▶ sufficiently sensitive to know when to pull back, i.e. not pressure the customer.

Activity

1. Choose a car that you would love to own.
2. Use a search engine to find the website devoted to selling that car.
3. Select three features of the car that you think would make the car appeal to a young family with one small child. Explain how you would present each feature to this type of car buyer.

Processes in sales and after sales

Sales

The sales process follows the following pattern:

▶ *Initiate the sale*: this might be by cold calling or might be through advertising, to get the customer to make a phone enquiry.

▶ *Make the customer interested*: by showing the customer how the product fits their needs.

▶ *Close the sale*, i.e. get the customer to commit: if this commitment is made in the person's own home, they have 14 days in which to change their mind. This is a legal 'cooling-off period'.

▶ **Upselling**: encouraging the customer to buy more. The person buying jeans is asked: 'Have you thought about a belt to go with that?' and so on. Generally, sales staff receive extra bonuses for upselling.

After-sales care

After-sales care includes the following pattern:

▶ *Delivery*: making sure the right number of the right product arrives on time and in perfect condition.

▶ *Warranty*: usually 12 months for electrical items, though John Lewis adds an extra 12 months' free warranty.

▶ *Follow-up*: a clever way of providing customer care and getting customer feedback is to follow up a sale with a friendly phone call. The new TV arrived 2 days ago and the salesperson phones to ask whether it's all set up satisfactorily.

▶ *Handling complaints*: when a customer complains, a good salesperson will apologise, promise to follow it up, and send a money-off voucher. This could turn a complaint into an extra sale.

? Did you know?

In 2008 two 'hoopla' stalls in Blackpool were closed down after customers complained that the sales people were intimidating and were conning them.

Recording information

Most sales today will be put through a scanning and computer system that will record all the necessary information. The system may even order a replacement item from the supplier. If no such system exists, the salesperson will need to write down what has been sold and to whom, in case of complaints later – or in case the customer wants to buy a matching item. Good record keeping is especially important in the case of items sold on **Interest-free credit**, i.e. to make sure that the money arrives when it should.

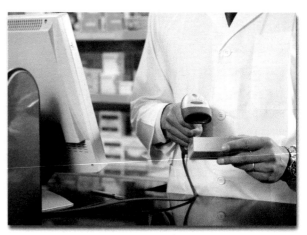

Liaison with other departments

In the same way, most computer systems will communicate sales information to the departments that need to know about it: dispatch, purchasing and accounts. Only if there is no computer system would it be necessary to go and tell the relevant staff. But every salesperson must make sure that the customer receives what they ordered when they wanted it delivered. So the responsibility for liaison clearly rests with the salesperson.

Conclusion

Personal selling can be a very effective way of retailers ensuring sales in a competitive market, but if they get it wrong it can have the opposite effect. Retailers have to ensure that they consider all aspects covered in this chapter before they let staff loose on their most precious commodity – the customers!

 Case study

First Choice travel agents in West Sussex was fined £25,600 for displaying fake holiday deals in the windows of four of its branches.

Trading Standards brought about the prosecution and believe the ruling will act as a warning to other agencies.

First Choice is retraining its shop staff to stop it happening again.

A spokesperson from Trading Standards stated that the malpractice of putting a card in the window advertising a holiday that isn't available or is more expensive than advertised has been an issue in the area for years and is misleading for customers.

1. Which law have the travel agents broken?

2. How would you train staff to ensure this didn't happen again?

Assessment activity 10.1 (P1, P2, P3, M1)

You work as a trainer for a national high street retailer. You have to devise a training programme for new sales staff explaining their role and the skills they need.

1. Give a presentation to the trainees explaining the role of personal selling.

2. Create a guide for staff about the techniques used when making a sale.

3. Write a report about the knowledge and skills that sales staff use when making a sale.

Assessment activity 10.2 (P4, P5, M2, D1, D2)

1. You have to be able to demonstrate your skills in personal selling. For the following situations you need to prepare to make the sale to a member of your class. For each situation you will need to research the product/service and then carry out a role play/presentation to demonstrate your skills.

Situation 1

You work for an electrical retailer. A customer has come in the shop and is looking at LCD TVs. You need to sell them a 32-inch LCD TV, arrange delivery and sell them an extended warranty.

Situation 2

You work for a clothing retailer. An angry customer has returned a pair of jeans they claim have shrunk despite following the washing instructions. What will you do?

Situation 3

You are a holiday rep – host a welcome meeting to the resort making sure you promote the local attractions. Complete a booking form for a trip and take a payment from the customer. A customer has booked a coach tour of the resort but you need to try and upsell them a limo tour.

Situation 4

You work for a furniture retailer and sell a leather suite. The customer would like to buy it on a buy now, pay later deal and wants it to be delivered. Which departments will you need to deal with?

2. Write a report comparing and evaluating the preparation, selling skills and processes you used in each of the four situations. Conclude the report with an evaluation of which skills and processes proved the most important.

Topic check

1 Why do salespeople need to seem warm and friendly in dealing with customers?

2 Why might it be dangerous for a university student to buy a lot of items using interest-free credit?

3 How might a good salesperson handle a customer complaint?

4 Why is liaison important between a firm's departments?

5 In the past, bank staff have 'mis-sold' complex financial products to customers who didn't need them. Should this be made illegal?

Assessment summary

The overall grade you achieve for this unit depends on how well you meet the grading criteria set out at the start of the chapter (see page 173). You must complete:
- all of the P criteria to achieve a **pass** grade
- all of the P and the M criteria to achieve a **merit** grade
- all of the P, M and D criteria to achieve a **distinction** grade.

Your tutor will assess the assessment activities that you complete for this unit. The work you produce should provide evidence which demonstrates that you have achieved each of the assessment criteria. The table below identifies what you need to demonstrate to meet each of the pass, merit and distinction criteria for this unit. You should always check and self-assess your work before you submit your assignments for marking.

Remember that you MUST provide evidence for all of the P criteria to pass the unit.

Grading criteria	You need to demonstrate that you can:	Do you have the evidence?
P1	Describe the role of sales staff	
P2	Identify the techniques used when making personal sales	
P3	Describe the knowledge and skills when making personal sales	
P4	Prepare to make personal sales	
P5	Use selling skills and processes to make sales	
M1	Explain the role of sales staff and the sales technique they use	
M2	Compare the selling skills and processes used in different situations	
D1	Demonstrate the confident use of personal selling skills when making sales	
D2	Evaluate the preparation, skills and processes used in different situations	

Always ask your tutor to explain any assignment tasks or assessment criteria that you don't understand fully. Being clear about the task before you begin gives you the best chance of succeeding. Good luck with your Unit 10 assessment work!

11 Customer relations in business

Unit outline

Developing good customer relations is critical to the success of every business. A happy, satisfied customer will keep returning and, through word of mouth, attract new customers.

Learning outcomes

1 **Know how customer service is provided in business.**
2 **Be able to apply appropriate presentation and interpersonal skills in customer service situations.**
3 **Understand how consistent and reliable customer service contributes to customer satisfaction.**
4 **Know how to monitor and evaluate customer service within an organisation.**

Grading guide

To achieve a **pass**, you must show you can:	To achieve a **merit**, you must show you can:	To achieve a **distinction**, you must show you can:
P1 Describe three different types of customers and their needs and expectations	**M1** Explain how different customers' needs and expectations can differ	
P2 Outline the benefits of good customer service in a selected organisation		
P3 Demonstrate presentation, communication and interpersonal skills in different customer service situations	**M2** Display confident presentation, communication and interpersonal skills when demonstrating customer service in a range of customer service situations	**D1** Anticipate and meet the needs of different customers in three contrasting situations
P4 Explain what contributes to consistent and reliable customer service	**M3** Analyse the importance of customer service to different businesses	
P5 Describe how customer service can be monitored and evaluated	**M4** Explain how monitoring and evaluating can improve customer service for the customer, the organisation and the employee	**D2** Analyse how monitoring and evaluating can improve customer service for the customer, the organisation and the employee
P6 Outline how improvements to the customer service in an organisation could be made		

How customer service is provided in business

Getting started

There are two main types of customer service: a) based on human contact and b) based on efficient technology. A parent coming to school expects to be treated with care and respect. But often, customers want a simple, quick transaction with as little human contact as possible – hole-in-the-wall money, or booking a flight on the internet. To know how to provide good customer service, the business must start by knowing what the customer really wants.

When you have completed this topic, you should:

- understand the different types of customer service
- understand how each type can be provided by well-run organisations.

Key terms

Customer expectations: things that make a customer choose one business over another

Customer needs: basic customer requirements

Performance indicators: measurable signs of how well customers are being served, e.g. queuing time per customer, or 'X% very satisfied' from a customer survey.

Customer needs and expectations

The biggest problem in providing good customer service is that different customers want different things. A lonely pensioner might want a chat, whereas a busy businessperson wants a super-fast transaction. As with most things in business, intelligent flexibility can be hugely helpful. When there's a long queue at a checkout, speed represents good service. When there's no queue, a chattier approach may work better for meeting customer needs and expectations.

What is customer service?

Customer service relates to the things organisations do to ensure that customers are happy and satisfied. It is vital to the success of an organisation, as suggested by this quote from Sam Walton, the founder of Wal-Mart (the biggest retailer in the world, and owner of ASDA): 'There is only one boss – the customer. And he can fire everybody in the company from the Chairman down, simply by spending his money elsewhere.'

In order to offer excellent customer service, organisations need to understand and ensure they satisfy two things:

▶ what their customers really *need* (i.e. **customer needs**)

▶ what their customers *expect* from them (i.e. **customer expectations**).

Consequently, most customer service departments have organisational targets, otherwise known as **performance indicators**.

Examples of customer service targets include:

▶ to respond to all telephone queries within 2 minutes

▶ to ensure delivery of goods within 5 working days.

Customer needs

The starting point is identifying customer needs and then seeing how these can be met. They will vary depending on the product/service offered and for different customers. However, there are some customer needs that all organisations have to meet, as shown in Figure 11.1.

Over to you!

Come up with three performance indicators for your school or college. These could be based on:

- students
- visitors
- parents
- staff.

Ask your teacher what their and your performance indicators are.

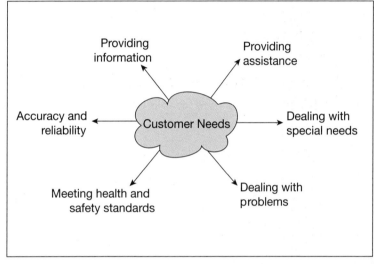

Figure 11.1 Customer needs

Accuracy and reliability

Customers will not be happy if a product and/or service they need is not delivered as promised. There can also be serious legal consequences if an organisation is seen to be selling a product or service which it cannot deliver. Therefore, organisations need to ensure that the products or services they provide are reliable (i.e. consistent with what they have provided in the past) and accurate (i.e. consistent with the promises they have made to customers). For example, what would you think if you bought a new watch but it did not tell the correct time?

Providing information and advice

Customers need sufficient and accurate information from organisations to be able to decide if their needs can be met. For example, they need to know exactly what service and/or product they are getting for their money, how much the product will cost, where and when they can buy the product and how long the product will last.

Years ago, the only way to get this information was to ask a member of staff – in a shop or on the phone. Today, many people prefer to look up the information on the internet. They can find out the official company view of its products – then check a comparison website to see what customers say.

Activity

Locate the 'contact us' pages on the following websites (you will often find they are in the 'help' sections of the website):

www.game.co.uk

http://store.nike.com/uk

www.mcdonalds.co.uk

What are the different ways the websites offer customers to find out information and help? Think about FAQs, email, addresses and links to other pages.

Did you know?

Most organisations rely on customers leaving their organisation happy and telling their friends. This is also known as 'word of mouth'. Word of mouth is by far the largest single influencer of purchasing decisions.

Customers often need advice on what product or service best meets their needs, especially when a business sells complex or several different types of products. For example, banks have trained specialist advisers for each of their financial products (e.g. student accounts, pensions, mortgages). They can answer any question a customer is likely to ask (but remember, their job is to sell, not to inform).

The quality and availability of advice is also important. B &Q sales assistants have extensive product knowledge and are clearly identifiable by their orange aprons. Each assistant wears a name badge so that customers feel comfortable approaching them to discuss the different products that will meet their needs.

Case study

The following is an online customer review for Couriers Express Ltd.

'I felt the need to write a review as I have just had the most unpleasant dealing with Couriers Express Ltd. Today is Christmas Eve, and I was guaranteed that my parcel would be delivered by 22 December. It was a Christmas present I had ordered for my wife. As the order had not arrived I decided to call up and find out where it was and when I could expect it. I was informed that my parcel was in storage some 30 miles from their depot and that I would not receive my parcel in time for Christmas. They admitted to errors on their behalf and that they had basically taken on too much. My item was alongside thousands of other Christmas presents that will not be under trees in the morning. When I asked when I could expect delivery I was told they were closed until 5 January and that I would get it that week.'

1. What does this paragraph tell you about the importance of good customer service?

2. Outline two things Couriers Express Ltd could have done differently.

Providing assistance

As well as information and advice, customers will often need assistance when buying a product or after they have bought a product. This can consist of:

▶ helping the customer find the product in the store

▶ ordering products if items aren't in stock

▶ providing help lines and after-sales service. For example, if you buy an oven or dishwasher, the retailer may provide an engineer who will come and install it for you. Also, many organisations provide help lines or online help pages so that customers can find help after they have purchased a product.

Dealing with special needs

It is important for organisations to tailor their products to the specific needs of their customers, examples of which are given in Figure 11.2.

 Over to you!

Think of all of the different ways that shops like Tesco cater for the needs of the following customers:

- blind customers
- foreign language speaking customers
- customers in a hurry
- parents with children.

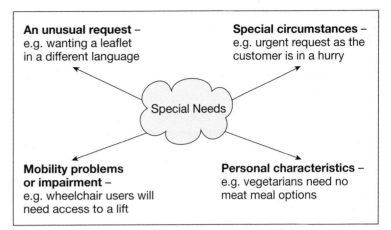

Figure 11.2 Possible special needs of customers

There are several different types of special need that customers may have, which organisations have to meet. These are outlined in Figure 11.3.

Figure 11.3 Ways of meeting special needs

Type of customer	Ways to meet their needs
Deaf/hard of hearing	Most deaf people can lip read, so it's important that staff look at the customer when they are talking to them, and speak slowly.
Blind/visually impaired	If a visually impaired person asks for help, lead them gently and warn them of obstacles.
Foreign speaking	If a customer's first language is not English, speak slowly and clearly and use simple words. Writing things down may help as they may be able to read English better than they can speak it.
Mobility impaired	Know what facilities are on offer so that you can advise customers with impaired mobility. Many of these facilities are compulsory under the Disability Discrimination Act, e.g. disabled parking, disabled toilets, ramps, lifts. Staff should also be ready to assist where necessary.

Meeting health, safety and security needs

Organisations need to ensure that the health and safety risks to their customers are minimised. They do this by showing evacuation procedures in the event of a fire alarm, performing regular risk assessments and training employees to deal with health and safety issues such as medical emergencies.

Organisations also need to take account of security issues. This may include: having security guards, CCTV, panic buttons, online secure payment processes and ways to protect data on staff and customers.

Over to you!

Think of all the ways your school or college meets:

- the health and safety needs of all its users
- the security needs of all its users.

Consider staff, students and visitors.

Did you know?

Legally, all organisations have to abide by the Health and Safety at Work Act 1974. Find out more about it at www.hse.gov.uk/legislation/hswa.htm.

Customer expectations

Meeting customer needs is a basic requirement of an organisation if it wants to attract customers. However, to succeed a business must do more than meet customer needs – it must match or beat their expectations. For example, to get to work, I *need* a train, but I *expect* (want) a seat on the train. Success in beating customer expectations is what creates customer loyalty. This enables an organisation to be better than its competitors. Sir Terry Leahy, Chief Executive, Tesco Plc, says: 'Follow the customer – if they change … we change'.

Customer expectations can be influenced by a large number of different factors, including:

▶ *Price* – expectations change depending on price. In India you can find a hotel charging $4 a night – or one charging $200! Expectations of service will, naturally, be far greater at an expensive 5-star hotel.

▶ *Competitors* – if customers have experienced good levels of service on Air France, they will expect the same or better on British Airways.

▶ *Previous visits to the same organisation* – when customers revisit an organisation, they will base their expectations on any previous visits they have made. Customers hate to think that standards are slipping.

▶ *Reading media reports* – if the customer reads a very positive newspaper article on an organisation, they will expect to receive the same level of service from the organisation themselves. With the use of the internet, media reports are playing a bigger part than ever in moulding customers' expectations of organisations. It is very easy for customers to review products and service they have bought and post them on websites such as www.ciao.co.uk. An example is shown in Figure 11.4.

Over to you!

In groups, discuss how your expectations have led you to choose one product over another.

We purchased a Dansai DVD at £99.49 from Tesco local store.

Reasons for purchase:

1) Recommended by a relative
2) The price at under £100 was good value for money
3) This model is only available from Tesco as own brand.

Up until recently the machine has worked OK, no problems, but then we noticed that it started to jump and slow down while watching films.
My husband rang to report the problem, thinking it would be a lengthy process. We were pleasantly surprised by the result. They agreed to send a replacement direct in the next 2 days and if the exact model was not available the nearest equivalent would be sent... Two days later a friendly man arrived with a new machine which works better than the original!

Well done Tesco – 100% achieved for prompt service and customer kindness

http://www.ciao.co.uk/Tesco_Customer_Service__Review_5329591

Figure 11.4 Tesco customer review

Different types of customers

For 'front-line' staff to provide good service to customers, they need good backup from many other people in the business, e.g. IT support. Therefore, organisations like to get every member of staff to treat others as their customers, even if they are simply co-workers.

Internal customers

Everybody within an organisation works with and for other people. Just as customers expect goods to be delivered on time, so a manager expects staff to deliver a report on time or arrive at a meeting on time. Staff should regard all colleagues as 'internal customers'. They are called customers because they depend on the services provided by each other.

An organisation can only achieve excellent customer service if all employees are working together as a team, regardless of whether they actually deal directly with external customers. This means that staff should work to the same high standards within the business, whether or not they are dealing with external customers. For example, the staff canteen should serve food fit for real customers.

At school or college there are lots of different staff who work together to ensure that you receive a good education and have a good experience. These include teachers, education welfare officers, administrative staff, cleaners, dinner ladies and the caretaker.

In most businesses the key internal customers are: colleagues, supervisors, managers and staff teams. They are called 'internal' even if they work elsewhere, e.g. Tesco Head Office is an internal customer of Tesco Brighton branch.

External customers

External customers are the people who buy or use the products and/or services of an organisation. Their needs and expectations can vary widely. As a result, an organisation needs to tailor its customer services to meet the needs and expectations of the customers it wishes to attract.

Here are some examples of factors that affect different external customers' needs and expectations:

▶ *Gender* – men and women have different needs, such as toilets and changing rooms, and different wants.

▶ *People in groups, on their own or families* – the organisation may offer group discount tickets and family parking bays.

▶ *New versus existing customers* – the organisation may offer promotions to new customers and rewards to loyal customers, e.g. loyalty cards offering discounts on certain products.

▶ *Different ages* – organisations may have to cater for both the young and the elderly, for example, they may have a play area for children and baby changing facilities. Some organisations play music in their stores that they think will attract their target customers.

- ► *Business customers* – the organisation may offer special accounts or special facilities to business customers.
- ► *Customers with special needs*, e.g. disabilities – organisations have to cater for people with special needs. They can do this, for example, by having ramps, wide aisles, disabled parking and lifts.
- ► *Different nationalities* – people who are from different cultures or have different nationalities may have different needs. These may be met, for example, by having leaflets and signs in different languages.

Over to you!

Using your favourite shop as an example, explain what it does to meet the needs of each of the different external customers listed above. For example:

Customers with disabilities – lifts and ramps and staff to assist.

Benefits of good customer service

Benefits of good customer service to the customer:

- ► Pleasant experience – they are more likely to return and look forward to repeating their experience with the organisation, and to tell their friends of their pleasant experience.
- ► Able to rely on service – if a customer can rely on the service, they can save time when making their next purchases as they do not have to shop around.
- ► Confident about purchase – customers feel confident, so they can enjoy their purchase, feel valued and important.

Benefits of good customer service to the organisation:

- ► Enhanced reputation.
- ► Repeat business – customers return because their needs and expectations were met.
- ► Attracts more customers – therefore higher revenue and more opportunities for staff to shine.
- ► Increased profits – the more customers there are the higher the profits – as long as costs are kept under control

Benefits of good customer service to the employee:

- ► Pleasant working conditions – if the organisation offers good customer service, fewer customers will complain and therefore staff will be less stressed.
- ► Satisfaction of pleasing customers – employees can build positive relationships with both internal and external customers and therefore achieve high working standards.
- ► More secure employment – this comes from pleasing customers and meeting or exceeding targets. Also, happy customers mean that the organisation will be a success, which is good news for the employees as profits will increase, leading to better staff bonuses and promotions!

Assessment activity (P1, P2, M1)

JD Sports is a retailer of fashionable sports brands. It started in 1981 with one shop in Bury called John David Sports. Now there are 400 stores and JD is the leading UK retailer of fashionable sports and casual wear. It has separated itself from shops such as JJB through innovative shop layout and the most exclusive and stylish ranges. This means that customers enjoy a pleasant experience in their stores. Whereas Sports Direct and JJB focus on low prices and clothing such as football kits, JD is more to do with Saturday night than Saturday afternoon.

JD Sports also has a new e-commerce business. This provides customers with their branded fashion needs online. They can feel confident in JD online because they can see and visit the shops. They can also track their orders so they can rely on the service offered to them.

JD Sports has the largest selection of branded, fashionable sportswear. The choice encourages customers to return – and customers often tell their friends of the good service and range of products. Due to this, JD Sports' profits have been increasing year on year.

The rapid growth of JD Sports has given employees with the right qualities and ambition opportunities to progress quickly. The company challenges staff to be creative and forward thinking and suggest ways that the business can improve. Staff have the satisfaction of happy customers and secure employment.

1. Describe three different types of customers who might want buy sportswear.

2. Explain how their needs and expectations can differ.

3. Outline the benefits that JD's good customer service brings to their customers.

4. Outline the benefits that JD's good customer service brings to the business.

5. Outline the benefits that JD's good customer service brings to its staff.

6. Explain how their different needs and expectations might lead to some customers being unable to find what they want at JD Sports.

Applying presentation and interpersonal skills in customer service situations

Getting started

When dealing with customers face to face, the skills and personalities of staff are crucial. This is particularly the case in high-value situations, such as Reception at a posh hotel, or the sales floor at an Armani store.

When you have completed this topic, you should:

- identify the key presentation and interpersonal skills
- understand their importance – especially when recruiting staff
- be aware of how organisations try to improve these skills among their staff.

Key terms

Difficult customer service situations: customer service situations that do not occur often and as a result you are not sure how to deal with the customer's need

Interpersonal skills: 'inter' means between, so these are 'skills between people', such as a warm smile and good eye contact

Jargon: the technical or slang terms used widely within an industry (e.g. in football, 'the gaffer' is often used to mean the team's manager)

Routine customer service situations: customer service situations that occur on a daily basis within organisations

Presentation skills

Presentation skills help ensure that people feel comfortable around you. Many organisations issue uniforms to staff so that they are easy to spot and show a consistent image to customers. Other organisations have strict dress codes so that employees always look smart and presentable.

There are certain standards that all organisations expect of their employees with regard to their presentation. These include:

▶ Having good personal hygiene (e.g. tidy hair and clean fingernails) shows that you care about the way internal and external customers see you.

▶ Hairstyle, make up and jewellery must fit in with the business image, e.g. subtle for Marks & Spencer; younger and funkier for Topshop and HMV.

▶ Having a clean and tidy working space shows that you care about the working environment and about the way internal and external customers see you. Being tidy also suggests that you are organised and efficient. So, personal items

Did you know?

Children always show their feelings through their facial expressions, as they haven't yet learned to cover up their emotions, whereas adults are expected to mask them.

should be kept out of the way, walkways and corridors kept clear, paperwork that can be seen kept to a minimum and always following instructions for using equipment.

Did you know?

Foxtons, the estate agents that operate in the south east of England, have a very strict dress code. Although they do not issue uniforms, they do expect employees to wear a suit. Ties have to be tied in a Windsor knot and men must always be clean shaven.

It is important to keep your work area clean and tidy.

Over to you!

In pairs, take it in turns to perform the following actions and discuss what each communicates to customers:

- fold your arms
- cross your legs
- lower your head
- lean forward
- sit upright
- raise your eyebrows
- make eye contact
- tilt your head
- nod
- shake your head
- twist your hair
- shrug your shoulders
- put your hands on your hips
- clench your fists
- tap your foot or fingers.

Not only is the way you look important, but also the messages you convey to customers through your body language. Different types of body language include:

▶ *Facial expressions* – these are expressions on your face that can give away your thoughts and feelings about someone or something. It is important that staff do not display any inappropriate feelings towards their customers, such as boredom! Smiling is extremely important as it shows customers that you are approachable and willing to help them.

▶ *Posture* – the way you stand and sit is important when communicating with customers. If you slouch and hunch your shoulders you look uninterested and bored. Sit upright and straight and you look confident and interested.

▶ *Gestures* – these are ways we communicate with people using our bodies. We often use them to emphasise what we are saying, perhaps by pointing or shrugging our shoulders. Having eye contact with customers is one of the easiest ways to let them know that you are interested in what they are saying and that you are confident in your ability to help them.

Did you know?

Most organisations spend thousands of pounds ensuring that their reception areas – usually the first area of the business that customers see – are impressive, as they recognise the importance of first impressions!

Interpersonal skills

Interpersonal skills are shown in the way you behave with other people, especially those you are meeting for the first time. Are you friendly or cold? Are you chatty or do you go quiet? When you are dealing with customers, it is important to be polite and show interest at all times.

Interpersonal skills include:

▶ *Attitude and behaviour* – this is influenced by what you are thinking at the time. When you are dealing with customers, you should always show a positive attitude and behaviour, regardless of what you are feeling inside.

▶ *First impressions and greeting customers* – everybody has heard of the saying that 'first impressions count', and they really do! Most people make a judgement about the type of person you are in the first minute of meeting you. Therefore it is extremely important, when greeting customers, to make an excellent first impression. Greet them in a professional and polite manner. Many organisations train their staff how to greet their customers, e.g. shaking their hand, introducing themselves and giving their position within the company.

▶ *Showing respect for customers* – this is done through being polite, showing concern for customer needs, showing interest in helping them, listening to them, asking questions if you do not understand something, being efficient in dealing with their request and being tactful (i.e. sensitive to people and not showing any true negative feelings you may have).

▶ *Responding to the different customer behaviour* – different customers behave in different ways of behaving. If a customer is in a rush they will behave very differently from if they have all the time in the world. Employees therefore need to watch the body language of their customers (both internal and external) and respond to them appropriately.

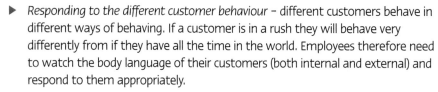

Over to you!

In pairs, with one of you as the customer and the other a sales assistant, take it in turns to act out the following scenarios:

- Dealing with a customer in a rush.
- Dealing with a happy customer.
- Dealing with a stressed customer.
- Dealing with an unhappy customer.
- Dealing with a customer who has a lot of time.

Communication skills

Skilful communication can turn a grumpy customer into a fan. Poor communication can turn a small problem into a gripe that is blogged worldwide.

Communication skills include the following:

▶ *Tone of voice* – the way you speak to your friends is very different from the way you may speak to your teacher. Your tone of voice depends on who you are talking to – whether you are formal or informal, concerned, apologetic, persuasive or grovelling!

▶ *Pitch of voice* – this is the sound of your voice, i.e. whether it low or high. Varying your pitch when you talk makes you sound more interesting and people will be more likely to listen to you.

Over to you!
Listen to the news on the TV tonight. Take note of the different pitch the newsreaders use relative to the stories they are talking about.

▶ *Language* – It is very important to use the correct language – only use slang when talking to your friends.

Activity
Schools and colleges are full of technical **jargon** that people who do not work in education would rarely understand. Make a list of any jargon members of staff at your school or college use. Find out what the different terms mean and write a 'jargon glossary' for someone who might not be familiar with them.

▶ *Pace* – the speed at which you talk is also important. A fast pace is acceptable as long as you are sure that the people you are talking to understand what you are saying. If you are unsure, it is important to slow down your pace so that the listener can take in what you are saying.

▶ *Listening skills* – being a good listener is extremely important when dealing with customers efficiently and effectively. This means not interrupting them or letting your mind wander. Being a good listener means you should be able to repeat back nearly everything that a person says to you. This is extremely important if you are to meet the needs of customers.

▶ *Appropriateness to customer/situation* – it is important to match the way you communicate with the people or the situation you are dealing with. Being polite to customers goes without saying, but sometimes you must be firm with them, for example when there's a fire alarm and they need your help.

Over to you!
Read one of the paragraphs about communication skills to a friend. Do not let them read it. After you have finished reading it aloud, see how well they have listened by asking them to write down everything you said.

Customer service situations

Figure 11.5 summarises the different skills required to match different types of communication.

Figure 11.5 Matching communication skills with different situations

Type of communication	Presentation skills	Interpersonal skills	Communication skills
Face to face	Having a professional appearance is essential; this includes using professional body language.	Good first impressions are very important, as is being friendly and interested in customers' needs.	Speaking clearly, using appropriate body language and tone of voice, avoiding slang – especially with external customers.
On the telephone	Sounding friendly is important when communicating on the telephone.	Your attitude can be shown verbally, so it is vital to sound interested.	A clear voice and appropriate pace is important because body language cannot be seen.
In writing	Neat writing and accurate spelling are essential.	Must be professional, formal, polite and precise.	The key is to be clear in what you are saying, and to address precisely the customer's needs.
Email	Always follow the format that is standard in your organisation.	Must be professional and courteous.	Should follow organisation rules, but always write formally to external customers.

For **routine customer service situations**, it is important not to be complacent, but to treat the customer the same way as you did the first time – the best way you can, using appropriate presentation, interpersonal and communication skills.

For **difficult customer service situations**, the most important thing to remember is not to panic. Always use your line manager as a source of help if needed. They will always be able to take control if you do not feel you are able to deal with the situation.

Dealing with different customers needs

As discussed earlier, different customers have different needs and these needs to be dealt with in different ways.

Sometimes customers can be difficult or abusive and demand things that perhaps the organisation is unable to offer. For example, a customer may demand a product that the organisation simply does not have. In these situations, it is always important to remain polite and professional – always call your manager if you are not able to handle the situation on your own.

When dealing with disabled customers, you may have to adapt your interpersonal and communication skills in order to deliver effective customer service. Remember that disabled customers include those who are mobility impaired, blind or visually impaired and deaf or hard of hearing. It is important not to be patronising with these customers, but be patient and polite. You may need to adapt your communication skills to ensure that you are understood, for example, for a customer who is hard of hearing you may need you to display more hand gestures to explain what you mean, or you may need to slow your pace so that they can lip read.

Some customers need technical information, so, depending on what they need to know, you may have to adapt the language you use. Ensure that you are able to explain any technical terms, as external customers may not be familiar with all of the jargon involved in products such as mobile phones or laptops.

Assessment activity 11.1 (P3, M2, D1)

Read the three role-play scenarios below. In pairs, act out each role-play.

In order to achieve P3 you must demonstrate presentation, communication and interpersonal skills.

In order to achieve M2 you must display confident presentation, communication and interpersonal skills.

To achieve D1 you must anticipate and meet the needs of the different customers.

Role-play 1 A complaint from a disabled customer

You work in the gift shop at a museum. A group of customers has just come into the shop after being on a tour. One of the customers is in a wheelchair.

The person in the wheelchair complains that the aisles in the shop are not wide enough for the wheelchair to pass through. Furthermore, there are gifts on the top shelves that he cannot reach. He is very angry and feels that the gift shop is not well equipped for disabled customers.

You need to deal with the customer's complaint and ensure that he leaves the shop satisfied.

Role-play 2 A request for information from a non-English speaking tourist

You work on the information desk at a museum. A Japanese tourist approaches who does not speak very good English. She would like a tour of the museum, but due to language difficulties needs assistance to understand the tour.

Role-play 3 A customer is drunk in the museum

You work in the canteen at a museum. You have noticed that one customer in particular has had too much to drink. He is disturbing other customers and they are leaving. You have to make sure he is dealt with appropriately.

Topic check

1 Why may the posture of a receptionist be important?
2 Identify two interpersonal skills that would be helpful when dealing with a stressed customer.
3 Explain the difference between 'tone of voice' and 'pitch of voice'.
4 Explain the importance of presentation skills when going to a job interview.
5 Identify two interpersonal skills that would be helpful when dealing with a blind customer.

How consistent and reliable customer service contributes to customer satisfaction

Getting started

Some businesses say that customer satisfaction is not enough. They want 'customer delight'! Most customers, though, as they grab their morning paper, or get a lunchtime sandwich, are happy enough with consistent, reliable service: not much of a queue, the right products in stock, and reasonably polite service. These points will keep most customers satisfied and keep them coming back.

When you have completed this topic, you should:

- understand why customers want consistency and reliability
- understand how organisations attempt to provide reliable service
- understand the link between customer service, customer satisfaction and business success.

Key terms

Confidence: when a customer trusts the service because they have always been given reliable goods and services in the past

Jargon: the technical or slang terms used widely within an industry (e.g. in football, 'the gaffer' is often used to mean the team's manager)

Value for money: this does not mean that the goods are the cheapest, but that the package of product and services (e.g. helpful staff, delivery, installation, guarantees etc.) is good for the price paid

Making sure service is consistent and reliable

Customers expect to experience the same high levels of service no matter who deals with their needs. Achieving consistency requires a lot of money to be invested in staff training. The training focuses on the following areas:

▶ *Scope of the job role* – employees need to be trained on what they can and cannot do as part of their job. They need to know the situations where customers should be passed on to their manager.

Activity

What is the difference between being consistent and being reliable?

In pairs, think of and discuss EITHER a footballer OR an *X-Factor* star who has been consistently poor in his or her performance recently. Come up with your own definition of consistent. Why is it important that customer service is consistent?

In your pairs, think of EITHER a make of car OR a computer games console that has a reputation for being unreliable. Why is this make or brand seen as unreliable? Why is it therefore important to have reliable customer service?

▶ *Knowledge of products and services* – staff must understand the different products and services so that they can offer reliable assistance and advice. Employees should know where they can get information on the products, e.g. manuals or catalogues and understand the terms (the **jargon**) used within them.

▶ *Type and quality of products and services* – employees need to be able to identify the best product and/or service to satisfy the different needs and expectations of different customers.

▶ *Staff attitude and behaviour* – employees need to understand the importance of having a positive attitude and being polite and professional.

▶ *Timing* – customers hate having their time misused, e.g. by having to wait in unnecessarily long queues. Similarly, being aware of how much time they have and when to approach them to offer help is also important. If you have kept customers waiting, make sure to apologise; deal with their problem as quickly and effectively as possible.

▶ *Accessibility/availability* – it is important that employees know what products are available and the procedure for helping customers if the product they want is not in stock. This may include putting the customer's name on a waiting list and calling them when the product comes into the store.

▶ *Meeting specific customer needs* – staff need to know the correct questions to ask customers so that they can identify and fulfil their needs as quickly as possible.

▶ *Working under pressure* – employees should be able act appropriately towards customers even when they are busy and under pressure.

▶ *Confirming service meets needs and expectations* – organisations trying to improve their customer service may check that their customers are satisfied. This might involve phoning them to check that they were happy with the service, or asking them to complete a customer service questionnaire.

▶ *Dealing with problems* – when customers are unhappy and have a problem, staff need to know how to deal with them. Is the customer *always* right? Staff need to know what they can offer an unhappy customer: money back? Or some other form of compensation? The Case study on page 202 shows the value of empowering staff to make quick decisions about customer problems.

 Did you know?

Dissatisfied customers tell an average of 10 other people about their bad experience. Twelve per cent of customers will tell up to 20 people. It's true what they say about bad news spreading quickly!

On the other hand, satisfied customers will tell an average of 5 people about their positive experience so, unfortunately, the good news doesn't spread so quickly – in fact, bad news spreads twice as fast!

Case study

After seeing a BBC series on the opening of a 'Rock 'n' Roll' hotel in London, Sian and Julia went there for a Saturday breakfast. They were the only people there, yet found service slow and the fry-up quite poorly cooked. When they complained, the waiter was brilliant. He apologised, explained that the breakfast chef was off work, sick, and gave a 50% discount on the bill. Sian and Julia went away happy.

1. Briefly explain why it is so important to deal quickly and effectively with customer problems.

2. How might the hotel's management make sure that the problem doesn't happen again?

Customer satisfaction

A satisfied customer:

▶ has **confidence** in the product and/or service received

▶ feels they have received **value for money**.

The benefits of a satisfied customer are:

▶ repeat purchases, because customers will return if they are happy with the product and/or service they have received

▶ word-of-mouth recommendations to others – this is often the most effective way of enhancing a firm's reputation.

Customer satisfaction is also important for internal customers as it leads to job satisfaction. It also benefits teamwork and communication within the organisation, helping to make the organisation more efficient. Ultimately, this means the organisation is more likely to fulfil its aims and objectives and meet the needs and expectations of its external customers.

It is important to note the negative effects of poor internal communication. If staff have a faulty understanding of what customers value, future plans may prove unsuccessful. At a restaurant, the waiters may assure the chef that everyone loves his food, but if they're only saying that to keep the boss happy, the future of the restaurant may be in peril.

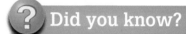

? Did you know?

It costs five times more money to attract a new customer than to keep an existing one.

Codes of practice

These are voluntary guidelines that identify standards of service that customers can expect. They may also provide advice to customers on what to do if they are not satisfied. Codes of practice can be made at different levels. These include:

▶ *Industry codes of practice* – these set out minimum standards expected throughout an industry, for example banking and finance.

▶ *Organisational codes of practice* – these are guidelines written by specific companies on their own standards and ways of dealing with customer complaints. For example, retailers with high standards, such as John Lewis, are likely to have 'no-quibble' money-back guarantees.

▶ *Professional codes of practice* – these are the guidelines that all professional workers should abide by, e.g. doctors or solicitors. They are drawn up by professional institutions such as the British Medical Association.

▶ *Ethical standards* – these are standards saying that organisations should trade fairly and honestly with customers and suppliers. The institute of business ethics provides guidance: www.ibe.org.uk.

Assessment activity 11.2 (P4, M3)

When people visit London, most use the Tube (London Underground). Most customers' basic needs and expectations include a reliable service, value for money, a safe, comfortable and clean area to sit and staff that are helpful. However, this isn't always the case. Most customers will complain of engineering works affecting the reliability of the service, high ticket prices and cramped and hot conditions.

However, there are plans to improve the customer service offered to Tube users. The introduction of the Oyster Card ensured cheaper journeys on all London Tubes and buses and, in light of the 2012 London Olympics, this will soon be offered on other train journeys and ferries on the Thames. They are also planning to increase the reliability of the service and there are talks of air-cooling systems being fitted in the future. Newer Tube lines also offer better facilities for the disabled.

1. Identify four aspects of customer service that customers see as important when using the Tube in London.

2. Describe how the Tube is trying to meets the needs of all of its customers.

3. Describe what other services customers may want in the future as more and more people use the Tube, especially with the increase in tourism related to the London Olympics.

4. Using the information above, describe how consistent and reliable customer service contributes to customer satisfaction of customers using the Tube.

5. Complete the table below explaining why good customer service is important to both JD Sports and the Tube.

	Why is customer service important to their customers?
JD Sports	
The Tube	

Topic check

1 Why do businesses love to have regular customers who 'repeat purchase'?

2 Briefly explain why reliability might be important to customers of:

   a) a low-cost airline   b) a bus service.

3 Briefly explain why consistency might be important to customers of:

   a) McDonald's   b) an expensive London hotel.

4 What is meant by 'an industry code of practice'?

5 Explain what is meant by 'ethical standards'.

Monitoring and evaluating customer service within an organisation

Getting started

Managers like to measure whether staff are achieving the goals set out for them. Therefore, they check on the level of customer service. One way of doing this is by using 'mystery shoppers' who may find staff who are failing to perform in the way they have been trained.

When you have completed this topic, you should:

- understand why customer service levels are monitored and evaluated
- understand the main ways in which monitoring takes place.

How do organisations monitor customer service levels?

Organisations need to monitor their customer service so that they know:

▶ what their customers think

▶ what they are doing well

▶ what needs to be improved.

Did you know?

Providing high-quality customer service can save businesses money. The same skills that lead to increased customer satisfaction also lead to increased employee **productivity**. The same things that make customers happy make employees happy!

 Key terms

Productivity: staff efficiency, e.g. how many telephone calls a receptionist answers per hour

Quality control: measures to check on the quality of the finished product before it is sent to the customer

Organisations use several different methods to monitor customer service levels, including the following:

▶ *Informal customer feedback* – for example, when you eat a meal in a restaurant, the waiter asks if everything was all right so that, if necessary, any problems can be sorted out.

▶ *Customer comment cards* – many hotels supply comment cards for their customers to complete on the service they have received. This allows customers to suggest how the business can improve its service.

▶ *Customer questionnaires* – these are more detailed than comment cards and ask specific questions about the service the customer has received. Not only do questionnaires serve as feedback, they also find out the typical customer that

the business attracts (such as age, gender and occupation). This helps the business decide how to cater for different customers' different requirements.

▶ *Employee feedback* – it is important to know what your employees think about the service the business is offering. This is because employees are the people who deal directly with the customers and therefore know all of the positive and negative comments that customers make. Staff feedback is also important because they are internal customers and keeping them happy is important for their job satisfaction.

▶ *Mystery customers* – this is when businesses employ customers to visit their stores to assess their staff. They may also go to competitors' stores to compare the service they have received. They then write a report which is given to the business. The mystery customer assesses the quality of the service, the speed of the service and the staff's attitude. Gordon Ramsay hires 'mystery diners' to keep a check on the standards at his many restaurants worldwide.

▶ *Complaints and compliments letters* – if several complaints are made about the same thing, it indicates that something needs to be done to solve it quickly. Letters or emails giving praise are also important for businesses – they are often put up on notice boards or websites.

Did you know?

If you are interested in becoming a mystery shopper, check out the following website:

www.grassrootsmysteryshopping.com.

How do organisations evaluate customer service levels?

Evaluating customer service is also important: if all the feedback a business is getting is positive, it should be doing very well overall. However, it is important to check that this is the case by looking at indicators, including:

▶ *Level of sales* – if the service offered to customers is good, sales should be rising and the business can check this by looking at its sales turnover figures.

▶ *Repeat customers* – if customers keep returning to a business, it means they are happy. Businesses can check if customers keep returning by looking at how many times they reorder goods, or looking at market share statistics.

▶ *New customers* – if the service offered is good, the number of new customers should be increasing. This will be reflected in increased sales turnover.

▶ *Level of complaints/compliments letters* – if the service offered is of a good standard, complaints should be falling and compliments rising. Trends in complaints and compliments should be evaluated to see what needs to be improved and what is doing well.

▶ *Staff turnover* – this should be falling if the service offered is good. If staff are not leaving it usually indicates that they are happy. If employees are leaving, it is important to interview them before they leave to check their reasons for leaving. In 2009 Morrison's boasted on their website that staff turnover had fallen by 7%. This was, rightly, a matter of pride for management.

What can organisations do to improve customer service levels?

Once customer service levels have been monitored and evaluated, it is important for a business to identify where it can improve so that it ensures it has satisfied customers. Improvements can include:

▶ *Improvements to quality of service* – there may be a need for extra staff training, or a need for new policies, e.g. scrapping an impersonal call centre and allowing customers to phone staff or managers directly.

▶ *Reliability* – better **quality control** before products are sold will make the customer experience far better.

▶ *Improvements to the organisation* – increased management focus on customer service (perhaps including staff empowerment) will help keep staff happy, attract new customers and increase sales and – it's hoped – profits.

▶ *Improvements to the employee* – improving job satisfaction and the working environment can help staff motivation. Satisfied employees are less likely to leave, which means hardworking employees are retained and the cost of recruiting and training new employees is reduced.

"CONGRATULATIONS! . . . YOU'RE OUR ONE MILLIONTH DISSATISFIED CUSTOMER!"

Assessment activity 11.3 (P5, P6, M4, D2)

Selfridges is a chain of luxury department stores across the UK. The flagship store is on Oxford Street in London, and is the second biggest store in the whole of Britain. Selfridges has always been forward thinking. The London store was the first shop to display merchandise so customers could examine it, as all department stores do nowadays. It was the first to use the phrase 'the customer is always right', which was used extensively in its advertising campaigns.

Selfridges checks that its customer service is of the highest standard by using mystery shoppers. Anyone can sign up to be a mystery customer on the website (www.selfridges.com). Their aim is 'to provide a world-class shopping experience and we believe that our customers are the best people to tell us how we are doing. We would therefore like feedback on your "real" shopping experiences.'

Selfridges asks customers to register online and complete a short questionnaire online after their next visit. Customers are encouraged to do this as they receive £10 for each completed questionnaire.

The responses to the questionnaires are then analysed to see what action should be taken to improve the service offered to customers.

Not only are the views of their customers important to Selfridges, but also the views of their employees. To Selfridges, 'shopping is about entertainment, inspiration and above all, fun. And while our innovative window displays set the tone for what's in store, it's our people who really make the difference. We know it's their passion that keeps our

Assessment activity 11.3 (P5, P6, M4, D2) *continued*

customers coming back for more. That's why we've made sure that Selfridges is the number one choice for ambitious retail professionals.'

Selfridges also offers customers other ways to provide feedback, both positive and negative. There is a Customer Relations team to phone, and also an online feedback form that customers can complete.

1. Describe how the views of staff and customers are monitored by Selfridges.

2. Suggest three types of business information Selfridges could check to evaluate its customer feedback and the trends it would want to see.

3. Describe any improvements or recommendations that you could offer to Selfridges in order to improve their customer service.

4. Explain how monitoring and evaluating customer service has improved customer service for Selfridges itself, its employees and its customers.

5. Complete the tables below, analysing how providing effective customer service benefits Selfridges' customers, its employees and the organisation itself.

	Benefits to Selfridges' customers	Benefits to Selfridges' employees	Benefits to Selfridges (the organisation)
Mystery shoppers			
Online customer feedback forms			
Unique shopping experiences			
Add any more here…			

	Limitations to Selfridges' customers	Limitations to Selfridges' employees	Limitations to Selfridges (the organisation)
Mystery shoppers			
Online customer feedback forms			
Unique shopping experiences			
Add any more here…			

Topic check

1 Explain why Harrods might employ 'mystery shoppers' to visit the store from time to time.

2 If a store manager is frequently on the shop floor, talking to staff and customers, is there a need for regular customer surveys?

3 If sales are rising, is there a need for customer service to be monitored regularly?

4 How may staff motivation affect customer service?

Assessment summary

The overall grade you achieve for this unit depends on how well you meet the grading criteria set out at the start of the chapter (see page 185). You must complete:

■ all of the P criteria to achieve a **pass** grade
■ all of the P and the M criteria to achieve a **merit** grade
■ all of the P, M and D criteria to achieve a **distinction** grade.

Your tutor will assess the assessment activities that you complete for this unit. The work you produce should provide evidence which demonstrates that you have achieved each of the assessment criteria. The table below identifies what you need to demonstrate to meet each of the pass, merit and distinction criteria for this unit. You should always check and self-assess your work before you submit your assignments for marking.

Remember that you MUST provide evidence for all of the P criteria to pass the unit.

Grading criteria	You need to demonstrate that you can:	Do you have the evidence?
P1	Describe three different types of customers and their needs and expectations	
P2	Outline the benefits of good customer service in a selected organisation	
P3	Demonstrate presentation, communication and interpersonal skills in different customer service situations	
P4	Explain what contributes to consistent and reliable customer service	
P5	Describe how customer service can be monitored and evaluated	
P6	Outline how improvements to the customer service in an organisation could be made	
M1	Explain how different customers' needs and expectations can differ	
M2	Display confident presentation, communication and interpersonal skills when demonstrating customer service in a range of customer service situations	
M3	Analyse the importance of customer service to different businesses	
M4	Explain how monitoring and evaluating can improve customer service for the customer, the organisation and the employee	
D1	Anticipate and meet the needs of different customers in three contrasting situations	
D2	Analyse how monitoring and evaluating can improve customer service for the customer, the organisation and the employee	

Always ask your tutor to explain any assignment tasks or assessment criteria that you don't understand fully. Being clear about the task before you begin gives you the best chance of succeeding. Good luck with your Unit 11 assessment work!

12 Business online

Unit outline

Twenty years ago if you wanted to watch a film you would hire a video from *Blockbuster* or buy one from *Virgin Megastore*. If you needed a loaf of bread you would nip to the corner shop. The face of retailing has radically changed – music and films can be downloaded, supermarket shopping carried out online and more and more consumers are using the web for their selling and buying. Will all retailing be carried out online one day?

Learning outcomes

1 **Understand different online business activities.**
2 **Understand the issues relating to doing business online.**
3 **Be able to create web pages or a website for a stated business need.**
4 **Know the impact of an online business presence.**

Grading guide

To achieve a **pass**, you must show you can:	To achieve a **merit**, you must show you can:	To achieve a **distinction**, you must show you can:
P1 Describe three different business organisations which operate online	**M1** Compare the features of three business organisations operating online	
P2 Explain how they operate their activities online		
P3 Explain the issues a business organisation would need to consider to go online	**M2** Analyse the benefits to businesses and customers of conducting business online	**D1** Make recommendations for a business organisation considering going online
P4 Explain the operational risks for a business operating online		**D2** Suggest ways in which a business could deal with the operational risks associated with an online presence
P5 Create web pages to meet user need	**M3** Explain how the website assists in achieving the aims and objectives of the business user	**D3** Justify the use of different construction features in the design of a website
P6 Describe the benefits to a business organisation of marketing a product or service online		
P7 Outline the impact of online business on society	**M4** Analyse the consequences on society of an increase in online business	**D4** Evaluate the benefits and drawbacks to society of increasing business online

Understanding different online business activities

▶ Getting started

We all know about online retail shopping, such as Amazon or ASOS. There are also 'business-to-business' online activities such as automatic ordering of extra supplies. A top student understands the range of different online activities.

When you have completed this topic, you should:

■ know about different online business activities

■ understand their importance for business efficiency.

Range of online activities and sectors

Think of a business you know of that operates online... in fact, make a list of as many as you can in two minutes. How many did you get? Who were they?

Who operates online and why?

When we consider online business, most of us immediately think of large retailers, privately owned, who use the web to make a profit, such as Play.com, Amazon, ASOS, Oli and so on. These private sector businesses see huge advantages in online selling, such as:

▶ Cutting out a physical high street presence saves a huge of money amount in terms of property and labour costs, e.g. Amazon v Waterstones or Asos v Topshop. This enables the online supplier to choose to either charge lower prices or offer a broader service, e.g. stocking 50,000 different book titles instead of 8,000.

▶ Suppliers of services, such as Thomas Cook holidays, can save paying commission to travel agents. This helps their profits.

▶ Selling online allows a much wider group of people to buy, such as people in rural Cornwall or people in Belgium.

▶ It allows a business to control every aspect of the shopping process. Luxury goods companies want to protect their brand image, for example, Chanel would not want its perfume to be sold for £9.99 at Superdrug. Online, the producer can control the shopping environment.

Many other organisations also have an online presence – but they may not want to sell us anything. These include:

▶ The NHS is part of the public sector. It has a website (http://www.nhs.uk), but this only provides information.

▶ Voluntary, not-for-profit organisations, such as Oxfam, also use the web. Oxfam uses its website (www.oxfam.org.uk) to inform people about its work providing education resources for schools, to make sales through its virtual shop and to encourage web-based donations.

 Key terms

Active website: a website where customers can act on what a website provides, e.g. order and pay for items

Passive online presence: providing online information that neither allows the user to interact nor to shop online

- The digital photo company Snapfish (www.Snapfish.co.uk) allows its customers to upload images, share images, order prints and create their own customised gifts. This is an example of an **active website**.

- Other businesses, like Hotel Rural El Criadero (www.elcriadero.es), use the web as a brochure, allowing web users to browse the range of goods and services they offer. It is not possible to make bookings and purchases online – instead, contact details are given so that people can make telephone or email enquiries.

The type of online presence a business has will depend very much on its aims and objectives, the type of business activity, its ownership and, most importantly, its budget, i.e. what the business can afford.

Types of online presence

Different businesses use their online presence in different ways. Many sites provide information only (e.g. a restaurant giving opening times, a sample menu and contact details). This is known as a **passive online presence**. It is genuinely useful, though some customers might want to be able to take things further. They may want to book online or even pay online (make an online transaction). These services are possible, though many small firms are reluctant to spend the extra money on both the website and on the payment systems themselves. Online payments are received through systems such as Paypal or credit cards. In both cases, the banks take a cut.

Did you know?

Over half of British Adults have used the internet for shopping.

Some firms originally began as mail order businesses, and have used the internet as a way of complementing their offline (catalogue and postal) services.

Case study

Screwfix was a successful small mail order business specialising in supplying builders. In the early 1990s Screwfix boomed, as builders could use their mobile phones to place an order from a building site, then have the materials delivered there. Since 2000 the boom has been in online ordering. Today, an increasing number of the online orders are from mobile phones or Blackberries.

1. Does Screwfix have a 'passive' or an 'active' online presence?

2. Explain why Screwfix may be especially well suited to mobile online access, e.g. texting or sending emails.

A further boom area for online activity has been digital image processing. This provides businesses with the opportunity to offer interactive customisation, i.e. to allow customers to design and fit their own clothes or glasses online. The producer is able to charge extra for the customisation – yet it is the customer who takes all the time and makes all the effort!

Assessment activity 12.1 (P1, P2, M1)

You need to investigate three different businesses that operate online. Select:

- a public sector business (e.g. the local library)
- a private sector business (e.g. Amazon)
- a voluntary/not-for-profit business (e.g. One Water).

In your report, explain:

- the aims and objectives of the business in having their site
- the service the business offers through its online presence
- the type of presence the business has (e.g. passive brochure ware, information, online transactions etc.).

The issues relating to doing business online

Getting started

It is easy to understand why firms want to be online, but how is it done? This section looks at the main factors in creating an online presence.

When you have completed this topic, you should:

- understand the main issues in planning an online presence
- understand the problems and opportunities involved in implementing an online presence.

Key terms

Domain name: the name of the website, e.g. www.bbc.co.uk

E-commerce: when a website enables a customer to complete an order and pay for the item automatically online

Interactive: a two-way process, i.e. instead of looking at information (one-way process), you are able to ask more, find out more or do more, e.g. place an order

and get a reply: 'Thank you, the order is complete and will be delivered within 4 days'

Phishing: when an online message invites you to take an action that will reveal your bank details to crooks who will then steal electronically from your bank account

Supply chain: the links between a business and its suppliers, e.g. Tesco dealing with Cadbury, which in turn deals with farmers producing cocoa and sugar

Planning issues

The first issue to consider is the suitability of the business for an online operation. In other words, would it be better to have a physical, perhaps high street, presence? Selling online works fantastically for easyJet, ASOS and Amazon, but most online shopping is done with businesses that also have a reassuring high street face, such as Tesco, Next and Comet.

Starting an online business is genuinely difficult unless you have the technical knowledge to do it yourself. After all, there are so many other things to do:

- ▶ Form your company or find your partners.
- ▶ Arrange finance for start-up costs and to fund the first few months' trading.
- ▶ Decide on your precise range of products/services.
- ▶ Decide who to buy them from; negotiate prices and terms.
- ▶ Hire and train staff.
- ▶ Plan an advertising or PR (public relations) campaign to get the website known.

Case study

Mari Williams is a web-based entrepreneur owning the company 'gabeandgrace.co.uk', a business supplying organic and natural baby and children's products.

Mari could have opened a high street shop in her home town of Preston, but instead chose to be web based. By researching online competitors she was able to draw a flow chart of the **supply chain**, including manufacturers, distributors, wholesalers and retailers. Through her research she was able to identify gaps in the market and then formulate a business plan. Being web based meant she expected low start-up costs – having a high street presence would have meant paying rent on a building, buying shop fittings, employing sales staff etc.

Before she could decide on her **domain name** Mari had to first make sure the name wasn't already being used. Checking which domain names are available can be done though sites such as www.123domainnames.co.uk. Mari wanted a name

that was catchy, and chose one that sounded friendly and suggested boys and girls.

Mari's set-up costs proved higher than planned. She needed a web designer, a hosting company, a photographer (for the product shots) and a merchant account with a bank. Not being very technical, Mari hired a website design company. She had to change web providers and hosters several times before she felt comfortable and confident in the work being done. She says, 'It's easy to be blinded by technical issues, so having a contact that you can trust and who understands your company is vital (but rare).'

1. Outline one case for and one case against a business such as 'gabeandgrace' having an online presence only.

2. Marie wanted a web address that was catchy. If you were trying to find a domain name for a posh fashion clothing business, outline three factors you think are particularly important.

Implementation issues

Before the site could start operating, Mari needed to sort out some crucial issues:

▶ *Customisation*: Should the site be built to her exact specifications, or should it be based on an existing software package? As a custom-made site would have cost five times as much, she opted to use existing software.

▶ *Extent*: Were the online operations to be passive (information/brochure only), or partially or fully **interactive**? Mari opted for a fully interactive service, including **e-commerce**, i.e. allowing customers to order and pay for items online.

▶ *Changing user specifications*: Who would be allowed access to the site? At first it would be just Mari and the 'webmaster' (the person in charge of a website). In other words, only these two would have the password required to change the text on the site. As the business gets bigger, Mari may wish to change the specifications to allow more of her staff to have access.

▶ *Availability of technical and design skills*: Although Mari initially needed to hire outside experts, as she hires more staff she will look to recruit full-timers who can provide the expertise she needs.

▶ *Relationship with partners*: What online links would Mari need with her bank, her suppliers and her distribution and delivery services? Would an order to her website immediately feed through to distribution and delivery, and trigger an extra order from her suppliers? And would she have an online link for her financial services? There were a variety of issues Mari had to consider.

Mari needed a site that was easy to navigate, 100% secure and enabled purchases to be made with only a few clicks. In addition, she wanted her website to rank high on search engines such as Google (this is called 'search engine optimisation'). This means she has to keep employing her outsourced 'webmaster', even though the site is completed.

Activity

Visit Mari's site www.gabeandgrace.co.uk. How easy is it to navigate?

Operation risks

There are risks involved in any business. Shops have to worry about shoplifting and being robbed (perhaps violently) of their cash takings. There are also risks to running an online business, such as credit card fraud. Breakdowns in service can also occur in a number of ways – a lost parcel, a late delivery, loss of data and problems with stock supply. All these can be out of a business owner's control, but Mari has systems in place to limit their impact.

▶ A big risk is the security of payment both for the customer shopping online and for the online business. The customer worries about whether the online seller really exists, and whether someone could access their card details. The business worries whether the credit or debit card is stolen and whether the money will be transferred correctly. To overcome these worries, Mari uses WorldPay, which is backed by the Royal bank of Scotland. Using the WorldPay service means that if a customer tries to make a purchase with a stolen card, Mari gets an instant email

Did you know?

PayPal manages over 184 million accounts.

warning her that the transaction is high risk. Other services, such as Paypal, are another way of protecting both the business and customer from non-payment for goods.

▶ Buying from suppliers online can also be a risk, so Mari only buys from suppliers she has met personally, particularly as many expect payment in advance.

▶ Another risk is losing goods in the post, so Mari sends all her goods by recorded delivery or via a courier. If a parcel gets lost or damaged she can trace it and make a claim, protecting herself from loss of income.

▶ It can sometimes be easy to make mistakes when placing orders online. The 'Gabe and Grace' website has been designed to try to avoid this, but when errors in ordering occur, they can be put right.

▶ All online businesses are unfortunately vulnerable to hostile attacks. These come in many guises. There are a large number of '**phishing**' sites that claim to be from banks or the Inland Revenue requesting personal data and bank details. To avoid being victim to this financial fraud Mari has installed anti-phishing, anti-spy and antivirus software to alert her to any problems. Mari tries to overcome these problems by dealing with local businesses that she has met and has built up a relationship with, so she is more aware of bogus emails.

▶ A website is the shop window of an online business. The home page represents everything about the business and tells customers a lot about you. It is important to keep this up to date, as a good website will encourage customer loyalty. Out-of-date information will have the opposite effect. It may mislead customers and misrepresent the business. It is therefore essential for Mari to keep her website up to date, both by adding new material and by deleting old information.

▶ Websites can open businesses to the global market. Language problems can be an obstacle, but one that can be overcome with online translation sites. Mari has found that many European customers do speak a good level of English, but having a good knowledge of languages can help the business to develop (Mari has a degree in French and Italian, which helps). For websites with a global customer base, such as British Airways, the sites have to be translated professionally into many different languages.

▶ Hardware and software failures are something many online businesses face. Mari Williams makes sure that she backs up all her files at the end of each day. She is also insured against losing data and against equipment breakdown, in case the worst should happen.

▶ Whatever country an online business trades in will have its own business regulations. When she first started 'Gabe and Grace', Mari contacted trading standards, which advised her about the rules and product labelling requirements for the UK. It is the manufacturer's responsibility to ensure that the products are tested to the relevant safety standards, which is why a good relationship with suppliers is essential. As and when Mari starts selling overseas, she will have to research labelling requirements in other countries.

 Activity

Tickets for the World cup in South Africa in 2010 were initially only available to purchase online from the FIFA website. This meant that many South Africans who had no access to the internet and no credit card could not purchase match tickets. FIFA were criticised for this and did, in April 2010, make tickets available to buy over the counter.

What other products would be unsuitable to buy online? Why?

Staffing issues

One complaint by customers of online businesses is the lack of personal contact. If customers have a complaint, they may have to deal with call centres whose staff know (and seem to care) little about the products or the customers' needs. Mari is a sociable person and finds the lack of personal contact with customers a real source of frustration. She always follows up an order with an email and sometimes a telephone call, and attends consumer fairs to meet customers face to face. She says that the fairs are a platform for ideas and for product development purposes where customers may ask you for something you haven't thought of. She has added a blog to her website, where customers can report back about their purchases. She believes that feedback is crucial part of an online business's success.

It is also important to consider the training needs of any staff Mari employs. Staff who are unfamiliar with the technology could hold the business back, so it is important that they are trained in the systems that Mari uses. There is a risk that untrained staff might make mistakes that lead to breakdowns in service like those mentioned earlier. These could be costly. In addition, everyone must understand the way the online transactions work, and must be well informed about the products and services so that they can respond appropriately to phone calls and emails.

The 'About Us' screen on the Gabe and Grace website

Financial issues

The initial investment costs of setting up a business can, in some cases, kill off a great business idea before it gets started (think about all those entrepreneurs who enter the *Dragons' Den* with a great idea and leave disappointed because the sums don't add up). Over-investing at the start-up can cause cash flow problems later; under-investing can mean there is no money for marketing or PR to launch the business. Thorough research will give a true picture of the start-up costs, and reviewing suppliers regularly will make sure an online entrepreneur has the best deals.

Sometimes online businesses can be the victims of their own success – being accessible to a global market can lead to higher demand than anticipated, leading to insufficient stock and insufficient cash flow for further stock purchases. Mari was prepared for this and had researched cheap local warehousing facilities so that she could keep a good level of stock. By having a good working relationship with her suppliers she was able to maintain her cash flow and avoid disappointing customers.

Another issue that must be considered is possible tax liabilities for international transactions. As an online business, you may be selling overseas and have to charge the duty (tax) that applies in that country. Whisky, for example, is taxed differently across the world. In Britain a bottle of whisky carries £6.34 of tax duty. In Norway the figure is £12.50! Similarly, goods from suppliers overseas may be subject to import duty.

Distribution issues

Depending on the nature of the product, distribution can be a headache. Large bulky goods can be expensive to transport, especially to overseas customers. Fragile goods can easily be damaged in transit, while other goods and services are much easier and cheaper to distribute, for example:

▶ online insurance quotes can link the web user to the insurance company website and a purchase can be made with the click of a mouse

▶ you can book a flight and receive an e-ticket, then check in without moving from your armchair.

Topic check

1 What is a domain name?
2 Name three risks of running an online business.
3 What is one of the main complaints customers have of online businesses?
4 Why would customers prefer to pay for goods using Paypal or WorldPay rather than enter their details online?
5 A blog is a useful way of communicating with customers. What is a blog?

Creating web pages or a website for a stated business need

Getting started

Today, so many businesses have websites that it is hard to stand out. It is not enough to provide information, the site must be created to make a good, strong impression. It needs to offer the customer enough interest to make them keen to return.

When you have completed this topic, you should:

- be able to see how to create an effective website
- be able to identify the type of site required for a specific business need.

Web development software

There are many different types of software that can be used to create websites (e.g. MS Frontpage, Dreamweaver, Mediator) or they can be created in Word or Publisher.

Hypertext mark-up language (HTML) is the language used to create web pages. HTML codes are written within the less than (<) or greater than (>) signs.

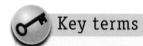

Key terms

Intranet: an internal in-house internet, i.e. one for staff to use

Figure 12.1 Some examples of HTML code

HTML tag	Meaning
< >	These are the brackets you put round the HTML code
/	This ends an action
<HTML>	This begins your HTML document
<HEAD>	This contains information about your page
</HEAD>	This ends the information about your page
<TITLE>	This is the title of your page
</TITLE>	This ends the heading
<P>	This is a new paragraph
<BODY>	This is the start of the body of the text
</P>	End of paragraph
<centre>	This centres text/objects

Web pages contain all different types of information from different sources, e.g. clip art, digital photos. Part of the HTML code for the page below is shown in Figure 12.2.

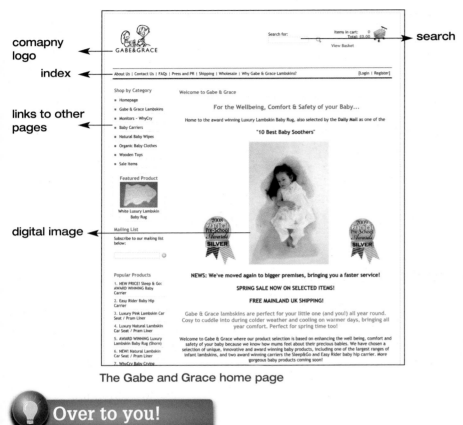

comapny logo →

index →

links to other pages →

digital image →

search →

The Gabe and Grace home page

```
<!DOCTYPE html PUBLIC "-//W3C//DTD
XHTML 1.0 Transitional//EN"
"http://www.w3.org/TR/xhtml1/DTD/xhtml1-
transitional.dtd">

<html
xmlns="http://www.w3.org/1999/xhtml">

<head>

<meta http-equiv="Content-Type"
content="text/html; charset=iso-8859-1"/>

<title>Gabe and Grace</title>

<meta name="description"
content="Lambskins, Gabe & Grace Natural,
Organic & Innovative Baby Products.
Lambskins"/>

<meta name="keywords"
content="Lambskins, Gifts for newborns,
Gabe & Grace, Christening Gifts, ethical baby
products, Eco baby products, organic baby
gifts, baby shop, sheepskin rugs, sheepskin
pram liners, lambskin pram liners, lambskin
pramliners, sheepskin pram liners, sheepskin
rugs, sheepskin footmuffs, sheepskin booties,
sheepskin baby booties, baby hip carrier, baby
hip carriers, baby crying monitor, baby whycry
montior, baby crying monitors, whycry baby
monitor, lambskin uk, lambskin baby rugs,
lambskin footmuffs, lambskin baby slippers,
booties, eco friendly toys, wooden baby toys,
organic baby toys, hip baby carrier, easy rider
baby carrier, organic baby clothing, organic
baby bedding, organic babies playmat,
natural baby wipes, clearly herbal baby wipes,
baby wipes wholesale, bamboo maternity
wear, yoga maternity wear, jute bags, jute
shopping bags" />
```

Figure 12.2 Part of the HTML code for the web page

Over to you!

Decode the HTML in Figure 12.2.

Review

Before the site goes live, it is important to get a few potential users to have a go at using it and then comment on it. What seems 'cool' to you may irritate them. Among the things to look out for are:

▶ *Appropriate for purpose and audience*: it must communicate an image that fits in with the business; if it's a nightclub website, dark colours and sharp music may be spot on; if it's Marks & Spencer then bright colours and no animation seems about right!

▶ *Problems*, e.g. unnecessary animation, inappropriate or unclear graphics: animation can add interest, but only a customer can tell you whether they find it irritating or unprofessional. Poor graphics (e.g. light coloured type on a white background or a weird font) could also be off-putting. People expect the companies they deal with to be reliable and reassuring – not funky!

▶ *Slow download speeds*: clearly the point of a website is to make the customer's life easier, so good companies test the download speeds of what's offered on their website. It is better to forget about video clips than provide them at annoyingly slow download speeds.

Did you know?

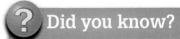

iTunes have details of over 200 million customers.

Publishing

Although it will be a huge matter emotionally for an entrepreneur, 'going live' with a website requires nothing more than clicking an icon. This changes the site from being offline to being online. Putting the website online is known as 'publishing'. This will automatically upload files to the server of the site that is hosting your software. Or, for bigger firms, it may upload to your own server that is being used to host an **intranet** site.

If the site has been set up sensibly, it should be quite easy for staff with the right security access to maintain the content by updating it regularly. This is likely to be a daily task, and may eventually require several full-time members of staff. Old information must be deleted and new material added. File management (e.g. naming and renaming files, changing the folder structures to keep things tidy and understandable, and moving and deleting files) is also an ongoing and continuous task.

Assessment activity 12.2 (P3, P4, M2, D1, D2, P5, M3, D3, P6)

Imelda's is a high street shop selling a wide range of shoes for men, women and children. At the moment it has no website and the manager is keen to investigate if they should begin conducting their business online.

1. Produce a presentation for the owners of Imelda's advising them of:

   • the issues they would need to consider (e.g. the suitability of the business for online operations, set-up issues, domain name and the resources they need)

   • the implementation issues (e.g. technical skills, design skills, type of online operation, changing user specifications, relationship with partners such as banks)

   • the risks they face from operating an online business (e.g. security, unfamiliar trading conditions, errors in ordering, potential use of personal information, updating information, language problems, hardware and software failures, loss of data, global business regulations)

   • staffing issues (lack of personal contact with customers, breakdowns in service, training needs to use the new technology)

   • financial issues (start-up costs, tax liabilities, ability to cope with global demand)

   • distribution issues (how will they deliver the shoes?).

2. The owners of Imelda's are concerned about the risks. Produce a report for them detailing the potential benefits of operating online and suggesting ways that they could deal with the associated risks.

3. The owners of Imelda's have asked you to design a website for their business. They would like it, at this stage, to be an information-only site advising customers of where to find them on the high street. You can use any software of your choice to produce this.

4. Present your completed site to the owners and explain to them how this site helps them achieve the aims and objectives of the business. Also explain:

   • why you have selected that particular software

   • why you chose the design features you have included

   • the checks you have carried out on the site.

5. The owners love your site and are thinking about proceeding with your design. But they are still not sure how their business will benefit from marketing their products and services online. Produce a report outlining the possible marketing benefits. Think about their market presence, the potential marketing benefits, the levels of response and effects on customers and the financial advantages it offers.

Topic check

1 To start a web page in HTML you would use brackets like this { } around the HTML codes.

   a) true

   b) false

2 A disadvantage of web-based companies is that they need a lot of staff.

   a) true

   b) false

3 Having a web presence allows you more contact with customers than you would have in a shop.

   a) true

   b) false

4 Paypal is a popular way of paying for goods bought online.

   a) true

   b) false

The impact of an online business presence

Getting started

Years ago it took a lot of time and money to build from a business idea to a national presence. It took The Body Shop 15 years. Now it's possible to turn an idea into a worldwide phenomenon in months. Facebook went from 1 million users to 300 million users in 2 years. Going online can have quite an impact.

When you have completed this topic, you should:

- understand the scale of the potential impact of an online presence
- understand the speed with which online impact can be felt.

Market presence

There are enormous benefits for the online retailer. How could 'Gabe and Grace', a new company in Preston, manage to have a global presence if the business was operated via a high street shop? The internet removes consumer ideas about size and scale of business operations and allows shops to keep their doors open 24 hours a day. Consumers can compare prices via online comparison sites at the click of a mouse; business owners can do the same and keep a close eye on their competitors. Response to customer interest can be instant – if I am interested in booking a flight I can see instantly if seats are available, how much they are and the times they fly, and can at the same time check out alternatives dates, airlines and prices.

Marketing benefits

Online business offers a wealth of opportunities for both the supplier and the customer. Customers can complete transactions via their PC or mobile phone and the business can keep customers informed of special offers, new products and sales via text messaging and email, allowing them to tailor their message to customers' prior purchases. Online enquiries give a wealth of marketing data (location, age, gender) that businesses in the past would have spent enormous amounts of time and money collecting. The business can attract customers from remote locations, for example 'Gabe and Grace' sell to customers across the UK, including the Isle of Mull – those customers would not have been able to travel easily to Preston.

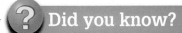

Level of response

The nature of the internet means that customers can buy a book from Amazon at 10 p.m. on Sunday night in the UK, receive an email within minutes confirming their order and giving an estimated delivery date, and can track their order through their Amazon account until the goods are delivered to their door (or the door of their place of work if they prefer). Amazon would struggle to provide this level of service through high street shops and would also struggle to have stores large enough to hold all their stock – being web based means they hold less stock as they supply only what customers demand.

> **? Did you know?**
>
> A high street book shop stocks around 10,000 different titles. Online Amazon is able to stock over 500,000, giving 50 times the choice.

Financial advantages

The financial advantages of online business are massive:

▶ the business has better cash flow because customers pay for goods at time of ordering

▶ the business can be operated from anywhere and does not need expensive town-centre offices

▶ fewer staff are required, lowering labour costs

▶ the business has low overheads, e.g. Mari operates 'Gabe and Grace' from her office at home, with the future option of working from her warehouse when necessary.

Effects on customers

There are enormous benefits to customers from shopping online:

▶ they can shop 24 hours a day from their mobile phone or PC

▶ they have a wider choice of products and suppliers, allowing them to find a better deal

▶ having the goods delivered means they don't even have to carry them back to their car or struggle home with them on the bus.

However, critics argue that consumers can in some cases get a worse deal because they have no direct contact with the company and can't test the products before they buy. This lack of interaction can mean they don't have a relationship with the business, ruling out goodwill or discounts.

> **⚙ Activity**
>
> Create a glossary for a web-based entrepreneur who doesn't understand technical terms. Identify ten key terms they need to understand and briefly explain the meaning of each one.

The impact on society

So far in this chapter we have examined the pros and cons to a business of operating online. We also need to consider the wider impact that online business has on society. Will the internet kill off the high street? There have already been some casualties, e.g. Dixons has closed its electrical retail stores and now operates solely online. Shoppers have always shopped around for the best deal, but can now do that in their own home on their PC, which could impact not only on high street retailers but on ancillary services such as transport and cafés. Will this lead to a breakdown of communities as more people lose their jobs, being replaced by web-based businesses that need fewer staff, and removing town centres as a community hub? What about consumers? If they work from home for a web-based business and complete all their shopping, banking and holiday bookings online, will they become socially isolated?

 Case study

According to a watchdog report, a lack of consumer confidence is preventing online retailing from reaching its full potential.

The Office of Fair Trading report stated that a third of internet users are not shopping online because they don't trust the internet, and are most concerned about their personal security, with one-fifth of users citing this as the main reason they choose not to shop online and 15% turning down the chance of internet shopping because they did not trust the retailers.

The report believes that online retailing is the future for many businesses and is very important to the UK Economy, so these consumer worries need to be addressed to allow e-tailing to grow.

However, the figures also show that consumer confidence in the internet has grown in the last 3 years.

Among the people who do shop online, 54% felt it was as safe as shopping in store, compared with 26% in 2006, and as a nation the UK buys twice as much over the internet as other European countries.

1. Almost a third of internet users don't trust the internet for shopping. Explain why you think this is.

2. Why might UK consumers buy almost twice as much over the internet as shoppers elsewhere in Europe?

Assessment activity 12.3 (P7, M4, D4)

Not everyone believes that conducting business online is a good thing. In the final assignment for this unit you need to produce a leaflet for small businesses advising them of the impact of online business on society. This should look at both the benefits and the drawbacks.

Topic check

1 Other than those mentioned in this chapter, identify two other UK businesses that have built a major UK presence online.

2 Identify two financial advantages for a manufacturer from encouraging customers to shop online.

3 Identify two possible benefits to customers from shopping online.

4 How might society be affected if more and more consumers bought online from supermarkets?

Assessment summary

The overall grade you achieve for this unit depends on how well you meet the grading criteria set out at the start of the chapter (see page 209). You must complete:

- all of the P criteria to achieve a **pass** grade
- all of the P and the M criteria to achieve a **merit** grade
- all of the P, M and D criteria to achieve a **distinction** grade.

Your tutor will assess the assessment activities that you complete for this unit. The work you produce should provide evidence which demonstrates that you have achieved each of the assessment criteria. The table below identifies what you need to demonstrate to meet each of the pass, merit and distinction criteria for this unit. You should always check and self-assess your work before you submit your assignments for marking.

Remember that you MUST provide evidence for all of the P criteria to pass the unit.

Grading criteria	You need to demonstrate that you can:	Do you have the evidence?
P1	Describe three different business organisations which operate online	
M1	Compare the features of three business organisations operating online	
P2	Explain how they operate their activities online	
P3	Explain the issues a business organisation would need to consider to go online	
M2	Analyse the benefits to businesses and customers of conducting business online	
D1	Make recommendations for a business organisation considering going online	
P4	Explain the operational risks for a business operating online	
D2	Suggest ways in which a business could deal with the operational risks associated with an online presence	
P5	Create web pages to meet user need	
M3	Explain how the website assists in achieving the aims and objectives of the business user	
D3	Justify the use of different construction features in the design of a website	
P6	Describe the benefits to a business organisation of marketing a product or service online	
P7	Outline the impact of online business on society	
M4	Analyse the consequences on society of an increase in online business	
D4	Evaluate the benefits and drawbacks to society of increasing business online	

Always ask your tutor to explain any assignment tasks or assessment criteria that you don't understand fully. Being clear about the task before you begin gives you the best chance of succeeding. Good luck with your Unit 12 assessment work!

13 Business enterprise (Unit 16)

Unit outline

Starting their first business is one of the most exciting things people ever do in their lives. In Spring 2010 Julian Dunkerton received £80 million in cash when his Superdry fashion chain became a plc. He had started his business on a market stall in Cheltenham. Now he was a multimillionaire. That's real business enterprise.

Learning outcomes

1 **Understand how to prepare for business.**
2 **Know how different aspects affect preparation for business.**
3 **Understand how to start and run a business.**

Grading guide

To achieve a **pass**, you must show you can:	To achieve a **merit**, you must show you can:	To achieve a **distinction**, you must show you can:
P1 Explain how knowledge of personal strengths and weaknesses can be applied to preparing for and contributing to a business	**M1** Explain, using examples, the benefits of starting a business	**D1** Evaluate the issues that need to be considered when starting a business
P2 Identify how regulations and laws for small businesses can affect preparation for business	**M2** Analyse the different aspects that will affect preparation for business	
P3 Describe how small businesses prepare to market and sell products or services		
P4 Describe the financial issues that can affect preparation for business		
P5 Outline the contents of a business plan for starting and running a business		**D2** Justify recommendations made for starting a business
P6 Explain the sources of advice and support available when preparing for business		

How to prepare for business

▶ Getting started

Many businesses start and then close down because their owners have failed to prepare. They have a dream, but haven't checked whether it's a dream shared by customers. To succeed, a start-up requires the right business idea developed by the right businessperson. Do you have the desire to run your own business? And have you the right skills? This chapter will help you find out.

When you have completed this topic, you should:

- know the skills and abilities required for start-up success
- know which of these skills and abilities you already have
- understand the main objectives of those starting a business.

Own strengths and weaknesses

Adejere Docherty started The Whole Leaf Co in 2007 after getting bored as a recruitment consultant. The business sells plates and bowls made from palm leaves collected from the ground in rural India. It provides work for some of the world's poorest people, and gives Westerners a natural, recyclable alternative to paper plates. Adejere, in December 2009, told a group of business students: 'My great problem was that I didn't know what you know. I didn't study business, so every mistake I've made has cost me money.' For a video clip of how the products are made, go to: www.thewholeleafco.com.

Key terms

Credit crunch: the banking crisis that led to the sharp economic downturn in 2008–09

Entrepreneur: someone who makes a business idea happen, either through their own effort, or by organising others to do the work

To give yourself the best chance of starting a business successfully, you need to know your own strengths and weaknesses. Having identified your weaknesses, you can either work on them, or look for a partner who is strong where you are weak. Figure 13.1 shows two people who started a business running adventure holidays. See where they fit (and where they don't).

In many business start-ups, the factors discussed below are where strengths and weaknesses are important.

Personal circumstances

Start-ups are costly in terms of two things above all else: cash and time. Customers rarely flood in from day 1. It takes time to build up regular custom, and in that time the business may run out of cash. Banks are rarely generous with new, small firms, so it is hugely helpful to come from a family wealthy enough to help out.

In business, time is money, but some people have more time available than others. Young, single people can afford to put 12- or 16-hour days into building the business they hope will make them rich. So, in fact, can 50-year-old couples whose kids have left home. But for young couples, perhaps with small children, the hours taken in the early days of the business might put a great strain on their relationship and hence on the business.

Figure 13.1 Strengths and weaknesses of partners in a new business

Personal quality	Lisa Burton	Jay Parfitt	Combined?
Full of bright ideas	Strength	Weakness	
Enthusiastic	Strength	OK	
Highly knowledgeable about adventure holidays	Strength	Weakness	
Copes well with setbacks	Strength	Weakness	
Anticipates problems	Weakness	Strength	
Efficient at organising	Weakness	Strength	
Careful with paperwork	Weakness	OK	
Good at financial planning	Strength	Weakness	
Willing to work hard	Strength	Strength	
Cares for customers	Strength	Strength	
Dealing with tax issues	Weakness	Weakness	

Activity

1. How well matched are Lisa and Jay?

2. In which two areas may there still be weaknesses?

3. How might the business be affected by one of the weaknesses?

 Case study

In 2007 Matteo Pantani opened 'Scoop' ice cream parlour in London's Covent Garden. Fresh from Pisa, Italy, Matteo would make 20 flavours of real Italian 'gelato' every day! For the first 8 months of the business, he arrived at 6.30 a.m. to make fresh ice creams until the store opened at 11.30 a.m. Then he worked in the shop until it closed at 7.00 in the evening, 7 days a week! Later, at home, he had to do the paperwork (e.g. make sure his suppliers got paid). Luckily for Matteo, his wife backed him all the way.

Summary

Key issues in personal circumstances: money and time. Has the **entrepreneur** got deep pockets financially, or a family that can provide financial back-up? And can the entrepreneur cope with the time demands of the start-up phase?

Experience, skills, knowledge and abilities

For Matteo Pantani, working in London was difficult, but at least he knew how to make, display and serve ice cream. He had been managing the family ice cream parlour in Pisa for several years. So all his experience was essential, including:

▶ Knowledge of suppliers, such as where to get the best ice cream-making machines (and what price to pay for them – many naïve new businesspeople are overcharged by suppliers).

▶ Knowledge of the space required for a successful ice cream shop; the yearly rent on Matteo's small shop is nearly £50,000! If he had taken a bigger shop, an even bigger rent bill might have crippled the business.

▶ Skills: making ice cream that is consistently delicious is the key to a successful ice cream business. With the British climate, Matteo needs regular customers who will come in November, not just August. Consistent excellence comes from learning ice cream-making skills over many months, and being trained by top Italian ice cream makers.

▶ Abilities may require more than simply learning skills. Matteo has been taught the same skills as others, but has combined them with his own talents to create a level of ability that few can match. Top fashion designers create business success in the same way.

 Did you know?

Every year, more than 400,000 new businesses start up in Britain. That's more than 1,000 every day.

▷ Experience is valuable, not only in making the best product, but also in running the business. New, young entrepreneurs can struggle to manage staff effectively. They may not realise that staff are rarely motivated by money alone – they also need to feel part of the business.

Summary

Business success is affected by experience, skills, knowledge and abilities. Young people are bound to have weaknesses in some or all of these qualities, though one super-strength can outweigh the others. Take Hannah Marshall, a star fashion designer who started her own fashion label at 26. Her creative abilities outweigh her lack of experience.

Activity

1. Complete the table below, giving yourself a score from 1 to 10 where 1 is a serious weakness and 10 is a super-strength. Then ask your parents to give you a score for each quality. Finally, use a scale of 1 to 5 (where 5 is very important) for how important each quality is for a business you would like to start (e.g. for a new night club, 'Know useful contacts' might have a rating of 5).

Personal quality	Your view	Your parents' view	Importance in your business
Creativity; bright new ideas			
Skilled at chosen business			
Good at managing money			
Cope well with setbacks			
Experienced in chosen area			
Know useful contacts			
Hard working			
Strong abilities, e.g. cooking			
Good at working with others			
Cares for customers			

2. Choose one area for which you have a low score. How might you improve on it?

3. What marks out of 5 would you give these two businesses in terms of the importance of each of the above when starting up?

   a) a sweet shop   b) a computer games development company

Areas for development and improvement

Even after starting a business, it is important to find ways to improve and develop continuously. When football striker Louis Saha first came to Britain, he only ever shot with his left foot. Today people talk about him as two-footed. Good though he was, he worked continuously to improve his weaker foot.

The same applies to anyone considering opening their first business. They need not only to analyse their strengths and weaknesses but also to act on them. In some cases, working on the weaknesses may be the right approach. But it can be clever to work hardest on key strengths, to push yourself from being great to being a superstar. Hannah Marshall will only ever be judged in the fashion world by the fashions she creates. Sometime soon, she might take a year off to spend time in Japan, in Rio de Janeiro and in Milan – all great fashion cities. This might give her further insights that will make her an even stronger creative force.

Suitability for self-employment or a small business

Some people hate the thought of working for others. Therefore they want to be their own boss. But they do not necessarily want to be the boss of other people. Therefore they may want to be self-employed. In effect, this means running yourself as a small business. You have to find clients to hire your services, and you have to send them bills – instead of getting a regular salary. Self-employment can be very well paid in good times – but the risk is that work may dry up completely when times are hard. Actors are a good example of the self-employed. Even those with regular work on *Neighbours* know that they could be killed off tomorrow!

Often, people who want to start a small business begin as self-employed. For example, starting a high street estate agency will cost a lot in rent and wages. So why not start from home, with an online business offering to bring buyers and sellers together? You can work for yourself until there's enough work to open an office and hire staff.

Summary

Self-employment can either be a way of life (such as for actors) or it can be a stepping stone to starting a business. Either way, it has an element of risk and uncertainty that is rarely present for people who earn a monthly salary.

Contributing to a business

A variety of different people and organisations can contribute to a business.

The entrepreneur's contribution

The entrepreneur's main single contribution is likely to come from market insight and passion. Thirty years ago, the Brompton Bicycle was designed by Andrew Ritchie. It took nearly 10 years to finance a serious level of production for this folding bicycle. Today Brompton Bicycle is Britain's biggest bicycle manufacturer and the Brompton is the favourite bike for London's commuters. Andrew Ritchie saw the need and the opportunity for a commuter bike – and had the passion to keep the business driving forward.

A Brompton Bicycle

Despite Ritchie's passion, the business would never have got going without capital. Ritchie could provide inspiration and a huge amount of time and effort – but he had no money. It actually took 5 years – and a lucky meeting with entrepreneur Julian Vereker – to finance the opening of Brompton's first factory.

In addition to time and money, Ritchie provided the direction for all Brompton employees. They learnt that Ritchie was passionate about the environment, and therefore hated waste – especially of materials. Staff learnt to work to the highest quality level, so that hardly anything would have to be scrapped. This, in turn, helped customers to love their Bromptons.

Summary

The person who starts a business will always need to devote time and effort, but will also – ideally – provide insight and passion. Finding the money to start up is also a critical part of the entrepreneur's task.

Contribution from professional advisers

Most businesses start with just two types of advice: from their bank and from an accountant. In both cases it is important to realise that the bank manager's and the accountant's first priority is to look after their own business – not yours. Many people who start new businesses are very critical of their bank. In the case of Brompton, though, the bank put up half the money for the start-up. With a lot of its own money at stake, the bank gave Ritchie good advice on taking care of cash in the early days of the company.

Like bankers, accountants are likely to recommend taking a cautious approach to financing the start-up. Accountants will urge (and may help in) drawing up a cash flow forecast in order to see when there may be difficult months ahead. All new businesses are at risk of failing: without the advice to be cautious financially, failure rates would be even higher.

Barriers to starting a successful business

Successful start-up requires the ability to turn a business idea into reality – and then persuade people to come to see and try for themselves. The biggest barriers, therefore, come from:

▶ Entrepreneurs who have the ability but not the personality to persuade bankers to lend, suppliers to deliver and customers to come. There are not many types of business cut out for shy entrepreneurs.

▶ Customer caution – customers may dislike their current supplier, yet be reluctant to change. The holiday company may provide poor service, but at least they've been around for years. Why would I switch to your new business? What if you go bust?

▶ Tough competition – the entrepreneur may underestimate the quality of the companies already in the market. She may have visited the local Indian restaurant and thought the food poor; but locals may love the chicken balti that she didn't try.

Barriers to running a successful business

Start-up is hard; long-term success is even harder. In the start-up phase, every entrepreneur is excited and hard working. But when the business is up and running, some start to lose their drive and determination. Standards may slip. Barriers to running a successful business include:

▶ Failure to make the best use of staff; the person who started the business may want to make every decision about 'my baby'. Brighter staff get fed-up with a job in which their views count for so little. They leave, and are replaced by weaker, duller staff.

Did you know?

Twitter started up in 2006 in San Francisco, California. For its first three years it made no profit. It survived as more and more investors put money into the business. In April 2010 it announced that it had over 100 million users. At the same time it announced that it would be accepting paid-for advertising.

▶ Winning customer loyalty is different from winning customer trial. Getting people to come for the first time may require good advertising. Getting people to come regularly requires top products delivered consistently, e.g. terrific, good-value food every time you come to a restaurant. The barrier is when quality standards are variable.

▶ If an entrepreneur has a bright idea, others quickly copy, so your new shop 'iPhone Heaven' is imitated by others – pushing down your customer numbers. If there is no way to protect yourself from competition, it is hard to stay successful for long.

Summary

The main barriers to starting a successful business are a weak personality, customer caution and tough competition. The barriers to running the business are poor management of staff, poor management of quality and no protection from copying by others.

Benefits of running a business

There are a whole range of advantages to running your own business.

Personal objectives

The main motive for starting up something new is desire. People want satisfaction from a sense of achievement. If they could get it from their normal workplace, they might not bother. Terry Leahy, Chief Executive of Tesco, has become wealthy, famous and powerful from a lifetime spent climbing up the career ladder at the one company. Many others find frustrations at work, and want to break out; to give themselves a challenge.

The next most important motivator is the desire to be your own boss. Independent decision-making allows the individual to do things in the way they think is best. Most jobs involve a degree of compromise. When running something for yourself you may not be able to afford the best, but at least you know that you will get the best you can afford. So the chef who hates working in a cramped kitchen with second-rate ingredients may long to be in a position to make all the decisions.

Then, of course, there is money. A person may start a burger bar because of the conviction that it will make a fortune. Such a person may dream of retiring early, with a beachfront house and a huge fridge packed with beer. The typical business to go for in this case would be a franchise, in which the individual buys the rights to open a local branch of a business that already exists (and makes good profits). The Subway sandwich chain works in this way.

Business objectives

Every business has financial objectives, but they are not all the same. ShakeAway – the milkshake business – wants to make enough profit to finance its rapid growth (doubling in size every year). For a new business, a common objective is to try to break even by Year 2. Some businesses start with social objectives, i.e. they are set up to achieve charitable purposes. For One Water, the goal is to give all profits from selling bottled water to build clean water wells in Africa. For The Whole Leaf company, the plan is to give 15% of profits to schools in India and Africa.

For most businesses, the only other major objective is for growth rather than profit. This is especially true of online businesses, where founders of businesses such as Amazon or eBay took the view that they *must* become the Number 1. They believed there would only be room for one big business and therefore coming second would be no better than coming last. Amazon.com started in 1994 and took 7 years before it made its first small profit. But founder Jeff Bezos – who invested $40,000 to start the business – now has shares worth over $1 billion. He was right to focus on growth, make sure of becoming the world's biggest online bookseller, and only then worry about making a profit.

Summary

Personal objectives for starting a business can be psychological or financial. An entrepreneur might want to become rich, or may just want to prove him or herself to doubters. Business objectives are usually financial or related to growth. But is important to realise that the true objective behind the finance might be to achieve something for society, such as clean water in Africa.

Profitability of the business

'Dragon' Duncan Bannatyne often mumbles a business cliché in the 'Den': 'Turnover is vanity; profit is sanity'. This means that making lots of sales (turnover) is useless unless the revenue more than covers the costs. Without profit (revenue *minus* costs) no business can survive for long. Day by day, it may be fine if revenue and costs are in balance, i.e. the business is breaking even. But what happens when a key piece of machinery breaks down and has to be replaced? If you are only breaking even, how can extra cash be found to buy extra things?

Some businesses can seem to be making vast profits, such as an ice cream van on a hot day. But is it making enough to cover the winter months when hardly any cash is coming in? Profitability is therefore measured over a period of time, usually one year. If the year's revenue more than pays for all the business costs, the business is profitable. Therefore it should still be around in a year's time.

Case study

In Autumn 2008 Woolworths was struggling with the sharp sales downturn caused by the **credit crunch**. So were most other shops. But whereas others survived, Woolworths was allowed to die. The reason was that the business had barely been profitable for years. In 2007/08 it made less than 1p profit per £1 spent in its shops. So, when the banks were deciding whether to lend any more to Woolworths, they all decided against. If a business barely makes a profit in good times, it is unlikely to survive bad times.

Other considerations

Although the start-up phase requires long hours and a great deal of stress, running a business may prove wonderful for family life in the longer term. The owner of a successful business can appoint managers who deal with the day-to-day issues, leaving the owner free to enjoy family life or a playboy lifestyle. Topshop owner Philip Green is famous for his long summers in the South of France, his parties and his wealthy friends. Virgin owner Richard Branson has built a lifestyle around adventures such as being one of the first tourists in space.

Running your own business can be hugely enjoyable without being hugely hard work.

Summary

A business simply has to be profitable over the course of a year. That is the only way to survive. When the business is profitable and successful, it may be that the owner can start to enjoy the rewards. He or she may be able to take longer holidays and will always be able to have flexible working hours.

Assessment and grading masterclass

Read this account of the start-up of One Water. Note the explanation of where Merit and Distinction grades can be achieved.

The start-up of One Water	Merit and Distinction opportunities
In 2004, Duncan Goose quit his highly paid (£85,000 a year) marketing job. His vision was to use the profits from selling bottled water in Britain to fund roundabouts in Africa. When children played, the turning roundabout would pump clean water from deep wells. Each roundabout well would cost £7,000 but would provide fresh water for thousands of villagers for many years.	Merit: 'Explain, using examples, the benefits of starting a business': Duncan wanted a new challenge, but one that would provide more meaning to his life. He loved his previous job, but it left him feeling empty. He wanted to make a difference to the world. Starting his own business was a way to do this.
One Water needed to be from a pure water source, and bottled in hygienic conditions to conform to the Food Safety Act. He found a family-run water business in Wales that was willing to supply him at a cost of about 13p for a small bottle. Duncan had to make sure that the labelling on the bottle met the Trades Descriptions Act. He says that he was able to find out all that he needed within 1 day. By contrast, it took 2 years to get the Co-op to stock One Water (since then it has become one of his biggest customers).	Merit: 'Analyse the different aspects that will affect preparation for business': Starting a business involves so many things that it is understandable that entrepreneurs may moan about regulations and laws. Yet Duncan had to do no more than ask his supplier for advice, and then talk to the Trading Standards officer in Wales. Duncan is clear that his start-up faced far more difficult problems than rules and regulations. And what is the alternative? Risking customers' lives with dodgy water?
Duncan's business plan was to keep overhead costs to the absolute minimum, by running the business from his home and using contacts to provide free advice and help. He planned to take no salary for the first 3 years! The revenue would come from selling the water to supermarkets and other retail chains. In fact this proved very difficult. Even after One Water was adopted for the massive Live8 concerts, retail chains would not commit to stocking the brand. Fortunately, Total petrol stations started stocking One, and proved very supportive.	Distinction: 'Justify recommendations made for starting a business': No one could recommend that a business be started on the basis that the boss takes zero income for 3 years. Duncan went ahead because his passion and determination made him ignore the downsides. He knew how tough it was going to be, so his business plan proved right. Where he was lucky was in getting the Live8 publicity – and in Total's support.

Activity

In early 2010 a new Yorkshire food producer called Darnton spotted an opportunity. Although sales of instant pot snacks (such as Pot Noodle) were booming, the Chinese 'Blue Dragon' brand suffered a 25% sales collapse in 2009. Research suggested that there was room for a tasty Chinese noodle alternative. So Darnton launched 'Shanghai Sensation'.

1. Name two groups of people Darnton might have interviewed in its research.

2. Is it a good or a bad idea to compete with a product with falling sales?

Assessment activity 13.1 (P1, M1, D1)

First, you need to identify someone who has started up their own business within the past 5 years. Then pin them down to an interview. Start the process by asking questions about the entrepreneur him/herself, i.e. study their talents, motivations and achievements.

1. a) Ask them to analyse their personal strengths and weaknesses within the process of start-up.

   b) How did they use their knowledge of their strengths and weaknesses in preparing to start up?

2. Ask them to explain, using examples, the benefits of starting their business.

3. Ask them what they have learnt about the issues that need to be considered when starting a business.

By making comparisons between business theory and reality, it should be possible to conduct effective analysis. Given the context, such analysis should span written and numerical techniques. As an example of the latter, it would be great if the proprietor still had a copy of the original business plan. Comparing actual cash flow and profit against the forecast level would generate excellent scope for analysis and evaluation.

Despite the great scope for a top grade project, bear in mind that success will depend upon the entrepreneur's willingness to provide facts and figures. This is particularly important if there is no possibility of obtaining a range of views upon the start-up process. This is less of an issue if there are people who were there at the start who can comment and criticise from a different perspective, such as the bank manager, accountant, any staff employed from the start or, perhaps most revealingly, the spouse, children or other family members. A period remembered by the entrepreneur as thrilling may be recalled by the family as stressful and unpleasant.

Candidates could consider:

- the business(es), its market and its competitors

- the context and process of the business start-up

- the proprietor's motivations through motivation theory

- the extent to which the entrepreneur uses business methods such as cash flow forecasting and break-even analysis

- the future of the business through a survey of its customers

- the survey findings in relation to other evidence

- the role and the rewards of being an entrepreneur.

Topic check

1 Identify two features of limited liability.

   a) It guarantees that no business investor can end up losing their money.

   b) It helps owners in taking bolder business decisions.

   c) It always applies to shareholders in companies.

   d) It only applies to public limited companies, not small private ones.

2 Identify two qualities required by people starting their own business.

   a) determination

   b) sense of humour

   c) humility

   d) hard working

3 What is an entrepreneur?

4 Explain briefly two skills that would be useful to someone opening a café.

5 A new competitor is about to open alongside Zayka, an established Indian restaurant. Outline two actions the manager of Zayka might take before the competitor opens.

How different aspects affect preparation for business

Getting started

It is possible to start your first business tomorrow, simply by renting a stall at a local market. But it's important to check the law. If the stall sells sandwiches, you are breaking the law if you have no food hygiene qualifications. And if you do not tell Inland Revenue that you've started a business, you could end up with problems over tax. It is also time to decide the right type of business organisation you are going to be: a sole trader? Or perhaps a private limited company.

When you have completed this topic, you should:

- understand the basics of starting a business
- understand the importance of meeting regulations.

Key terms

Limited liability: if a company collapses, with massive debts, the owners (shareholders) can only lose the money they invested – nothing more

National Insurance: a form of tax, set at 11% of an employee's earnings – it is the worker's contribution towards the unemployment and the pensions pay pots

Unlimited liability: the business owners are liable personally for every penny of debt within the business; the owners must repay the debts, even if it means losing their house

Regulations and laws for small business

The government's Business Link website says that:

To put your business on a proper footing with HM Revenue & Customs (HMRC) and other authorities, you need to make sure that it has the right legal structure. It's worth thinking carefully about which structure best suits the way that you do business, as this will affect:

▶ the tax and **National Insurance** that you pay

▶ the records and accounts that you have to keep

▶ your financial liability if the business runs into trouble

▶ the ways your business can raise money

▶ the way management decisions are made about the business.

There are several structures to choose from, depending on your situation. This guide will help you understand the differences between them. If you are not sure which legal structure would best suit your business, it's a good idea to get advice from an accountant or solicitor.

Figure 13.2 Rules applying to the different forms of business organisation

	Self-employed	Sole trader	Partnership	Private limited company (Ltd)
Before starting	Register as self-employed with HMRC; set up a record-keeping system	Register as self-employed with HMRC (Inland Revenue); set up a record-keeping system	All partners must register as self-employed; best to draw up a partnership agreement	Application must be made to incorporate the business as a company; register it at Companies House
Minimum number of people involved	One only	One only	Two or more	One or more
Financial liability	Not applicable	**Unlimited liability** faced by one person	Unlimited liability shared between partners	**Limited liability** (owners can only lose their investment)
How are profits treated?	All business costs can be offset against business income	All business profits are treated as the owner's income, and therefore taxable	All business profits are treated as owners' income, split between them, and then taxed	Profits attract corporation tax; what's left can be held in the business for reinvestment
Dealings with Inland Revenue	Fill in an annual self-assessment tax return	Fill in an annual self-assessment tax return; be prepared to show records of income and expenditure	Fill in an annual self-assessment tax return; be prepared to show records of income and expenditure	Actual profits are taxed; any salary payments or dividend payments are also taxed
Importance of keeping business records	For evidence of the costs that should be set against the income (to avoid paying too much tax)	For evidence of the costs that should be set against the income (to avoid paying too much tax)	For evidence of the costs that should be set against the income (to avoid paying too much tax)	As part of the process of drawing up accounts that must be submitted annually to Companies House

The importance of limited liability

Anyone can start a business today, by buying some fruit and selling it at a street market. There are two problems, though, of starting an informal business:

▶ If the taxman does not know what you are doing, there is a temptation not to tell him. By the time he catches you, the consequences can be severe – quite apart from the risk of a jail sentence, there is a likelihood that you will end up paying taxes and fines that are difficult to cope with.

▷ Unlimited liability means that if you start an informal business, the finances of the business are treated as your personal finances – the business profits are your profits, but so are the losses; worse still, so are the debts. In other words, if the business crashes, with £120,000 of debt, you are liable personally for that debt. The court can strip you and your family of everything but the clothes you stand in.

Generally, it is wise to start a limited company and therefore enjoy the protection of limited liability. Even if you own 100% of the shares, the finances of the business are treated separately from your personal finances. A horrible crash into £120,000 of debt may push the business into liquidation – but you will only lose the money you put into the business in the first place.

Forming a private limited company

If the founders of a business decide they want the legal and financial protection offered by limited liability, they will want to form a private limited company. This is quick and easy to do, and should cost no more than £150 to £200. If you do everything yourself, the cost should be less than £100.

Business Link (www.businesslink.gov.uk) sets out the following process for incorporating your business as a company.

To set up as a limited company in the UK, you – or the agent acting for you – will need to send several documents and completed forms to Companies House:

▷ a Memorandum of Association, giving the name of, and authentication by, each subscriber

▷ Articles of Association, describing how the company will be run, the rights of the shareholders, the company's objects (unless they are unrestricted) and the powers of the company's directors

▷ form IN01 (Application to register a company), giving details of the company's registered office and the names and addresses of its directors and company secretary.

> **? Did you know?**
>
> Start-ups of private limited companies have boomed, even during the recent recession. In the first 10 weeks of 2010, the number rose by 25% compared with 2009.

Regulations affecting businesses

Many entrepreneurs criticise the British government for 'red tape', meaning the number of rules that govern businesses. In fact, in 2010 Britain was ranked 5th out of 180 countries for 'Ease of Doing Business' (www.doingbusiness.org). By comparison, Germany came 25th and China came 89th.

Many of the rules are to protect the companies themselves. When starting a business, most companies register their trading name. This is to prevent it being copied by others. After all, if you founded Scoop ice cream and made it a huge success, you would not want others to call themselves Scoop. Nevertheless, there are some regulations that small businesses hate. These include:

▷ The Health and Safety at Work Act forces all firms with five or more staff to have a written health and safety policy, available for inspectors to look at.

▷ Careful procedures for recruitment, training and promotion to avoid discrimination in the workplace. Firms must fit in with the rules set out by the Equality and Human Rights Act.

▶ Allowing paid and unpaid maternity and paternity leave, leaving jobs open for the staff once they return to work. This is clearly beneficial to the employees, but may be very difficult (and costly) for a small employer.

Summary

Businesses are quick and easy to start up, but there is a lot to decide before making a decision. The key is whether or not to accept the protection of limited liability by forming a company. If the entrepreneur decides against this, a choice needs to be made between sole trader or partnership, though pure self-employment can also be considered. Despite the grumbles by employers about 'red tape', there is no evidence that Britain is over-regulated.

Activity

Look at the data in the graph, then answer the questions. (Q = quarter)

1. Why may company liquidations have been rising so sharply in 2008 and early 2009?

2. Discuss whether the government should 'bail out' firms about to enter liquidation, such as Woolworths in 2008.

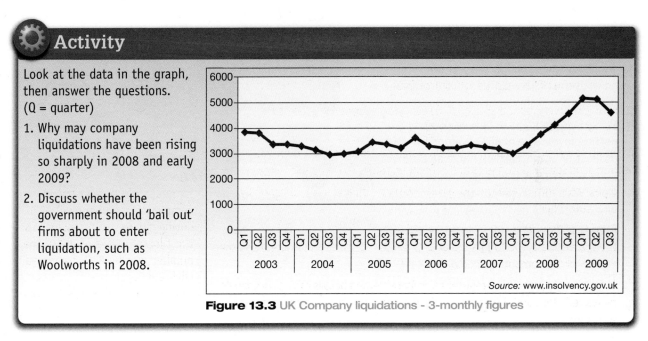

Source: www.insolvency.gov.uk

Figure 13.3 UK Company liquidations - 3-monthly figures

Marketing and sales

There are really only three ways to start up a successful business:

▶ do something really new (and that people want)

▶ do something that already exists, but do it better

▶ do something that already exists, but at lower cost.

All three rely on learning what people want and what they need, then combining this with a full understanding of what existing businesses are supplying. Any gap between what people want and what they currently get gives rise to an opportunity. Unfortunately, many gaps that look significant prove very hard to fill. One example is banking. A recent survey showed that 10 million people were dissatisfied with their current high street bank, yet few make a switch. Research might make a new bank account sound a winner, but customers might be too lazy to switch.

Reaching and retaining customers

When a firm has identified a product or service that people want, it has to get the message across to customers. Well-run businesses are good at promoting products or services. There are three ways to reach customers for the first time:

▶ *Location*, e.g. a new clothes shop opens in a busy part of the high street; effective window displays are all the 'advertising' that is needed. A manufacturer might also achieve success through location. When TicTacs were launched, there was no advertising – shopkeepers started to display the little boxes near their tills because they were being offered large profits per sale.

▶ *Advertising*, e.g. through media such as local newspapers or local radio, through direct methods such as leaflets or sandwich boards, or online. Whichever way, the secret to success is targeting, i.e. making sure the advertisements are placed in front of the people most likely to buy your product.

▶ *Public Relations (PR)* means working hard at getting favourable media coverage for your product or brand. Fashion handbag business Bobelle gets huge coverage because owner Claire Watt-Smith spends one afternoon a week writing to newspapers and magazines. Pre-Christmas 2009 she enjoyed a sales boom when a write-up in *The Times* was followed a week later by a write-up in *The Sunday Times*. The only cost to Claire is her time.

Retaining customers means keeping them loyal. This is best achieved by providing terrific service to go with a terrific product. In other words, quality is the key. It also helps to think about building customer relationships. This can be a face-to-face relationship, in which the customer enjoys hearing, 'Good morning Mrs Simpson' and trusts that anything wrong will be put right immediately. Or it may be online, where companies such as Amazon programme their computers to learn the type of books the customer is interested in. Therefore, when a Liverpool supporter logs on to buy a children's book pre-Christmas, the programme tells him there's a new book out on Steven Gerrard. This can help build a link between the customer and the company.

Summary

Marketing is crucial in persuading people to try your product. Retaining those customers requires more than good marketing – it depends on the quality of the product and the service. Clever businesses work hard to build customer relationships, in order to achieve customer loyalty.

Customer care and customer needs

It should be obvious that businesses should focus at all times on the customer. Yet this often doesn't happen. Sweetshop owners can seem irritated to have schoolchildren in the shop – yet who do they think buys sweets? Similarly, football supporters often have to queue for ages at half time to get an overpriced, lukewarm pie.

In a well-run business, customer needs and wants will be discussed regularly. The problem may be that different customers have different requirements. Being chatty with customers at a sandwich shop may please some people, but anger the person waiting behind in the queue. Effective customer care means finding out what people want – and giving it to them as quickly, efficiently and pleasantly as possible.

 Activity

In 2009 a business consultant from Imperial College (a London university) came to Scoop ice cream to give business advice to owner Matteo Pantani. Having looked around and asked some questions, the advice was to cut down the range of flavours from 20 to 8. This would save time and money. Matteo rejected this because, 'my customers love to see lots of flavours and occasionally taste something new; I would rather work harder to make sure I have happy customers'.

How might Matthew benefit from his focus on 'happy customers'?

Marketing information and market research

Matteo knows his customers because he sees and talks to them every day. But how can you get this understanding before the business has even started? In truth, you can't. Good businesspeople will try all they can, though, to learn as much as possible about the market they are about to enter.

A good start is to find out the marketing information that already exists. A visit to the City Business Library (at the Guildhall Library, Aldermanbury, London EC2V 7HH) will provide (free) information on many markets, such as:

▶ Is the pizza takeaway market growing or declining?

▶ What are the average weekly takings at sandwich shops in Britain?

▶ Which groups of people eat the most chocolate?

Having found out some useful general information, market research can be used to find out things that relate directly to your business idea. Examples might include:

▶ using a questionnaire in your high street to find out what price locals are prepared to pay for a restaurant meal

▶ phoning local shops to ask where they buy their supplies at the moment, and whether they would be happy to drive to a cash and carry to be opened on the edge of town

▶ running an online survey to find out people's favourite milkshake flavours.

Summary

Effective market research is invaluable in uncovering customer needs. Research can get answers to key questions about what people most need from their products. Then the business can work hard at providing the precise service the customers need.

Competition

A football team only plays as well as the opposition allows it to. In the same way, it is daft to think of starting up a business without thinking about the competition. Who are they? How good are they? And what exactly are their strengths and weaknesses? In one town in Devon, two rival fish and chip shops have been side by side for 15 years. Neither makes a good living, but either would get rich if the other closed down. How frustrating!

If the competition is strong locally, a new business will have to have an exceptional edge in order to succeed. Unfortunately, most new ideas can be copied by the existing businesses. And if they have been established for years, they may have deep enough pockets to cut their prices just as you are opening up. Nothing is riskier than taking on a strong, established competitor.

Unique selling points

When facing strong competitors, nothing is more important than a unique selling point (USP). Many adults prefer pizzas from restaurants that have wood-fired ovens. To be the first and only pizza place in town with a wood-fired oven would be a USP. Of course, others could copy, but it might take 6 months to get one installed. In the meantime you could hope to establish yourself as the original wood-fired pizza place. USPs among products today include:

- ▷ iPhone – the prestige of the Apple brand
- ▷ Bounty – the only chocolate bar featuring coconut
- ▷ Renault Megane (shaking that ****) – emphasising its uniquely designed rear end
- ▷ Magners cider poured over ice (though this was later copied by Bulmers cider)
- ▷ Ugg boots – authentic Australian heritage (plus the glamour of Kate Moss).

If the USP is strong enough, the producer is in a position to increase the price of the product without much impact on sales volumes. This can increase revenue and profit considerably.

Summary

Before starting a business, make sure to look carefully at the competition. Beware of dismissing it, because your business won't be perfect either. If the competition seems strong, only start up if you are sure that you have a real, sustainable advantage. Best of all is to have a USP. A unique selling point makes it possible to stand out from the crowd.

 Activity

Huggies nappies comes up with a unique new feature. It is then able to increase its price from £4 per pack to £5. This cuts daily sales from 20,000 to 19,500 packs.

1. What revenue was being made per day before the price change?

2. What revenue is made per day after the price change?

3. What is the percentage change in daily revenue?

Cost and price of products or services

Good products can be expensive to produce. They may require costly ingredients and may take time to get just right. As time is expensive (especially labour time) the final product may have a high production cost. This is no problem, as long as customers are willing to pay a high price. Figure 13.4 shows that one folding bike can cost seven times more than another. The expensive Brompton sells very well.

Figure 13.4 Prices for selected folding bikes, January 2010

	Price	Detail
Technix	£99.99	Imported folding bike
Ridgeback	£249.00	Imported folding bike ('of outstanding quality')
Brompton	£699.00	Custom-made in Britain, i.e. made to the customer's specification

When starting a business, it is vital to decide which part of the market you want to compete in. If the business is a restaurant, do you want to be 'All You Can Eat for £10'? If so, costs must be kept to the absolute minimum (cheap tables and chairs, cheap kitchen equipment and cheap food supplies), otherwise your costs will outweigh the revenues, pushing you into losses. Or do you want to be a 'fine dining' restaurant, with a posh design, superb service and fancy prices? If so, everything must look (and taste) the part. So you will buy in expensive steaks from organic farms, but still hope to charge high enough prices to make a good profit.

Selling

In a Tesco, customers help themselves to what they want, influenced only by the brand names and packaging on the products. For many businesses, though, there would be virtually no sales without people 'selling'. This may be because the product is too complicated to buy without more explanation. The customer may have lots of questions and only be willing to buy after these have been answered. A good example is a second-hand car. The car dealer will explain the good points of the car, and the customer must make a decision based on this.

Key methods of selling include:

▷ *shop sales*, such as at a clothes or a shoe shop, where the customer can be influenced (or persuaded) to buy; a good shoe shop salesperson achieves double the sales of a poor salesperson

▷ *telesales*, i.e. telephone selling – the phone rings and it is a double glazing company trying to get a householder to arrange a visit from a sales person

▷ *door-to-door sales* – perhaps the toughest job in the world, facing direct rejection time after time, helped only by the occasional sympathy sale

▷ *business-to-business ('B2B') sales*, such as JCB selling an excavator to a construction company. This usually requires building a long-term sales relationship, perhaps including trips to the pub or to Wembley. Only when the buyer trusts the salesperson is he or she willing to strike a deal. This personal selling can be very effective, but is expensive as it takes time and money.

Summary

Never confuse cost with price. The cost is what the business pays out; the price is the money it brings in. In some cases the price may depend on who is buying, and the quantity they want to buy. The art of selling is to find the right buyer who will offer a fair price; anyone can give goods away cheaply; good sales people sell the product, not the price.

Environmental issues

Today, almost every business sees the advantage of promoting itself as a friend of the environment. Often, this is a low-cost way of gaining a bit of extra credit with shoppers. So a company that has always made a bit of extra cash by selling waste or scrap products to dealers grandly announces '80% recycled' on the pack front. It may have made no change to its business practices, yet found something to boast about. Needless to say, this does nothing whatever for the environment!

The only things that can make a difference are real changes to business behaviour. These might include:

▷ cutting down on packaging, as Cadbury did with its Easter eggs in 2009; it says it cut its packaging by 350 tonnes (25%)

- changing the product fundamentally, as Toyota did when it introduced the Prius car (which has two engines, a battery one for zero in-town emissions, and a petrol one for fast motorway cruising)

- cutting back on the number of new model launches. Cars and phones seem old very quickly because there are so many new ones each year. So we scrap products that work perfectly well because we want the latest. This is good business sense, but lousy for the environment. There is no sign that Apple, Nokia or Toyota are going to follow this idea – it would be bad for business.

Summary

Many businesses claim to be environmentally friendly, but these may be empty words. Good firms change their behaviour to help the environment; others may just be making hollow boasts.

Financial issues

There is a whole range of financial issues to consider.

Start-up costs

Start-up costs are the one-off costs the business must finance in order to open its doors for the first time. For a clothes shop, this would include buying the property lease, paying for building and decoration work, buying shelving, equipment, security cameras and tills and, of course, buying the initial stock. For a new restaurant that opened in Wimbledon in 2008, the start-up cost was £180,000. For a shop, a more likely figure is £40,000.

For a new business, these costs can be estimated quite accurately, as long as the building work is tightly managed. The key things about the start-up costs are:
- all the money involved is being put at risk
- the money spent must reflect the business idea (cheap and cheerful or posh and pricey?).

Operating expenses and income

As soon as the business has opened, most costs (expenses) will be ongoing rather than one-offs. A wage bill of £1,000 a week might look small compared with £180,000 of start-up costs, but expenses keep coming. If there is not enough income to cover the expenses, the business may collapse.

 Did you know?

Rent can be a huge cost for shops or even stalls. Hiring a stall in the aisle of Wimbledon's 'Centre Court' shopping centre costs around £1,000 per week.

When planning to open a shop, an entrepreneur might forecast 200 customers a week, spending an average of £40 each. This would lead to an income of £8,000 a week. If expenses are estimated at £7,000, the result is a £1,000 profit. But what if sales revenue proves to be just £4,000, and expenditure £5,000? The result is a weekly loss of £1,000.

The key is to successfully control expenses and income, i.e. to actively ensure that costs are no higher than planned, and – where possible – to boost revenues to match or beat their forecast level. Cutting costs can involve tough decisions, such as making staff redundant or cutting out a helpful but expensive supplier. Figure 13.5 gives some ideas of what managers can do.

Figure 13.5 Controlling expenses and income

Action to boost revenue	Possible effect	Action to cut costs	Possible effect
Offer existing customers a special deal if they return soon.	May get customers used to deals; hard to stop running them.	Switching to a cheaper supplier, perhaps from overseas.	If quality standards slip, some customers will realise, and word may spread.
Persuade customers to spend more, e.g. by clever selling ('upselling').	May make customers reluctant to return when they see the final bill.	Staff are often the main cost, so it is vital to keep staff levels low.	Unexpectedly high customer numbers may leave the business struggling.
Ensure that all staff give 100%, so that the customer wants to come back as soon as possible.	Should work for customers; but staff may struggle to give 100% every day.	It may be necessary to move to cheaper or smaller premises.	For a shop, a poorer location can mean that sales fall sharply.

Cash flow forecasting

Cash flow is the difference between the flows of cash into and out of a business over a period of time. For example, if a firm starts up by spending £20,000 of cash on premises and stocks in its first month, but receives only £1,000 from sales to customers, its cash flow is *minus* £19,000.

Cash flow forecasting means predicting the future flows of cash into and out of the firm's bank account. In effect, it means forecasting what the bank balance will look like at the end of each month. A cash flow forecast will usually be for a 12-month period. Figure 13.6 shows the forecast cash flow for the first 6 months of a brand new nightclub, started with £250,000 of capital. The forecast is based on some key points:

▶ building work is finished by the end of September, so that customers can start coming in October

▶ that a launch party brings the publicity and the customers needed for success

▶ that costs prove as expected, so the cash flow is never negative.

Figure 13.6 Cash flow forecast for 6 months

Figures in £000s	Aug	Sept	Oct	Nov	Dec	Jan
Cash at start	250	65	10	20	25	55
Cash in	0	0	85	65	115	55
Cash out	185	55	75	60	85	60
Net monthly cash	(185)	(55)	10	5	30	(5)
Cash at month end	65	10	20	25	55	50

Successful cash flow forecasts require:

▶ accurate prediction of monthly sales revenues

▶ accurate prediction of when customers will pay for the goods they've bought

▶ careful allowance for operating costs and the timing of payments

▶ careful allowance for other flows of cash, such as cash outflows when purchasing assets such as land, and inflows from raising additional capital, perhaps from selling shares.

Record keeping and HMRC

Few businesses operate entirely on cash. Even if they do, the taxman (HMRC – Her Majesty's Revenue and Customs) insists that records should be kept, e.g. of how much cash was received per day, and how much was paid out. From day one, the clever entrepreneur keeps all the receipts for everything paid out to set up and run the business. If these records are kept, there will be plenty of costs to set against the revenues. If the early months are loss-making, HMRC will allow these losses to be set against future profits – cutting the tax bill.

It is important to remember that if the business is a success, the taxman is bound to notice that the business exists – and will therefore come after you. It works out much better to let HMRC know that you're starting up, and keeping records to make your tax affairs much simpler.

Measuring financial success

When a business starts up, the most important factor is the cash position. Positive cash flows ensure that bills can be paid. At the time of writing, Portsmouth FC, a Premiership football club, is faced with a court order to liquidate the business, following several occasions in which wage bills haven't been paid. Portsmouth has run out of cash.

As long as the cash flow is OK, a key measure of success is profit. If revenues are consistently higher than costs, regular profits will bring a steady stream of extra cash into the business. This will provide an ever-growing cash cushion to protect the business from a bad patch. Every business has its reasons why trading might be poor. Figure 13.7 shows some possible factors.

Figure 13.7 Short-term problems that might require a cash cushion

High-fashion clothes shop	Car manufacturer	Airline
Bad buys mean the autumn stock is very hard to sell and must be sold off in the sales.	A sharp rise in the oil price means that bigger (thirsty) cars are unsellable.	Terrorist alerts cuts air travel, causing revenues to plunge.
A new local rival is featured in *The Sun*, with pictures of Kate Moss shopping; your sales slip.	An economic downturn leads to sharp cutbacks in new car buying.	A large travel agency goes bust, owing the airline £20 million that will never be paid.

 Activity

1. Identify two possible short-term business problems that might affect the finances of a restaurant.
2. Explain how profits can lead to the build-up of a comfortable cash cushion.

Other ways of measuring financial success include:

▷ *Assets:* well-established businesses turn their cash cushion into a series of different assets that help to build the business. In February 2010 Scoop ice cream bought a lease on its second London shop; only by buying property (an asset) can it hope to expand.

▷ *Financial health:* in addition to measuring a firm's cash cushion, it is wise to check its debt level. In other words, it may owe the bank a lot of money. A financially successful business will have a cash cushion without being burdened by big bank debts. Therefore, cutting its debt level will be one of a firm's top financial priorities.

Risks

Every decision carries a risk – that the decision is wrong. For a PE teacher, the decision to teach tennis may prove a mistake – but no money is lost. In business, every decision can prove expensive. So it is important to weigh up the risk of failure against the rewards from success – and make a judgement. When Portsmouth FC decided to pay huge wages to top players, the directors (and supporters) saw the opportunity to win the FA Cup, but not the risk that the club would suffer financial collapse.

Among key business risks are that:

▷ if most of its income is from one source, the business is in peril if the customer cancels the order

▷ the business lacks the cash cushion to survive a spell of bad trading

▶ a new business may never make enough profit to give an acceptable income to the owners

▶ ambitious plans may lead to heavy debts and, ultimately, business failure.

Summary

Wise entrepreneurs know that they will have to struggle financially for the first year or two. Instead of taking profits out, they will have to keep every penny in the business, to ease it through to the time when it starts to make a profit. For some businesses, this may take three or more years. Up until then, cash flow must be watched with care, and income and expenditure controlled on a daily basis.

Assessment activity 13.2 (P2, P3, M2)

Ask the entrepreneur you interviewed in Assessment activity 13.1 to explain their business idea, covering these points:

1. the business, its market and its competitors

2. exactly how the start-up was planned – and how well it went in practice

3. how exactly they carried out their cash flow forecast – how accurate did it prove?

4. what legal rules they had to follow during the start-up phase – how easy or hard (and expensive) was it to deal with those rules?

Topic check

1 What is meant by the term 'retaining customers'?

   a) Teaching customers how to get the best from the products they buy.

   b) Persuading customers to come and buy for the first time.

   c) Keeping customers loyal, so that they return again and again.

   d) Giving customers the opportunity to work for the company.

2 Which is the best definition of 'limited liability'?

   a) A company need not repay its debts, no matter how high they may be.

   b) The owners have personal financial responsibility for any business debts.

   c) The owners are not liable, personally, for the debts of the business.

   d) The company must pay its debts, no matter how limited their cash position may be.

3 Why may it be hard for a sole trader to take a holiday?

4 Identify two possible business risks for a property company developing a new shopping centre.

5 Identify two risks for someone who stays in the same office job for 20 years.

Getting started

The key to business success is a great idea, i.e. identifying an opportunity that fits in with customers' lifestyles, then seeing how to create a business that matches the opportunity. But even great ideas can go wrong if they are badly managed. A carefully considered business plan can reduce the chances of things going wrong.

When you have completed this topic, you should:

- understand the value of a business plan when starting your first business
- understand how to prepare a business plan.

Key terms

Mentor: an individual with business experience who acts as the adviser to someone opening up their first business; a mentor may be paid or unpaid

Patent: legal protection for a technically new idea, giving the inventor up to 20 years in which copycats can be sued

Qualitative research: looks in-depth at the views of small groups of consumers, often looking at the reasons behind people's opinions and purchasing patterns

Quantitative research: measures the percentage of people who share views, e.g. 65% of over 35s prefer Cadbury's Dairy Milk to Galaxy

Business plans

A business plan is a document that sets out the goals, plans, finances and practical aspects of turning a business idea into a living business. Usually a business plan is prepared to persuade outsiders to invest or lend money to the business. The document has several sections that might include the following.

1 The business idea

This section should attract the reader with a short, clear statement of what the product does and which people will want it. Ideally, it should also explain why competitors will struggle to imitate the idea.

Section	Proposition	Comment
1. The idea	Solar-powered traffic lights: shining more brightly when the sun is bright; improving car and pedestrian safety. Target purchaser: the local authorities that buy traffic lights everywhere in the world. Protection comes from an already granted 20-year **patent**.	As suggested: short, clear and with obvious business potential.

2 Products or services

This sets out whether the business is selling a one-off product or an ongoing service. A solar-powered traffic light might be priced at £4,000, but will last for 20 years. Therefore you have to wait that long for the next £4,000. But if you can also sell a service contract for regular 6-monthly maintenance on the traffic light, you may be able to charge £250 a year on top.

Section	Proposition	Comment
2. Product or service	We plan to sell traffic lights plus the computerised light-switching system; then sell a separate service contract for 6-monthly maintenance. This will bring in a regular income stream and should be highly profitable.	This makes the full business potential clear to investors.

3 Possible customers

This should indicate the prime customers to be targeted at the time of launch, followed by the potential customer groups who can be targeted in future.

Section	Proposition	Comment
3. Possible customers	There are 200 local authorities in Britain. Each is, on average, responsible for 1,000 traffic lights, i.e. there are 200,000 traffic lights in Britain. After launching in Britain, environmentally aware countries such as Holland and Germany would come next.	This gives a clear idea of the vast potential, without making any exaggerated claims.

4 Customer needs

This should take the idea forward, to show the thought that has been given to how to make the business work. If the product was a chocolate bar, this would set out how the product is to be put in front of the consumer, e.g. by gaining distribution through sweetshops, and paying for special display stands to be put by the till.

Section	Proposition	Comment
4. Customer needs	We will appoint a small sales force to visit every council in Britain, to identify the key decision-makers at each council. Then work to persuade all future traffic light purchases to be of our superior, environmentally friendly product. Then the sales team will keep in regular contact with these decision-makers on a 6-monthly basis.	This shows a realistic understanding that councils will need to be persuaded; new business rarely comes easily.

5 Sales targets

Identifying realistic forecasts of what sales level can be expected – from which revenue and profit calculations can be made. Ideally, these targets would be set after market research; often, though, they will be rough estimates.

Section	Proposition	Comment
5. Sales target	By the end of Year 1 we expect to have customers among 5% of Britain's councils, i.e. 10 councils, and expect to have sales amounting to 50 lights per council, i.e. 500 lights. At a price of £4,000 each, that would amount to £2,000,000 (£2 million) of sales in the first year. The second year should provide £4 million.	Again, the key is to be modest, i.e. not claim a greater sales level than is realistic.

6 Forward planning

This will look beyond the start-up phase. A business might plan ahead for how many staff will be needed in 6 months' time, and how large a factory might be needed.

Section	Proposition	Comment
6. Forward planning	We expect to need four staff on day 1, rising to 20 staff by the end of the first year. As we recruit staff at the end of the year, we will look out for speakers of Dutch and German, in preparation for our growth plans.	This will help an outsider to see that the managers have thought ahead.

Figure 13.8 A business plan

Section	Proposition	Comment
1. The idea	Solar-powered traffic lights – shining more brightly when the sun is bright – improving car and pedestrian safety. Target purchaser: the local authorities that buy traffic lights everywhere in the world. Protection comes from an already granted 20-year patent.	As suggested: short, sharp and with obvious business potential.
2. Product or service	We plan to sell traffic lights plus the computerised light-switching system; then sell a separate service contract for 6-monthly maintenance. This will bring in a regular income stream and should be highly profitable.	This makes the full business potential clear to investors
3. Possible customers	There are 200 local authorities in Britain. Each is, on average, responsible for 1,000 traffic lights, i.e. there are 200,000 traffic lights in Britain. After launching in Britain, environmentally aware countries such as Holland and Germany would come next.	This gives a clear idea of the vast potential, without making any exaggerated claims
4. Customer needs	We will appoint a small sales force to visit every council in Britain, to identify the key decision-makers at each council. Then work to persuade all future traffic light purchases to be of our superior, environmentally-friendly product. Then the sales team will keep in regular contact with these decision makers on a 6-monthly basis.	This shows a realistic understanding that councils will need to be persuaded; new business rarely comes easily
5. Sales target	By the end of Year 1 we expect to have customers among 5% of Britain's councils, i.e. 10 councils; and expect to have sales amounting to 50 lights per council, i.e 500 lights. At a price of £4,000 each, that would amount to £2,000,000 (£2 million) of sales in the first year. The second year should provide £4 million.	Again, the key is to be modest, i.e. not claim a greater sales level than is realistic.
6. Forward planning	We expect to need 4 staff on Day 1 rising to 20 staff by the end of the first year. As we recruit staff at the end of the year, we will look out for speakers of Dutch and German, in preparation for our growth plans.	This will help an outsider to see that the managers have thought ahead.

Starting and running a business

There are many issues to consider in relation to starting and running a business, in addition to those already discussed in this chapter.

The needs of a business

A business is a group of people linked by a common goal and – usually – a common workplace. The greatest need (apart from cash to pay the wage bill) is for the people to work together – for the customer. If they can get that right, the results can be remarkable. Innocent Drinks grew from 3 to 130 staff in just 4 years. Regular Friday nights at the pub helped everyone feel part of the Innocent enterprise!

Research techniques

For a new small business, the two most important types of research are quantitative and qualitative. **Quantitative research** tries to find out the views of the majority, e.g. 60% of people prefer salted butter to unsalted, or 52% of people say they would try your new product. This is important when trying to make a sales forecast. Nevertheless it is important to remember that research only tells you what people say, not what they will do.

Qualitative research is often more useful. It doesn't try to ask questions to lots of people. It tries to probe in-depth among a small number of people who are in the target market. Why exactly do Galaxy-buyers choose it in preference to Cadbury's Dairy Milk? Is it really the taste? Or is it a desire to be different? And how much extra are they prepared to pay for the taste?

In both cases, the most important thing is to be clear about what exactly you are trying to find out. Small businesses often run surveys that tell them no more than they already know.

Planning techniques

The most important planning technique is the flow chart. This shows all the lines of activity that need to be completed – and by when. For example, if the business is to open a second shop in 3 months, many different things are needed: the shop must be decorated; new equipment must be bought and installed; new staff must be recruited and trained; new stock must be bought and displayed; and advertising must let customers know about the opening. Most of these things can be done at the same time, but everyone needs to know key completion dates. A flow chart can show this.

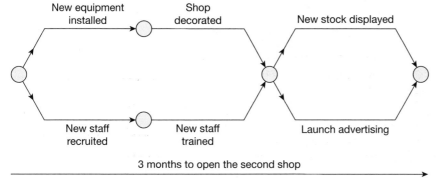

Figure 13.9 Flow chart of shop opening

Controllable and uncontrollable aspects

Controllable aspects of a new business should include staff recruitment and training, plus the quality of the product or service being offered. Even here, though, it is important to realise that things can get out of hand. Managers at a pizza restaurant in Birmingham were forced to sack the chef and his assistant when they were discovered drunk during the evening service (on the restaurant's booze). With no back-up plan, the restaurant had to close for a week before a new chef could be installed. This hit takings very hard.

More obviously uncontrollable aspects include:

- competitors' decisions, such as to run a 'mid-season sale'
- customers' tastes and habits, e.g. one TV programme on the calorie-laden sandwiches may wreck takings at your newly-opened Subway franchise
- the weather may wreck summer sales at your ice cream parlour
- timing may cause problems, e.g. a sudden upsurge in demand may leave you gasping as you wait for new deliveries from China.

Work needed to start a business

No one should start a business until they have discovered or created a significant gap or opportunity. For a start-up software business, there may be a huge amount of work involved in creating the software, plus the website required to market it. Only when the software is glitch free should the business start trying to take money from customers.

In other cases there may be a huge amount of building work, e.g. in converting a large house into a hotel, or a restaurant into a large shop. In all such cases, the key is to remember that time is money. The longer it takes to complete the work, the longer you are waiting to start getting some cash in from the business.

Most people starting a business think it will be easy to get supplies. After all, you are the customer and people will want to sell to you. In fact it can be hard. In the fashion world, successful labels do not want their clothes hanging in a new shop that might flop. So materials and supplies can be harder to get than you might expect. This requires careful research before starting up. Who is willing to supply you and on what terms? They will probably only supply on a cash-on-delivery basis, i.e. refuse to give you credit. This is understandable, but you will have to allow for this problem in your cash flow forecast.

Summary

Starting a business is hugely exciting and hugely stressful at the same time. Certain business clichés are helpful:

▶ 'By failing to prepare, you are preparing to fail.'

▶ 'When a business starts, cash is king.'

▶ 'In a start-up company, you have to rethink every 3 weeks.'

Advice and support

There are various sources of advice and support that you can turn to when you are starting out in business.

Government support for enterprise

Novice entrepreneurs believe that the government will be behind them all the way. They will soon find out that life is not like that. Over 40% of those thinking about starting a business believe that they will get a grant; in fact, only 2% get funding in this way, i.e. 1 new business in 50.

The government's main expenditure to support new business comes from the Business Link network. This offers advice for those starting up; all new businesspeople are entitled to one free consultation with an expert nominated by Business Link. Unfortunately, the quality of the advice is said to be very variable. Some entrepreneurs speak highly of their mentor; others criticise that 'mine hadn't run a business in his life; he was just a banker'. The government's own research shows that just 7% of recent business start-ups have gone to Business Link for support.

David Cameron has long believed that the key support for enterprise is to encourage an 'enterprise culture', in effect, to create a spirit among young people that being enterprising is 'cool'. The argument runs that if lots of people want to start their own businesses, perhaps Britain will develop as dynamically as America– the heart of the enterprise culture – has.

Mentoring

Especially for young entrepreneurs, it can be very helpful to have a more experienced mentor. This person will listen to your ideas, and will force you to justify your thoughts. Why do you think you will outsell an established rival? Do you really think people will work willingly for the minimum wage?

Business Link provides access to mentors, but you may be better off finding a family member who is willing to give you an hour a week for the first few months' of the life of the business.

 Case study

'Mimyne', an online retailer of children's products, started up with very little capital from the owner. She was able to persuade the government-funded East London Small Business Centre to guarantee a £10,000 bank loan. Looking back, though, she realises that she underestimated the cost of starting up.

Online support

The Business Link website (www.businesslink.gov.uk) is good for practical issues such as how to form a limited company. For practical advice on mistakes to avoid, though, there are much better sites. A good one is www.startups.co.uk. It regularly features interviews with entrepreneurs who are willing to own up to their failures as well as their successes. This is valuable advice. An advantage of this type of support is that it is general. No one is trying to make money out of you.

Perhaps the best of all is www.princes-trust.org.uk. This has 12 booklets that can be downloaded, telling you how to write a business plan or providing legal advice for start-up. The Prince's Trust is also one of the few places that might provide a small grant to help you finance your start-up (though this only applies to those who are unemployed).

Education and training

Of course, you are already studying a valuable course to prepare you for start-up. But you may feel the need for something more specific. Many local councils offer good courses, such as the East London Small Business Centre, which offers a free 4-day course for those who live locally. Regional Development Agencies such as Yorkshire Forward also put on free courses from time to time. They also claim to help with finding grants for start-up.

Summary

Does the government do enough to help entrepreneurs? Britain is one of the easiest, quickest and cheapest places in the world to start up a new firm. It comes as a shock, though, to find how little help there is out there. The government's huge spending on Business Link seems to achieve little. The most valuable opportunities are the online free materials together with finding a mentor you can trust.

 Case study

In early 2008 a brother and sister duo in their twenties started a design business. Their plan was to target small business customers with low-cost design work. They would produce logos, brochures and web designs from home – via their website http://sarabrown.co.uk. Working from home would keep fixed operating costs to a minimum. Their (rather wordy) mission statement is:

'A design force making effective visual communication solutions available to start-ups and small businesses without screwing up their cash flow.'

Two years on, Sara and her brother had won business from the Zambian Tourist Board and others. Comments from clients on Sara's Blog compliment her for a 'can-do attitude' and 'innovative' designs.

1. Explain why Sara's start-up seems likely to succeed.

2. Outline one possible advantage and one possible disadvantage in working from home when starting a business.

3. How might the pair's mission statement appeal to those who are starting up their own business and need design work?

Assessment activity 13.3 (P4, P5, D2)

Should the business you looked at in Assessment activities 13.1 and 13.2 have been started or not?

1. Outline the contents of the business plan for starting and running this business.

2. Justify recommendations as to whether the business should have been started or not.

Assessment activity 13.4 (P6)

Dominic Vey made his first million by the age of 15, importing collapsible scooters from America. He stumbled on the product when he typed 'viza' into a search engine when looking to see if you could get a credit card. Viza was the US scooter manufacturer, and Dominic has never looked back. Today he owns a magazine and has many other business interests. When he was asked about the help available for starting a new business, he replied:

'The other day I went into a local store opposite Waltham Forest Town Hall. I said to the owner,

"You've only been here six months, how's it going? Are the council helping a lot?" He said, "What? I only hear from the council when they want their fees paid."

I said, "Are there no forums, no networking groups, no grants, helping you out?" He said he wouldn't even know where to call and they probably don't know he exists.'

Explain to the store owner the sources of advice and support available when preparing to start a business.

Topic check

1 Which is the best definition of a business mentor?

   a) Someone who puts money into the business, to help it succeed.

   b) Someone who can take charge when things are getting difficult.

   c) Someone with experience who can provide advice, especially in the early days of the business.

   d) Someone who has the experience to deal with the media, even when things are going badly.

2 Which two of the following have no place in a business plan?

   a) A detailed list of the business ideas the entrepreneur has already rejected.

   b) A detailed cash flow forecast for the first 9 months of the life of the business.

   c) A full account of the business backgrounds of each of the directors.

   d) Email addresses of the potential customers the business intends to contact.

   e) A statement of what distinguishes the product from all its competitors.

3 Why does a brilliant business plan not necessarily mean a brilliant business?

4 Why do investors like to see that an entrepreneur has produced a business plan?

Assessment summary

The overall grade you achieve for this unit depends on how well you meet the grading criteria set out at the start of the chapter (see page 227). You must complete:

- all of the P criteria to achieve a **pass** grade
- all of the P and the M criteria to achieve a **merit** grade
- all of the P, M and D criteria to achieve a **distinction** grade.

Your tutor will assess the assessment activities that you complete for this unit. The work you produce should provide evidence which demonstrates that you have achieved each of the assessment criteria. The table below identifies what you need to demonstrate to meet each of the pass, merit and distinction criteria for this unit. You should always check and self-assess your work before you submit your assignments for marking.

Remember that you MUST provide evidence for all of the P criteria to pass the unit.

Grading criteria	You need to demonstrate that you can:	Do you have the evidence?
P1	Explain how knowledge of personal strengths and weaknesses can be applied to preparing for and contributing to a business	
M1	Explain, using examples, the benefits of starting a business	
D1	Evaluate the issues that need to be considered when starting a business	
P2	Identify how regulations and laws for small businesses can affect preparation for business	
M2	Analyse the different aspects that will affect preparation for business	
P3	Describe how small businesses prepare to market and sell products or services	
P4	Describe the financial issues that can affect preparation for business	
P5	Outline the contents of a business plan for starting and running a business	
D2	Justify recommendations made for starting a business	
P6	Explain the sources of advice and support available when preparing for business	

Always ask your tutor to explain any assignment tasks or assessment criteria that you don't understand fully. Being clear about the task before you begin gives you the best chance of succeeding. Good luck with your Unit 16 assessment work!

14 Managing personal finance (Unit 20)

Unit outline

Money is great when you've got it. Horrible when you haven't. There are so many things to buy; so many temptations. The key is to make money work *for* you. Most rich people are rich because they have been clever with money. It's not that hard to do.

Learning outcomes

1 **Know ways to manage personal finance.**
2 **Know common financial products and services.**
3 **Be able to produce a personal budget that takes account of personal remuneration and expenditure.**

Grading guide

To achieve a **pass**, you must show you can:	To achieve a **merit**, you must show you can:	To achieve a **distinction**, you must show you can:
P1 Outline ways of managing personal financial planning and accurate record keeping	**M1** Explain the reasons for budgetary decisions	**D1** Justify reasons for financial planning decisions
P2 Identify sources of advice for ways of managing financial products and services	**M2** Analyse the different features of financial products and services relating to to current and savings accounts	
P3 Describe financial products and services appropriate to self		
P4 Construct a personal budget that takes account of personal remuneration and expenditure		

The cleverest things you can do with money

▶ Getting started

The sooner you start managing your money, the earlier in life you'll have the wealth to live the life you want to live. Saving is simple, and has the potential to turn a poor 16-year-old into a rich 30-year-old.

When you have completed this topic, you should:

■ understand how budgeting can help avoid debt

■ understand the importance of starting to save as soon as possible

■ understand how to avoid making a big financial mistake.

 Key terms

Bankrupt: unable to pay your debts, leading to your assets being sold off

Inflation: the rate at which prices are rising, e.g. 10% inflation means that prices are 10% higher than they were a year ago

Management charges: banks that encourage you to invest with them may charge you up to 2% of your money each year; that adds up to a huge penalty over time

Personal budgeting – know what you're doing with it

Many highly paid film stars, footballers and TV actors have ended up **bankrupt**. They were earning plenty, yet never managed what they earned. Eventually it disappeared, and when the taxman came to call, they ended up in court (and in the papers). If it's hard to manage £40,000 a week, how much harder must it be to make everything work with £400? Or, like more than 10 million people in Britain, to cope on just £200 a week?

The answer is simple: budgeting. It's a three-step process:

1. How much have you got?

2. What do you want to do with your money?

3. How much of what you want can you afford?

John's ambition was a Fulham season ticket (yes, yes, jokes are in order). Under 16, the cost was £220 for the year. He had £60 at Christmas, and wanted to save £10 a week between then and June. So, from the £35 a week he earned working at his father's shop, he budgeted to spend no more than £25.

 Did you know?

- Slough is England's debt capital; households owe an average of £47,500.

- Self-employed people owe 219% of their yearly take-home pay.

- 18–24-year-olds who are 'debt-worried' increased by 19% in the year to August 2009.

Source: www.cleardebt.co.uk, 7 August 2009

Budgeting is about separating what you *must* have from what you *want* to have. And cutting out the things you buy that you don't even remember buying. In Britain, more than 40% of all the food people buy is thrown away – a complete waste of money.

This was John's budget (his parents gave him £3 a day for lunch):

Must have:

£40 a month for clothes (£10 a week)

£30 a month for phone (£7.50 a week)

£1 a day for me (£7 a week)

John's budget (end of 1st week)	Week 1		Week 2	
	Budget	Actual	Budget	Actual
Money in (shop and lunch money)	£50	£50	£50	
Money out:				
Food (lunch)	£15	£12	£15	
Food (snacks)	£7	£6	£7	
Clothes	£10	£15	£10	
Phone	£7.50	£7.50	£7.50	
Downloads	£0.50	£1.50	£0.50	
Total money out	£40	£42	£40	
Money saved	£10	£8	£10	

Over to you!

Choose two reasons why a family's finances might be helped by setting a weekly budget.

a) It will help them focus spending on what they really need.

b) It will help them spend more on all the things the family wants.

c) It may help them save, e.g. for the annual holiday.

d) It's a fun activity that everyone can enjoy together.

Know how to make it multiply

Paul Getty, an oil millionaire, once called compound interest 'the eighth wonder of the world'. It is the key to understanding money. If you had £1,000 and left it in a savings account that paid 10% a year, you'd expect to have £2,000 in 10 years' time. In fact you'd have £2,590. Leave it for another 10 years and it'll be £6,727. This is because the interest compounds on itself, boosting the total sum. Figure 14.1 shows the amazing effect of this over time. If you can start saving in a small way, early on in life, you'll end up with a pile of cash. If, at the age of 18, you could put away £5,000 and let the interest compound at 10%, you'd have £87,247 at the age of 48.

Figure 14.1 How compound interest works

	£1,000 invested at 10% compound	£5,000 invested at 10% compound	£10 saved a month at 10% compound	£25 saved a month at 10% compound
Value in 10 years	£2,593	£12,965	£2,048	£5,121
Value in 20 years	£6,727	£33,635	£7,594	£18,984
Value in 30 years	£17,449	**£87,247**	£22,605	£56,512

Avoid making a major money mistake

The biggest problem with money is that everyone wants to 'help' you with it. The big banks run huge advertising campaigns telling you to trust *them* with money. If only. In the 1980s they persuaded many of your teachers to buy 'personal pensions'. Big mistake. Banks are a fine place for saving money; but they want to 'help' you by selling you services that make extra profit for them. So do many others, including so-called independent financial advisers. In general, be careful of anyone who wants to help you with your money. The biggest money mistakes you can make are discussed below.

Borrowing to buy something you can't afford

If you can't afford it, the last thing you want is to have to pay a whole lot *more* for it. Yet that's what 'buying on credit' means. Instead of buying that iPod for £200, you buy it on credit and end up paying £300 for it. Or instead of buying a car for £18,000, you end up paying £50,000 for it (because your struggles to repay mean the interest charges keep going up).

Case study

£90,000 interest on a £500 loan

A loan shark who lent a couple £500 and forced them to pay back nearly £90,000 over 7 years escaped a jail sentence yesterday. Robert Reynolds, 39, had told Debra Wilson that there would be 'a bit of interest'. But the mother of four ended up suffering two strokes and a brain haemorrhage as she struggled with monthly repayments of up to £1,840.

By the time Reynolds – described as 'beyond contempt' by the judge – was reported to police, the interest rate was an alarming 2,500 per cent. Mrs Wilson and her husband Kevin could not pay their bills, survived on food leftovers, almost lost their home and came close to divorce.

Reynolds was convicted of harassment, but only given a 51-week jail sentence, suspended for 2 years.

Investing in something you don't understand

If you need an adviser to explain a financial idea to you, avoid it. Only invest your money in something you understand. If all you understand is a bank deposit account, that's fine. Keep your money there, safely. (But do check to make sure you are getting as high an interest rate as possible.)

Overpaying on 'management charges'

'**Management charges**' essentially mean people helping themselves to your money. Anyone offering you professional advice about money will charge for their service. Usually they charge a percentage upfront, plus an extra percentage each year. Over a number of years, they can often end up earning more from your money than you do! You should never pay more than 1% a year to an adviser.

Putting all your eggs in one basket

Many Head Office staff at Northern Rock bank were proud of its Newcastle roots. They were happy to buy subsidised shares in the business. It seemed a great way to save. But when Northern Rock went bust in 2007, staff lost not only their salary and their pension, but also their savings. They were wiped out virtually overnight – through no fault of their own. So, when you have a bit of money to invest, try to spread it around.

Ignoring inflation (price rises)

When **inflation** is about 2% a year, the value of £1 loses half its value in just under 40 years. If inflation is 10%, money halves in value in just over 7 years. So if you leave money in your current account, its value can have halved in 7 years. If inflation is high, beware of leaving too much in your bank account.

Topic check

1 Identify two serious financial mistakes people often make.

2 Identify two ways to avoid making serious financial mistakes.

3 Identify two reasons why families might benefit from budgeting.

4 Explain briefly how you might set about saving to buy your first (second-hand) car.

5 Outline two 'financial life stages' people go through.

Know ways to manage personal finance

▶ Getting started

Kai, a hotel worker in Thailand, earns £80 a month yet manages to save £20 towards his baby daughter's schooling. In Britain, families earning £500 a week often struggle to build any savings. Knowing ways to manage your personal finances can help you avoid struggling with money.

When you have completed this topic, you should:

- understand the basics of successful personal financial management
- see how these basics can help you build up your personal wealth over time.

Key terms

Contingency planning: thinking about what might go wrong in future, then planning how to cope; this might involve keeping cash in a savings account 'for a rainy day'

Credit rating: those who lend money 'score' customers on the basis of how reliably they repay their debts; those with a poor credit rating struggle to open a bank account, get a mortgage, or even get an 'interest free' sofa from DFS

Importance of managing personal finance

Much of this was covered in Topic 2.1. Additional points include:

▶ *Avoid getting into debt* – the problem of debt is that the solutions are usually very expensive, e.g. borrowing to repay the debt usually carries high interest charges.

▶ *Control costs* – see the emphasis in Topic 14.1 on the importance of budgeting.

▶ *Remain solvent* – this means keeping yourself in a position where you can always pay your bills. This requires some forward planning, i.e. thinking about what bills are coming up, and how you'll find the money to pay them.

▶ *Save* – remember the magic of saving when young and getting compound interest on your side: 'the eighth wonder of the world'.

It is sensible to seek advice before taking important financial decisions.

▶ *Maintain a good* **credit rating** – this is very important for when you want to move into your first flat; if your credit rating is bad, you won't be able to get water, gas or electricity without paying in advance! The rule is simple, don't borrow when you can't afford to repay; but if you do borrow, make sure to keep up the repayments.

Keeping financial records

Keeping financial records (perhaps in a shoe box) is very helpful in case the taxman calls. You may also want to check your bank statements (What's that payment of £74.15 for?). So records are helpful for you too. Among the most important are:

▶ Bank statements, which provide a full record of what's gone into and come out of your bank account over a period of time. ADVICE: when you set up a bank account, ask for monthly bank statements; this will help you keep a better track that the 3-monthly statements banks prefer to provide.

▶ Cheque stubs: you may never use a cheque book; indeed cheques are likely to disappear by 2018. If you do use cheques, though, remember to write down how much each cheque was for, and who it was to.

▶ Receipts and bills: it will be helpful to keep records if you are self-employed or start your own sole trader business. If you've bought a computer that is crucial to your self-employment, you can charge it against your income in order to reduce your tax bills.

▶ Pay slips: you may want to keep them all, but the only really important one is the March one. This sets out your earnings (and tax) for the whole tax year. This is helpful if you need to make a 'tax return'. This would be necessary if you have any extra earnings above your normal wages.

Keeping financial records is especially useful if things go wrong. For example, if a full-time worker is made redundant half way through the year, she or he would want to claim a 'tax rebate', i.e. get some of the money back that the taxman has charged already. Financial records make it easier to make **contingency planning** a realistic possibility.

Personal taxation

Some taxes are the same for rich and poor alike, such as the VAT tax on biscuits. Therefore, the poor are harder hit because a few pounds is nothing for a rich person, but matters to a poor one. Personal taxation in Britain is intended to be 'progressive', meaning that poorer people are hit less toughly than richer ones. Among the personal taxes are:

▶ Income tax – broadly, in 2010/11:

  • people earning below £6,750 pay no income tax

  • people at average earnings of £25,000 a year pay an income tax rate of 20%

  • people earning higher salaries pay 40% tax on the income above £45,000.

▶ National Insurance – this is charged at a rate of around 11% of salary.

The government's income from taxes is used to provide key services such as education and the National Health Service (NHS).

> **? Did you know?**
>
> American households spend 15% of their income on private health insurance, because they do not have a free National Health Service.

Keeping money secure

Money attracts crime. Electronic and plastic money is especially exciting for the criminal. To keep your money as secure as possible, follow these guidelines.

▶ *ATMs (automatic teller machines):* when using hole-in-the-wall cash point machines (ATMs) make sure to keep your PIN number hidden from view as you punch in the numbers.

▶ *PINs:* a card is no use to a fraudster without the four-digit PIN number. So it is important to keep the PIN number away from the card. Ideally you memorise it and destroy any record of it.

▶ *Standing orders* are a secure way to make regular payments; your bank simply makes a regular payment from your bank account, but only after you have signed to give authorisation.

▶ *Direct debits* are similar, but slightly less secure as the business you are dealing with (such as British Gas) has the authority to take whatever sum they say you owe them.

▶ *Online banking* is increasingly popular, but has its own risks. Fraudsters try to find out your bank details so that they can dip into your bank account. Take care to follow your bank's security instructions.

Skills needed to manage personal finance

▶ *Problem-solving,* i.e. the ability to identify what you need and then sift through all the different ways your needs can be met – remember that financial decisions are your decisions. Do not pass the decisions on to someone who will be only too happy to help. But help who?

▶ *Risk-taking* is part of problem-solving – the important thing is to have read enough to know what the risks are, and whether you want to take them. Buying shares in big businesses such as Tesco or Cadbury is risky, but far less risky than many other ways of investing or savings.

▶ *Decision-making* – when you are sure of what you want, make the decision quickly and firmly. Many people delay too long – or can never make a decision at all.

▶ *Time management* – make sure you find the time to budget and to research your financial decisions. Yes, it takes time to make the right decision, but that's far better than spending years regretting the decision you failed to make – or the decision you got wrong.

Assessment activity 14.1 (P1)

Roger Saul started a business called Mulberry with £500. Today its worldwide sales of handbags tops £75 million a year and its products are bought by celebrities such as Alexa Chung. Mulberry plc is worth over £120 million. Needless to say, Mr Saul is a very rich man.

To save £500, you are likely to need to do some careful financial planning. You would need to keep records to know how you spend (waste?) your money. Then you could plan how to and where to build your savings.

1. Outline how you would keep an accurate record of your spending.

2. Outline your financial plan for saving £500.

Topic check

1 Why may it be helpful to get a bank statement every month instead of once every 3 months?

2 What is compound interest?

3 Why is it important to keep a PIN number secret?

4 What is a direct debit?

5 Identify two possible concerns about banking online.

Know common financial products and services

Getting started

There are many products and services offered by financial organisations such as banks. And there are always new ones being introduced. But here is an explanation of the main ones.

When you have completed this topic, you should:

■ be able to identify the main products offered by banks

■ understand which may be suitable for your own financial needs.

Key terms

APR (Annual Percentage Rate): the calculation of the true rate of interest being charged per year on a loan or on goods bought on credit

Building Society: a type of bank owned not by shareholders, but by the members of the society (in effect, the customers), so there is less temptation to exploit customers for profit

Independent financial advisers (IFAs): these businesses are not tied to a specific bank, which is why they are called 'independent'; but it is crucial to be aware that their advice may be biased towards the bank that offers them the highest rate of commission

Financial service providers

There are a number of different types of financial service provider. They all make their living from your money, so you have to be cautious when dealing with them. They include the following.

▶ *Banks*, most of which have a high street presence, so you can pop in and ask for help or advice. Although banks are safe to deal with, they rarely offer the best value for money. The 2007–2009 'credit crunch' showed that the British government will not allow a bank to fail, so if you keep your cash in a bank, it is safe.

▶ **Building societies** may also be on your high street. Societies such as Nationwide pride themselves on being not-for-profit organisations that are there to provide a service to members. If you buy a product from the Nationwide you instantly become a member. Generally, dealing with a building society gives you better value for money than dealing with a bank. As with banks, the government will make sure that your cash is safe in a building society.

▶ **Independent financial advisers (IFAs)** – beware of the term 'independent'! It implies that these people provide unbiased advice. Unfortunately that is not necessarily so. A great deal of research has shown that IFAs tend to recommend products that yield high incomes to ... IFAs!

An IFA works for him or herself, i.e. is independent of any single bank or investment company, but they are not independent in a way that necessarily benefits the customer. The problem is that IFAs receive their income from commissions given by investment companies. So they are tempted to recommend that you buy a financial package that pays them the highest commission. As *Which?* (the Consumers' Association magazine) would confirm, the only IFA worth dealing with is a fee-only IFA, i.e. they promise to accept no commissions and therefore act in your best interest.

▶ *Financial companies* include those offering unit trusts and investment trusts – both ways of investing directly into the stock market. They are worth dealing with, as long as you follow the rules set out earlier: make sure that management charges are low and that your investment money is spread widely over many different types of shares.

▶ *Retailers* often offer credit to customers. Usually this is an expensive and risky way to buy anything. The first rule here is: if you can't afford to buy outright, you can't afford to buy on credit. In November 2009 the editor of *Which?* magazine wrote: 'Store cards have long been one of the most expensive ways to borrow'. He criticised stores for charging annual interest rates as high as 31.9% at a time when credit cards generally were charging 16–18%. Even DFS-style 'interest free credit for 4 years' offers must be treated warily. If you fail to make a payment on time, they hit you hard with extra charges.

The main purpose of these financial service providers is:

▶ *Providing savings accounts* – high street banks and building societies will usually be helpful with these products, but do be aware that offers online are often better, i.e. they may pay you a higher rate of interest on your money

▶ *Providing investment accounts* – this is where the advice from banks and IFAs must be treated with great caution. Remember: if you don't understand the product, don't buy it.

▶ *Providing insurance against sickness/loss* – beware of buying insurance products from banks – they are rarely good value for money. Go to a library and ask for a *Which?* magazine report on personal and on household insurance. It will provide independent advice and tell you which providers are the best value for money.

 Activity

The Citizens Advice Bureau is a government-funded, independent service that gives free advice on legal and financial problems. Go to its website (www.adviceguide.org.uk) and find out what sort of information and advice are provided.

List three sections that you might find useful, and find out what information the website gives about these.

▶ *Lending money subject to specific criteria*, e.g. a bank overdraft or a bank loan –
with some banks, going over your overdraft limit can lead to huge fees,
amounting to hundreds of pounds a year. If you must borrow, look to more
reputable lenders such as the Co-op Bank and the Nationwide building society.

▶ *Financial advice on managing money* – this is most likely to be helpful if you drop
in on a bank or building society, and your need is for advice on budgeting or saving.

Case study

In the last 10 years many people who have taken on bank overdrafts or loans have been persuaded to take out payment protection insurance, which seemed like a responsible thing to do. In fact, the protection provided by this insurance is very limited. And it's very expensive to buy – typically a customer ends up paying about £2,250. In 2009 Alliance and Leicester Bank was fined £9 million for mis-selling this insurance, i.e. selling it to people who could not receive benefits from it. Banks including Natwest, RBS and Lloyds have been forced to offer compensation to customers who should never have been persuaded to buy this product.

1. Why may banks be tempted to sell people financial products they do not need?

2. Why may it be safer to buy financial products from a building society than a bank?

Types of products and services

Bank accounts

Current accounts

Most current accounts provide a wide range of services to help busy people handle
their finances. Almost all the services involve ways of putting money into and paying
money out of the account. In most cases, current accounts pay no interest but most
of the services are not charged for. Among the key services are the following:

▶ *Easy cash withdrawals and payments*, either using a bank card (to draw money
out of a hole-in-the-wall 'ATM') or a cheque book*. Cash deposits or withdrawals
can also be made at a bank branch. (*Banks plan to withdraw cheques by 2018.)

▶ *Direct debits* allow services such as gas and electricity to take a sum regularly from
an individual's account, and top up when the actual bill is known (so that the bills
are paid on time, and relatively painlessly).

▶ *Standing orders* are similar to a direct debit, but a regular payment of a set sum,
e.g. if a mum wanted to put £100 a month into her daughter's bank account
while she was at university.

▶ *Overdrafts* are a convenient way for people to smooth out their financial ups and
downs by being able to pay out more than they have in their bank accounts, i.e. a
£1,000 overdraft allows bills to be paid up to that limit. Used sensibly, an overdraft
is the best way to borrow money from a bank. If you use an overdraft on a
Wednesday and receive your monthly pay on a Thursday, you will only be charged
interest for one day, i.e. a 365th of the interest rate of perhaps 15%.

(Note1: £1,000 borrowed for a year at 15% means a charge of £150; £1,000 borrowed for a day means a charge of £150 ÷ 365 = 41p.)

(Note 2: although overdrafts are a good way to borrow money for a short time, banks charge shocking rates on 'unauthorised overdrafts'. If your bank allows you a £1,000 overdraft but you go £1,200 'into the red', you may find penalties as high as £25 per day. Never, ever go beyond your overdraft limit.)

▶ *Unsecured loans:* usually given for a period of perhaps 18–36 months, a loan is a relatively low-cost way to finance a chunky purchase such as a car or new carpets. The interest rate is lower than on an overdraft.

▶ *Secured loans:* the difference here is that repayments on the loan are secured against a specific asset such as a house or a car. Be clear that means that if you don't keep up the repayments, you can have your house or car seized from you! So 'secured loans' mean security for the lender, not for you!

Deposit accounts

These are savings accounts that offer no extra services. All you can do is put money in, earn interest, then take the money out. Some provide 'instant access', e.g. via a debit card; others require notice, e.g. you may have to tell the bank 7 days before the time you want to make the withdrawal. These are accounts for saving money for months or years.

Figure 14.3 Advantages and disadvantages of overdrafts and bank loans

	Overdraft	Bank loan
Advantages	• Flexibility: borrow as much as you like for as long as you like (within agreed overdraft limit). • Ideal for running a small business, where the finances can be up and down within the day.	• Stability: once the loan is agreed, you have that money for, say, 3 years (as long as you pay the interest charges). • The interest rate is not too high, especially if the borrower can offer the bank some security.
Disadvantages	• The annual interest charges are usually relatively high, e.g. 15%, and extremely high (25% or more) for unauthorised overdrafts. • Your bank can demand that you repay the overdraft within 24 hours; this might be very, very difficult to do.	• If the borrower has no security (if they don't own a house), the interest charges can be very high. • Banks often charge a fee for arranging a loan.

Over to you!

Choose two reasons why an overdraft can be a better way to borrow than a bank loan.

a) Because the bank can't ask for its money back.

b) Because it's flexible – you don't need to borrow for long.

c) Because banks only charge interest on loans, not overdrafts.

d) Because you're only paying interest for the days you need the money.

Bank and credit cards

Solo

This card is available for users as young as 11 years old. It provides an easy way to pay for things, using the money from the user's bank deposit account. It can only be used when the money is available in the person's bank account, i.e. it is not a way to get credit.

Electron

This card can be 'charged up' with money. For example, parents could put £200 on an Electron card for their child to use on holiday. The child could keep spending up to the £200 limit, then there will be no more spending power. This is a great way to avoid running up debts.

Maestro

This is a debit card which enables the user to pay bills, withdraw cash or get up to £50 'cashback' when paying at shops. It makes withdrawals instantly from the person's bank account. It will not work if the person's bank balance is too low, therefore it is impossible to get into financial difficulty with a Maestro – or any other – debit card.

Credit card

A card that allows spending up to an agreed limit, e.g. £5,000. At the time the cardholder makes a purchase, there is no check on whether the money is available in their bank account. Therefore it encourages people to spend on credit, i.e. to buy things that they don't have the money for. If the credit card bill is not paid in full at the end of the month, the cardholder will be charged interest by the bank that has issued the card. At the time of writing, HSBC charges an interest rate of 16.9%, but the range of charges available varies between 14.9% and 34.9%. The higher the figure, the tougher it will be to repay. Usually a credit card is only available to those with a regular job.

? Did you know?

The average UK adult had £4,685 of outstanding debts via credit cards, store cards and overdrafts at the end of February 2010.

Store card

Many shops like you to take out a card such as a 'Debenhams' card. These are much the same as other credit cards, but usually charge an even higher rates of interest, such as the Argos Card, with 27.9%. This remarkably high figure was at a time that the Bank of England's interest rate was just 0.5%.

Think

Be safe: plastic is a convenient way to make purchases and withdraw cash. Solo, Electron and Maestro are cards that provide this convenience without any risks of running up debts.

Be sorry: credit and store cards are different – yes, they provide convenience, but with the risk of getting trapped in debt. A £1,000 purchase at an interest rate of 27.9% is tough to repay (£279 interest per year, plus repaying the £1,000 would mean paying £1,837 if the purchaser took 3 years to repay). Worse still comes for the person who cannot repay for a year or two. The interest compounds up, making the debts even bigger. Be wise, stick to Solo, Electron and Maestro.

Over to you!

Why might it be more worrying to lose a debit card than an Electron card? Choose one answer.

a) Because a thief could get at your whole bank account.

b) Because a debit card gives access to credit of up to £5,000.

c) Because an Electron card can only be used to pay fuel bills.

Conclusion and evaluation

Managing your money is vital to avoid the financial problems faced by so many families. It can also set you on the path to being free to do what you want, when you want to do it. The person with a chunk of cash in the bank is the person who can quit a bullying employer, or choose to go on a round-the-world adventure.

If you start now, when your finances are quite straightforward, it will be easy to manage your cash. Careful budgeting gives you the scope to start saving; and that can make it possible to start saving regularly. The earlier you can start, the earlier in life you'll have the cash to pay for a deposit on a flat.

When writing assignments on personal finance, make sure to learn fully about the individuals you are writing about. Distinctions come to those who show that they understand the needs and the difficulties of individuals when dealing with money. In a world in which top bankers recently made huge mistakes with money (in the lead-up to the 'credit crunch'), it is understandable that ordinary people often do the same.

 Case study

On 11 August 2009 the *Metro* newspaper featured a half-page colour advertisement for 'Oakam' and a smaller but still prominent one for 'PDUK'. The main part of each advertisement is shown below. Look at both advertisements, then think about the questions underneath.

Borrow £200–£5,000 with an Oakam Bonus Loan	**Cash When You Need It!**
If your bank says no, Oakam could say yes.	• £80 to £400 paid into your bank within 48 hours
£500 loan for just £15.71 a week*	• We charge £25 for every £100 borrowed
*Based on a total loan of £550 (including a £50 fee) over 1 year. Total repayment is £691.32 including a bonus cash back reward of £125.69 for making on-time repayments for the full term of the loan.	• Quick decisions online and by phone
	• 1737% APR typical
76.9% **APR** (typical variable)	**PDUK PayDay UK**
Oakam: Your local money store	

1. If you were desperate for £200 to buy a fantastic new product, which of the two loans would be the better choice?

2. What problems might you find when repaying:

   a) the Oakam loan?   b) the PDUK loan?

Assessment activity 14.2 Taking control of your finances (P4, M1)

The task is for you to a) set yourself a financial goal and b) budget for how you will achieve it. For example, you might want £300 for an iPhone before next summer's holiday. Your budget will show how you will generate that money. If you have no regular income, you'll have to talk to your parents about what jobs you might do to make (and save) some money. You must:

1. Decide how much money you want and when you want it by.

2. Spend a week making a note of everything you spend money on; then divide your spending into three: things you must have, things you want to have, things you bought without really wanting them.

3. Set out a budget on a spreadsheet (such as Excel), showing your income and your planned spending. Be realistic – don't give yourself nothing for fun spending.

4. Put the budget into action for a week, noting what you actually spent compared with your plans.

5. Explain the reasons for the budgetary decisions you have taken.

6. Explain the reasons for the budgetary decisions you have taken. How well did you do? What went right and what went wrong? A merit or distinction will come from your ability to draw conclusions from the process.

Assessment activity 14.3 (P2, P3, M2, D1)

At different times of their life, people need different financial services. Until the age of 18, most people need no more than a bank account with a card for withdrawing money. After leaving home, people need to have their weekly or monthly pay sent to their account, to pay bills – perhaps by direct debit – and perhaps to start saving. Soon enough the priority will be buying a house and perhaps paying into a pension fund.

As shown in the diagram below, most people will start with very little, then build up their assets in the early stages of adult life. By the time they are in middle age, their income is at its highest, and their children leave home. The adults have less to spend their money on, allowing them to spend more on themselves – and perhaps start saving seriously for their old age.

1. Interview someone between the ages of 25 and 50 about their financial life. Explain that they will need to tell you some personal information, but make it clear that you will change their name before writing up your notes. You must find out:

   a) Their current financial situation. Do they have any debts?

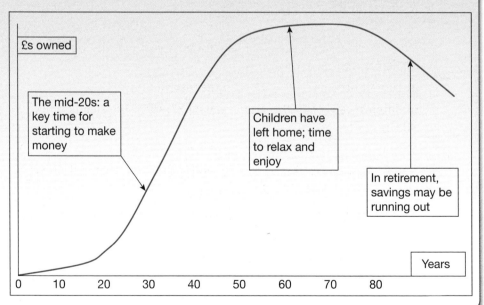

Assessment activity 14.3 (P2, P3, M2, D1) *continued*

If so, what are they? And what are their main assets, e.g. house, shares or money in the bank?

b) Their current financial goals, i.e. what they are hoping to achieve financially over the next few months or years (e.g. buy a new car or buy a new house).

c) When they are using bank and savings accounts, which features do they use most often and why? You will need to analyse the different features of financial products and services relating to current and savings accounts.

d) Ask them to describe a recent or current financial planning decision (e.g. taking on a mortgage, switching to a new pension or saving for a big event). How did they find the information they needed? What sources of advice did they use? And how long did it take to make a decision?

2. After completing the interview, identify and describe the financial products and services you think are most appropriate for you personally – both now and in 5 years' time.

3. Write a conclusion about how well or how poorly the interviewee has tackled the financial decisions they have faced. You need to explain and justify their reasons for these financial decisions.

Topic check

1 If you need to borrow to get through to payday, should you be looking for an overdraft or a bank loan?

   a) overdraft   b) bank loan

2 To pay a regular £20 a month into your bank deposit account, should you use a standing order or a direct debit?

   a) standing order   b) direct debit

3 If a business used a £50,000 overdraft for 3 days, and the interest rate was 14.6%, what would the interest charge be?

   a) £6   b) £60   c) £7,300   d) £21,900

4 Which bank account would be best for a 14 year old who wants to save up to buy an Apple Air laptop?

   a) current account   b) deposit account

5 An interest rate of 27.9% means paying 27.9% of the sum borrowed for every year you take to repay.

   a) true   b) false

6 A debit card is ideal for borrowing money that you need, but do not have.

   a) true   b) false

7 A credit card helps you buy goods you cannot afford to buy at present.

   a) true   b) false

8 An Electron card helps you control your spending, as you can't spend more than you have already got.

   a) true   b) false

Assessment summary

The overall grade you achieve for this unit depends on how well you meet the grading criteria set out at the start of the chapter (see page 261). You must complete:

- all of the P criteria to achieve a **pass** grade
- all of the P and the M criteria to achieve a **merit** grade
- all of the P, M and D criteria to achieve a **distinction** grade.

Your tutor will assess the assessment activities that you complete for this unit. The work you produce should provide evidence which demonstrates that you have achieved each of the assessment criteria. The table below identifies what you need to demonstrate to meet each of the pass, merit and distinction criteria for this unit. You should always check and self-assess your work before you submit your assignments for marking.

Remember that you MUST provide evidence for all of the P criteria to pass the unit.

Grading criteria	You need to demonstrate that you can:	Do you have the evidence?
P1	Outline ways of managing personal financial planning and accurate record keeping	
P2	Identify sources of advice for ways of managing financial products and services	
P3	Describe financial products and services appropriate to self	
P4	Construct a personal budget that takes account of personal remuneration and expenditure	
M1	Explain the reasons for budgetary decisions	
M2	Analyse the different features of financial products and services relating to to current and savings accounts	
D1	Justify reasons for financial planning decisions	

Always ask your tutor to explain any assignment tasks or assessment criteria that you don't understand fully. Being clear about the task before you begin gives you the best chance of succeeding. Good luck with your Unit 20 assessment work!

Index